GOD: EXPERIENCE OR ORIGIN?

GOD: Experience or Origin?

EDITED BY
ANTONIO T. DE NICOLÁS &
EVANGHELOS MOUTSOPOULOS

A NEW ERA BOOK

PARAGON HOUSE
New York

Published in the United States by
Paragon House Publishers
2 Hammarskjold Plaza
New York, New York 10017

A New Ecumenical Research Association Book.

Library of Congress Cataloging-in-Publication Data
Main entry under title:

God: Experience or Origin?

(God, The Contemporary Discussion Series)
"New ERA book."
Bibliography
Includes index.
1. Experience (Religion)—Congresses. 2. God—Congresses. 3. Spirituality—Congresses.
I. De Nicolás, Antonio T., 1932–
II. Moutsopoulos, E., 1930– III. Series.
BL53.G59 1985 291.4′2 85-12096
ISBN 0-913757-24-1 (hardbound)
ISBN 0-913757-25-X (softbound)

Contents

Introduction

Antonio T. de Nicolás

Papers written for a particular conference, seldom, if ever, overflow the interests of the sponsors of the conference or the sectarian limitations of the particular styles of scholarship of the participants. When the conference deals with religious subjects, the problem of universal appeal becomes even more questionable. In this latter case, the aim is often sectarian and dogmatic rather than universal and ecumenical. The writers are inclined to universal apologetics rather than to internal criticism or to internal criticism leading to universal apologetics. The cryptic slogan seems to pursue the same line of seduction: Follow us for we have the truth, or are very near to reaching it.

The conferences sponsored by New ERA (New Ecumenical Research Association), on the other hand, have added a new, and historically a first, change in style of religious conferences. The participants, seen from their papers published in this volume, come from all parts of the geographical and academic world. They belong to various styles learned through rigorous academic training. Yet, it will be obvious on reading the published papers, that none is concerned with paying tribute to the sponsors of the conference. More boldly stated, the sponsors of the conference do not act as an external inquisition in shaping the agreement or disagreement of the papers. Even more significantly, the internal inquisitions that normally belong to the styles of the particular writers are absent. Instead, each paper, and all the papers communally, transcend the internal and external limitations of style and dogma in, what appears to be, a search for a deeper communion and community that has been hiding behind the fears of external and internal dogmatism that accompany such free enterprise as academic performance. In short, for the first time in history a group of scholars has been able to meet, argue, and break new ground for what we might cautiously term the university of the future.

The university of the future, however, is linked in a particular way and with particular urgency with the future of the university. For the university to have a future, it cannot be linked to particular interests derived from any one particular methodology from the sciences or the humanities. The plurality of interests and methods, together with the responsibility of serious scholarship, has called into question the dogmatic tendencies of any one particular successful methodology universally applied to all the branches of research and teaching in the university.

Nowhere is this need and shortcoming more obvious than in the study of religion. The last fifteen years have seen a deep and disquieting change in the religious and public domains of the United States. For the first time public education and religion as a whole have come face to face. Religion has become an object of study, its umbilical cord cut from any ecclesiastical or dogmatic womb. The universities, however, in answer to this new situation, have been found wanting. They have been able to offer programs of religious studies closer to the methods of the social sciences, like history and linguistics, rather than hermeneutical programs able to handle religion on its own terms. For this reason many graduate programs in religious studies retreated, after a short public exposure, to the seminaries and ecclesiastical worlds, thereby cutting themselves off from the public domains and respectabilities controlled by the universities.

These problems and concerns are reflected in the papers in this volume. Though the participants are members of academic communities and therefore bound to particular styles or training in the development of their scholarship, their papers vividly exemplify the tension between that training or style and the search for the autonomous method in the study of religion. The search for method is in every case built into the criticism itself of the method used in the writing of the papers. More significantly, the thought habits of different styles are traced historically through the various styles, enabling the reader to follow the human steps of interpretation on the path of divine footsteps. For this reason the papers are organized under the titles of styles and grouped together in this fashion. Does it make sense to talk about the "experience" of God? Antoine Vergote traces the historical origin of that expression. Should we then opt for the "ultimate" instead? Evanghelos Moutsopoulos phrases this question to expand the human horizons even further than through the word "experience." In every case, in every paper, religion is grounded on a divine origin with many names, but with a set of particular practices similar across the board, even when theologies are so different across the same board. This is the lead of the papers dealing with Islam, African religions, Indian and Oriental religions, or even the individual struggles of Luther, Augustine, Hume and others. It is a surprising discovery, through these papers, the ease with which certain habits of thought introduced by people like Augustine have exerted more power over people's reason and bodily habits than any direct experience or origin claimed by numerous mystics. Ultimately the problem arises with the claims and practices of these same mystics. They pleased or tried to please the surrounding inquisition with their statements, while in practice they implied, rather than in theologies, bodily exercises as the way of preparation and the indispensable condition for the appearance of the divine. In this case, it might appear, practices bear a particular epistemology that religious studies have overlooked.

It is evident these papers are a first exercise in a new experiment in ecumenism. The theoretical praise of the similar gives way to a deeper scholarship in search of the radical and transforming difference. Religion might have come of age, but more significantly it may have found fertile historical conditions for planting the first seeds of a new scholarship and a new community.

Part One
ANALYTIC PROBLEMATIC STYLE

1

The Primacy of Experience in Spiritual Life and the Problem of its Interpretation

EMILIE ZUM BRUNN

"Grey, dear friend, is all theory—and green life's golden tree!"[1] Though it may seem a paradox, this mephistophelic verse applies excellently to our present subject, for what is of primary importance in our spiritual life, allowing it to be truly a *life,* is the experience of God. However we choose to name this mysterious Ultimacy, it transcends us and is within us. It is glimpsed by some and sought blindly, by many in the obscure night of faith, sometimes in a desperate barehanded fight against skepticism. (An agnostic's search for meaning in a world fraught with senselessness can be considered a preliminary experience of the Ultimate, even if that experience is only a perception of the "unknown God.")[2] Modern religious consciousness highlights the primacy of spiritual experience, that *passio* or *pati* of the soul which some great medieval mystics considered as the soul's supreme achievement.

The Primacy of Experience

Experience, as opposed to solely intellectual knowledge, allows us to participate in the nature and destiny of God/Ultimate, in the sense of the old philosophical word *eksis,* literally, having *participation.* Such is the meaning of Augustine's quest, as expressed in his *Dialogues.* How is it possible for us to *have God* (*habere deum*), to *be with* God (*esse cum deo*), or more simply to *be* (*esse*), since, according to the ontotheological tradition, God is 'Being itself' (*ipsum esse*)?[3]

Hoping to find such an experience of God, Augustine remained for years an adept of the Manicheans, until he finally realized that, in spite of his toilsome religious efforts, the revelation which his masters had promised him turned out to be a mere phantasm. Later on, Augustine was able to experimentally approach God through the aid of Bishop Ambrose's view of the spirituality of the soul and its Creator, which he interpreted with the help of "the books of the Platonists." However, Augustine was disappointed by the transient experience. It was an intellective insight which did not live up to what he had imagined. Finally, in moral desperation, he sought help in the Gospel. Christ then summoned him. Augustine wrote that from that very moment his heart and his life were thoroughly changed.[4]

In this confession, Augustine conveys that the condition for full conversion is an experience *of* and *through* the mediator, directly resulting from faith in him. He alone has the power to give man close and living access to God. Those who do not fulfill that condition, even the great Platonic masters, are doomed to contemplate him only from afar (*de longe*). However imperfectly conceived, this conversion experience—even on a Neoplatonist foundation—was much stronger than anything Augustine ever experienced as a Manichean. Thus he states that, from then on, he was more certain of God's existence than of his own.[5] The path which was to lead him to the Christian God was first and last, in great part, Neoplatonic doctrine and practice. It was a gnosis of the intellect, better suited to his cultural patterns and temperament than the Manichean gnosis of imagination. The former led him to the *ontôs on,* to what is truly real, the aim of the religious quest.

Meister Eckhart vividly expressed the paradox between outer knowledge and inner experience, between a conceptual God and a God existing as a living being in one's soul: *ein gewesener got.*

Such an experience of the living God reverses our sense of the real, for example, "For him who has ever for an instant thrown a glimpse on this *grunt,* for this man one thousand red *marks* of beaten gold are like a false *heller.*"[6] For Eckhart, and perhaps more so for Augustine, the true benefit of religion is centered on experience, on the birth of God in the soul. "If it does not happen (*geschihet*) in me, in what does this help me? But, that it should happen in me, everything depends on this."[7]

Practical Consequences: Freedom and Efficiency Such personal experience accounts for the superior mental balance of prophets, saints, and mystics, in spite of secondary symptoms presented by some of them when in trance. In *Les deux Sources de la Morale et de la Religion,* Bergson undertook an experimental spiritual quest and noted this superior balance in the cases he examined—especially those of Paul, Joan of Arc and Teresa of Avila. Contrary to reductive psychiatric analyses such as Pierre Janet's, Bergson states: "There is however a firmly set, exceptional intellectual health, which is recognized without difficulty. Is this not precisely what is found in the mystics of whom we speak? And could they not serve for the very definition of intellectual robustness?"[8]

Such an experience can be considered *self-validating* since the balance or robustness is due to an influence transcendent of ordinary personality. It is itself a *matter of experience* and thus a testimony to others, a foundation for hope in the anguish of the day. It testifies to the perfect *freedom* described by Meister Eckhart, of being totally at the disposal of God at all times, ready to do or not to do, in the all-consuming *now* of the man wholly detached from himself and any egotistic aims: ". . . your freedom to be at the disposal of God at this present moment and to follow him alone in the light by which he invites you to act or to omit, free and new at every present moment, as if you had, willed or could do nothing else."[9]

Recognizable in this freedom is the doctrine of action detached from the fruits of action, or the so-called Taoist nonaction, also expressed in the Bhagavad Gītā. Such is the nature of true freedom.

Otherwise, however free, active, efficient, and important we imagine ourselves, we are caught in the crossfire between the influences of the outer world and the "factors" of our mind and body, and become victims of that "myth of freedom" so clearly revealed in Buddhist psychology.[10]

In fact, this mental slavery is today mirrored in the world we have contributed to build, much like the beast in Kafka's story,[11] fast growing into a prison or death camp. This state of human affairs has been analyzed with great lucidity by Aldous Huxley. In modern terms, he expressed the traditional view that the times of lesser evil in history coincide with a flowering of mystical experience, and the times of greater evil coincide with its withering.[12] Other modern thinkers, such as Arthur Koestler, after adhering to a totalitarian creed, reached the same conclusion, and turned to the mystics, that is, to those endowed with deep spiritual experience, as the only hope for this world. Thus, despite modern cultural misconceptions to the contrary, genuine spiritual experience, is again considered by some as it was of old, that is, as the source of valid *practical* action—impossible to computerize, wherein lies the salvation and liberation of our world.

The Fundamental Criterion: Joy Without delving further into the phenomenology of spiritual experience, I would like to state that, to my mind, *joy* is the most fundamental result and criterion of such experience. This is proclaimed in the deepest religious and philosophic traditions as well as in the Christian beatitudes. Of course, according to the development and variations of cultures and temperaments, other aspects of spiritual experience may be put to the fore, such as awe in front of the *mysterium tremendum*. But at the outcome we find joy of a transcendent kind, "an inalienable spiritual beatitude,"[13] promised even in the midst of persecution to those who were faithful in the quest for truth and justice.[14] It is inalienable because it fulfills, by inward growth, the radical desire of the human soul, the *desiderium beatitudinis*. Augustine, in the Greco-Eurasian tradition,[15] identified this with the *desiderium essendi,* the desire to be, that is, to participate in the true reality of the spiritual world, as opposed to the reality of the created universe.

In my school years, during the general pessimism of World War II and the post-war period, especially in European academic circles, Renan's disenchanted remark seemed to correspond to reality: "After all, truth is perhaps sad." But then, as many others, I was attracted to Claudel's bouyant statement that "joy is superior and final," defying the sadness and horror of war surrounding us.

Later on, I learned to read the answer to my soul's innate questioning not only in Claudel's poems, but also in the smiles of archaic Greek statues and of Khmer Buddhas. I learned to follow the quest for joy in Augustine's *Dialogues* and *Confessions,* as well as in the Neoplatonic philosophy by which he interpreted Christian revelation. For such was the whole aim of ancient philosophy: to find *beata vita,* the happy life.

In that tradition philosophers were endowed, more than we are today, with the unity of knowledge and feeling, of theory and experience (*theoria* then meant vision). They were not tormented by the disassociation from which we suffer between science and spirituality, aesthetic enjoyment and morality, truth and joy. Arts and sciences were ordained to that common aim: *liberation* of the soul through intuitive participation in the Ultimate. Therefore *joy* was synonymous with being, as well as with truth (Cf. *sat-cit-ananda*). Such was the foundation of that ontotheology it has become fashionable to criticize after Heidegger—with reason only inasmuch as it has not kept true to the *togetherness* of joy and being, of *theory* and experience, and has lost itself in the greyness of overspeculation. Unfortunately, the Byzantinism of late scholasticism has been replaced today by others which are not more substantial though they are intellectually vogue. This is doubtless one reason why many people turn to the mystics of East and West. They want to find out if what was and is true for those mystics may still be found in, and in spite of, our present civilization: "This joy is near you and it is in you. There is none among you, however blunt, however faint be his comprehension and far from it, who cannot find this joy in himself, in truth, such as it is, with joy and comprehension, before you go out of this church today and even before I have finished preaching."[16]

The Royal Path of Passivity or Abandonment There is a path which remains when others have long disappeared, because it is the very condition of spiritual experience. This royal path is quasi-unanimously recognized by mystics to be receptivity towards God/Ultimate. The names given to that receptivity vary, ranging from passivity and obedience to detachment, abandonment, death to oneself, annihilation. Eckhart as an authority on this, quotes Denys the Areopagite's answer to his disciples asking him the reason why Timothy surpassed them all in perfection: "Because Timothy is a God-suffering man."[17] To "suffer" (*pati*) God, that is, in modern language to experience him, one must be passive or abandoned to him. This passivity allows God or the true Self to act without interference from the activity of the individual self pursuing its egoistic aims, even if those aims are "good" and "religious." Mystics recognize the necessity of a hard fight against one's passions, and especially against one's activism, before one attains the passivity which renounces enslavement to one's self. In many religions or dharmas, this receptivity is symbolized by the *feminine* attitude. This aspect is very strongly marked in Rheno-Flemish mysticism. Eckhart's evolution on this point is noteworthy. It is certainly due to the influence of the mystic tradition kept and experienced in the convents while it was chiefly a matter of theory for the university masters: "If the theme (of union to God) has with our beguines and nuns another flavour, another efficiency than in scholastic expositions, it is due to the inner life which animates them: it appears by them as an expression of what they experience."[18]

In accordance with the Dominican tradition, Eckhart first taught that the *Durchbruch* or "breaking through" of the soul to God was achieved by the intellect, called "the man in the soul." Later the Dominican master changed this theory into a transintellective conception of the *Durchbruch*. Therefore he said that "woman," symbolizing at once receptivity and fecundity, "is the noblest name of the soul."

Note the strong relation which unites this highest virtue of passivity and *negative theology*. Eckhart first said that we cannot love what we do not know—therefore there is a primacy of intellect over love, of John over Peter. Then, in the higher expressions of Eckhartian mysticism, the truly 'separate' or 'detached' or 'poor' man is said to be he who has nothing, wills nothing, and knows nothing. This is also the theme of one of Eckhart's rare statements concerning his personal experience, when he speaks of "a man" who became "pregnant with Naught as a woman is pregnant with child, and from this Naught God was born."[19]

This receptivity finds a parallel, among others, in the wisdom of Lao-Tsú: "What is softer surmounts what is harder, the feminine surmounts the masculine." As the Orthodox theologian Paul Evdokimov remarked, it is precisely in this sense that Christ uttered this fundamental spiritual principle: "I am meek and lowly in heart" (Mat. 11:29). "He refuses the masculine solution of the sword, as he rejects the masculine solutions to the three temptations in the desert and chooses the offering of himself, his own oblation, the figure of the immolated lamb."[20]

"Breaking Through" Temporality and Human Means Spiritual experience is centered on a *here and now* which is eschatological, partaking of another world. Therefore all other aspects of religion, of dharma, however important and necessary they may be along the way, are considered by many saints and mystics as *means* to this sole end. "Why do we pray, why do we fast, why do we accomplish all our works, why are we baptized, why has God become man—which was most sublime? I would say: for God to be born in the soul and the soul to be born in God. Therefore all Scripture has been written and God has created the world and angelic nature . . ."[21]

The Rheno-Flemish mystics considered the status of faith, dogma, cult, sacrifice, liturgy, even ethics in this manner.[22] When man has reached the perfection of his goal, these means are abolished because he no longer needs them. If he does not detach himself morally from them, they will become chains enslaving him. In other religions also "the way of tradition" is itself considered a chain on the way to realization.[23]

Such is the paradox of spiritual experience, whether perfection is considered attainable here and now, as in some Eastern traditions as well as in the ancient philosophy which influenced the young Augustine—or whether perfection is considered attainable only after death, as in the creeds centered on eschatology and resurrection.[24] In the latter case, spiritual experience is viewed at its best, as an analogy of future beatitude.[25] However, it must be noted that Christian mystics have a tendency to envisage as realizable "here and now" the promise of Jesus: "Today shalt thou be with me in paradise" (Luke 23:43). Hence their insistence on the present.

An integral part of the path of religious development is the spiritual guide. Though in most cases a single guide suffices, sometimes several are necessary on the way. Some traditions emphasize the necessity of a guide through the deification of their guru. But in a normal and complete (one is tempted to say adult) evolution, the Buddha himself must be "killed." According to a Zen teaching the outer guru must at some time be definitively replaced by the inner one. As it is impossible to directly transmit spiritual experience, one must finally tread alone "the way which is no longer a way," even though the mystic's chief effort is to try and help others dare this venture.

The Interpretation of Experience

Up until now, we have considered only the experiential aspect of a relationship with God/Ultimate. One question remains, since this participation in the divine cannot be wholly abstracted from conceptual thinking. *Who* or *what* is this God or Ultimate which is being experienced? What is the role of *genuine experience* and the role of *theory* or concept in approaching the divine? Let us look for examples inside a given church, school, or community. For instance, a new or unusual experience of God or the Ultimate often conflicts with the traditional representation of the socio-religious milieu in which it has been born. Due to the new *contents* which their experience as well as their reflection brought them to pour into "old bottles," some of the greatest saints and mystics—among them founders of religions—came to be considered as *destroyers* of religion.[26] The oneness or identity they proclaimed to share with the divine brought Jesus and Al Hadj to martyrdom for *blasphemy*—a plight shared by many of their followers and imitators. This comes from the *socio-ideological* aspect of instituted religions, the "religious" judgment, that is, the interpretation, focusing on the *ideological content* of the new doctrine or vision, more than on the experience itself. The latter is generally inaccessible to an "orthodox" jury in whom the relation of experience to conceptual thought is usually inversely proportional to what it is in those whom they judge.

The question of the *content* of spiritual experience has only been alluded to by the expressions "identification of" or "participation in" God/Ultimate. This alternative answers two different, although not opposite, *views* of spiritual experience—often in severe conflict. Augustine adopted the first view when he was a Manichean, and opposed it fiercely in favor of the second when he became a Christian. Therefore, if we scan the structure of spiritual experience, we are brought to consider its inevitable companion: *interpretation*.

Primacy of Cult and Religious Theory? How are theory and concept expressed within religious or spiritual experience? This process is complex, since every experience, in both hindsight and foresight, draws on subconscious as well as conscious rationalizations for its understanding and justification. This occurs in the sociological as well as individual frame of our determinisms (even though the experience itself is one of freedom, allowing the person to escape or to master those determinisms). Due to our individual outlook, we emphasize above all our own experience of God or Ultimacy, and tend to forget the influence of socio-religious and ethical teachings, including cult and rites. This was excellently illustrated during the last conference on "God: the Contemporary Discussion," in a paper entitled "*Qualis cultus, talis deus.*" The author emphasized "the fact that cult is much more than a 'factual appendix' of the Godhead, and plays a determining role in the *representation* of the Divine in a much broader sense than so far accepted by researchers and devotees . . . our formula intends to point out that the interdependence of Godhead from cult has the same *representative force* as myth and theological definitions in *moulding the aspect* assumed by the 'Divine' in a given tradition."[27]

Hence, we see that *cult* as well as *myth* and *religious theory* mold the aspect taken by the divine. But is it the religious ideologies, including cult and rites "which justify and, finally, validate mystical experiences"?[28] That is the whole question.

The Dialectic of Religious Tradition and Genuine Experience It is obvious that in many cases spiritual experience is *channeled* in order to be expressed in accordance with certain religious criteria or biases which form our thoughts on the matter. Therefore it is difficult and, in many cases, nearly impossible to distinguish clearly genuine experience from the predetermined categories by means of which this experience is expressed and understood. Nevertheless, it is feasible to some extent in cases of particularly strong and authentic experiences which do not fit the traditional pattern of the milieu where they have arisen—even if they are eventually woven into that pattern.

Even without resorting to the exceptional situations of great founders of religions, reformers, and "heretics," we see frequently around us a rejection of the established religious patterns. This happens for different reasons. One reason is change or exchange of cultures and religions, frequently happening today as it did during Rome's decline. Another reason may be due to an original quest for God/Ultimate. Sometimes there is a disparity between a person's individual perceptions of God/Ultimate versus that of his or her religious environment. Then he or she may respond to another religion, apparently more foreign. It may happen for philosophical reasons, such as in the case of Lama Govinda, who chose the Buddhist dharma over Islam and Christianity. Later he became one of Buddhism's greatest contemporary exponents.[29] In such cases, the motto of the paper just quoted may be reversed to become: *qualis deus, talis cultus.* But only to an extent, for the strangeness and beauty of Oriental cults and symbols attract doubtless as many adepts to them as the philosophy they contain—the same can be said, *mutatis mutandis,* of Catholic liturgy. In any case, after the choice, the former motto applies again. If our experience of God or the Ultimate tends to be channeled by conceptions and rites imprinted on us by our tradition, so it will be with the one we ourselves choose later on. So again: *qualis cultus, talis deus.*

Yet the central question still remains: How are the two treasures of *personal experience* on the one hand, and of *traditional faith and cult* on the other, to be reconciled? Ideal cases certainly have existed, such as Shankara's, that seem to show perfect continuity between the experience of God/Ultimate and the experience's doctrinal setting. This is possible when the religious structures are supple enough to assimilate renewal. But there are also cases in which a strong and genuine experience is in contradiction with the given structures. Though the experience, when authentic, might have proved stimulating for a re-examination and a revival of the said structures, it often turned tragic in dogmatic traditions in which one was easily condemned for heresy and burned *ad majorem gloriam dei!*

Towards an Explanation How are we going to discern this experience? Must we reduce it to a "smallest common denominator" and consider the differences as "overbeliefs" in the sense used by

William James? Nor are most modern phenomenological approaches enlightening, for they seem to identify the experience of God/Ultimate with the *ways of expressing* the experience. A recent typical example of this is Michel de Certeau's work *La Fable Mystique*. The title is a clear indication of his views on spiritual experience.[30] However brilliant that kind of explanation may be, it loses the essence of mystic language if the latter is an attempt to express, however imperfectly, the reality "before which words recoil."[31] Therefore they cannot satisfy those who do not want to minimize this experience in a new version of the psychiatric reduction against which Bergson and James already fought.

The only modern psychologist's attempt to explain spiritual experience in a nonreductive way is that of Carl-Gustav Jung. It can be accepted by believers because it emphasizes the importance of this experience for humankind. It can be accepted also by scientists because its conclusions, grounded in experience, do not jump over the frontiers of analytical psychology. Thus while studying the images used by the mystics, Jung discovered these images to be the same as the *archetypes* at the root of our collective unconscious (*Unbewusste*). These archetypical forms and, therefore, the mystical images expressing them, are not always orthodox, since a good part of this ancestral treasure has been censured or lost by religion in its present state, at least in the West. However, according to Jung, the function of religion is to express and reconcile the chaotic forces and figures dormant in us.

As an example of this loss, Jung points out that the Christian heaven is a masculine heaven in which the feminine element is merely tolerated. Thus the mother of God is not herself a Goddess, nor is she part of the Trinity. From the fifth century on, it was forbidden by the church to consider the Holy Spirit as a feminine Sophia, in accordance with the Gnostic view. It appears however that many Christian mystics have had experiences which diverge on this point from the orthodox position, even though they were quite ignorant of gnosticism. For example, one can cite the experiences of an analphabetic Swiss peasant of the fifteenth century, Nicholas von der Flue, who became a hermit. Among his visions were those of the Lord God (*Herr Gott*) and the Lady God (*Frau Gott*), with Brother Klaus as their son. Those visions were intended to initiate him into the state of child of God—and the Divinity appeared to him the first time as a kingly father, and the second time as a queenly mother. There are similar instances of this in the Catholic

Church, in which one finds a great number of visions and experiences whose archetypical character is still visible.[32]

It took Nicholas years to understand another vision, the most famous: that of a wrathful human face. It was so terrifying that he fell headlong, and from then retained himself some aura which deeply impressed his countrymen. With a booklet written by a German mystic, Nicholas interpreted his own vision as that of the Trinity understood as a revelation of love. But according to Jung, it was really a recurrence of the Yaweh archetype of the Old Testament, as it appears also in Revelation 1:13, in which wrath is not yet disassociated from goodness and love. We know similar instances in many other archetypical deities.

The living experience of an archetype is, in this view, an *original experience of the "not I"* or non-ego of the soul, of an inward "partner" who invites dialogue, discussion, and confrontation. It is understandable that in this situation the subject looks for something to lean on, such as comparable human experiences which offer helpful parallels. It may happen that in this search for signification, the primary event becomes wrongly assimilated to borrowed representations. Such was, according to Jung, the case for Nicholas—but that allowed him to recover peace and strength, for otherwise he might have been considered a heretic or a madman and would have had a very different destiny.

Concerning us, the most important and practical aspect of Jung's discovery is to let us know that such images are alive in all of us. This is why his theory makes sense to believers as well as to unbelievers, when he shows experience of God or the Ultimate as an answer to the fundamental need of men and women, the demand of their unconscious Self to be reconciled with its conscious partner. When the reconciliation of the 'I' or ego with the Self is accomplished through what is fundamentally a *religious* experience in the etymological sense of the word, our lives find a new center of gravity which allows them to be positive for ourselves as well as for others—i. e., our lives become theocentric or Selfcentric. Therefore experiences of God/Ultimate are certainly more frequent, and their realm is vaster than our philosophy, our faith, or our agnosticism could ever dream. For instance, the need to express and acquire understanding of their own inner experience seems to be the reason many cultivated people are attracted to theosophy and anthroposophy. Thanks to their Oriental roots, these gnostic systems know how to formulate those inner events, deprived of language, "better than any existing form of Christian religion." The latter never reached the fullness of old pagan symbolism, therefore it has survived in undercurrents which have not lost their vitality, and its forms continue to appear "to compensate the unilaterality marking the orientation of modern consciousness."[33]

This seems to become more visible today, for example, with the movements inside Christianity itself, concerning God's feminine aspect, and in relation to this, the revival of the old pagan Mother God symbols, not as anachronic as they may appear at first sight, if we consider them in this view of the archetypes. To return to Lama Govinda, for instance, he finally discovered that the deepest reasons for his conversion were not to be explained, as he had thought formerly, by philosophical considerations alone. He tells us in his fascinating autobiography how he, a follower of Hinayana, was definitively conquered by Tibetan Buddhism in spite of himself, and felt at home among those strange, "irrational" symbols which found an answer deep in his soul.

This difficulty of the mystics to fully understand and interpret their experience indicates that this experience comes from the unconscious or subconscious part of the soul,[34] and we ourselves may have been confronted with the same difficulty, however modest our experience may be. Therefore, we are here on a meeting ground with psychology, in its authentic sense of a "science of the soul." We must have the courage to explore this ground while repeating Augustine's famous prayer to know exclusively "God and the soul," this soul he deplored to be utterly ignorant of, a plight we still share today. For what is needed now as of old, as the different traditions tell us, is the daring and useful quest into our own inner abysses and paradises. We must explore them if we want to assign the meaning of our experiences of God/Ultimate—and discover what God or the Ultimate really means for us.

NOTES

1. Goethe, *Faust* (Stuttgart: Reclam, 1971), pt. 1, vv. 2038–39, 59.
2. See William Johnston, "The Experience of God in Christian Apophatic Mysticism," in *God: The Contemporary Discussion,* ed. Frederick Sontag and M. Darrol Bryant (Barrytown, N.Y.: Unification Theological Seminary, 1982), 371–72.

3. See Emilie Zum Brunn, *Le Dilemme de l'Etre et du Néant chez Saint Augustin* (Paris: Etudes Augustiniennes, 1969), 19ff.
4. Augustine *Confessions* 8.12, 28–29.
5. Ibid., 7.10; 7.17.
6. Eckhart, *Deutsche und Lateinische Werke* 1, (Stuttgart: Deutsche Forschungsgemeinschaft, 1963–). *Deutsche Werke* 1, *Predigt* 5b, 90.
7. Franz Pfeiffer, *Deutsche Mystiker des 14ten Jahrhunderts,* 11: 3, 7–8 (*PR.* 1). Cf. *In Iohannem, Lateinische Werke* 3, no. 117, 101.14–102.3.
8. Henri Bergson, *Les Deux Sources de la Morale et de la Religion* (Paris: Presses Universitaires de France, 1982, 1st ed. 1932), 241.
9. Eckhart, *Predigt* 2, *Deutsche Werke* 1: 28–29.
10. Chogyam Trungpa, *The Myth of Freedom and the Way to Meditation* (Berkeley: Shambhala Publications, 1976).
11. Franz Kafka, *Der Bau,* in *Meistererzählungen,* ed. H. Tauber (Zurich: Manesse Verlag, 1978), 300–47.
12. Aldous Huxley, *Grey Eminence* (London: Chatto and Windus, 1944, and Triad/Granada, 1982).
13. *Bhagavad Gītā,* chap. 6, v. 23, translation after Sri Aurobindo (Paris: Adrien-Maisonneuve, 1962), 67.
14. Matt. 5:3–12 and Luke 6:20ff.
15. See on the unity of the Eurasian traditions Hajime Nakamura, *Parallel Developments: A Comparative History of Ideas* (Tokyo, Kodansha, 1975).
16. Eckhart, *Predigt* 66, *Deutsche Werke* 3: 113–14.
17. Pfeiffer, *Deutsche Mystiker,* 11: 16, 1–9.
18. Fr. J. B. M. P. Introduction à Hadewijch, *Lettres Spirituelles;* Béatrice de Nazareth, *Sept Degrés d'Amour* (Geneva: Claude Martingay, 1972), 21–22.
19. On all this see Emilie Zum Brunn and Alain de Libera, *Maître Eckhart. Métaphysique du Verbe et Théologie Négative* (Paris: Beauschesne, 1984), chap. 3: "La Maïeutique du Non Savoir."
20. Paul Evdokimov, *La Femme et le Salut du monde* (Paris: Desclée de Brouwer, 1978), 155.
21. Eckhart, *Predigt* 38, *Deutsche Werke* 2: 227–28.
22. Marguerite Porete: "The annihilated soul gives their leave to the virtues." And Eckhart: "They have attracted in themselves the essence of all the virtues . . . so that the virtues emanate from them in a being way without their taking part in them." In Franz Pfeiffer, *Deutsche Mystiker des 14ten Jahrhunderts,* 11: 6.39–7.2. See Zum Brunn and de Libera, *Maître Eckhart,* 39ff.
23. "When a man follows the way of the world, or the way of flesh, or *the way of tradition,* knowledge of reality cannot arise in him. The wise say that this threefold way is like an iron chain, binding the feet of him who aspires to escape from the prison-house of this world. He who frees himself of the chain achieves deliverance." Shankara, in Aldous Huxley, *The Perennial Philosophy* (London: Chatto and Windus, 1946), 11.

24. "There are few who attain this knowledge here below, and even after this life it is impossible to surpass it." Augustine *De Ordine* 1.8.24. But, more in accordance with the teaching of the Church: "Whoever thinks that in this mortal life a man may so disperse the mists of bodily and carnal imaginations as to possess the undoubted light of changeless truth, and to cleave to it with the unswerving constancy of a spirit wholly estranged from common ways of life . . . he understands neither what he seeks, nor who he is who seeks it."

25. See Augustine *Confessions* 9.10.

26. "A destroyer is the ascetic Gotamo; and why is that? Because, as such, he goes against our principles," *Magandiyo* in Georg Grimm, *La religion du Bouddha, la religion de la connaissance* (Paris: Maisonneuve, 1959), 285.

27. Uma Marina Vesci, "Cultic Relationship between Man and his God as a Basic Element of Every Understanding of the Godhead", in a paper given at the second conference on "God: The Contemporary Discussion" (1982).

28. Mircea Eliade, *Méphistophélès et l'Androgyne* (Paris: Gallimard, 1962), 21–22.

29. Anagarika Govinda, *The Way of the White Clouds* (London: Rider and Co., 1974), 72.

30. Michel de Certeau, *La Fable mystique* (Paris: Gallimard, 1982). See a thoroughgoing criticism by Alain de Libera and Frederic Nef, "La Mystique, Fable ou Discours?", in *Littoral: Revue de Psychanalyse,* June 1983.

31. Shankara, *Commentary on the Gītā,* quoted by Rudolf Otto, *Mystique de l'Orient et de l'Occident,* trans. Jean Gouillard, (Paris: Payot, 1960), 33.

32. Carl-Gustav Jung, "Über die Archetypen des Kollektiven Unbewussten," in *Bewusstes und Unbewusstes* (Olten: Walter Verlag, 1971), 17ff.; *Les Racines de la Conscience,* trans. Yves le Lay (Paris: Buchet-Chastel, 1971), 19ff.; *Über Grundlagen der Analytischen Psychologie* (Hamburg: Fischer Taschenbuch Verlag, 1975), 106–7.

33. C.-G. Jung, *Psychologie de l'Inconscient,* trans. R. Cahen (Geneva: Librairie de l'Université Georg et Cie, 1972), 142–43.

34. "Mystics are human beings with a specially lively experience of the processes in the collective unconscious. Mystical experience is experience of the archetypes," C.-G. Jung, *Über die Grundlagen der Analytischen Psychologie.*

2

Mysticism: Some Methodological Remarks

CARL ALBERT KELLER

The Starting Point: Practice, Not Experience

Is it possible to say something new about mysticism? There is no dearth of serious research and scientific publications about individual mystics, about particular currents within mysticism—Hindu mysticism, Islamic mysticism and so forth—and about the phenomenon as a whole. A tremendous amount of labor has been spent exploring mystical religion. Various methods and points of view have been brought into focus. Philosophers, philologians, historians, psychologists, and analysts have added their contributions, and the variety of the results achieved is properly bewildering. If further progress is to be realized, it seems that some elementary methodological considerations are inevitable. Such is the argument of the present essay: its purpose is to clarify the nature and the method of the study of mysticism.

Having studied for several decades mystical texts from various religions—Hindu, Buddhist, Islamic, and Christian—and lectured about them, I am increasingly dissatisfied with general studies about mysticism. Such studies often lack a sound exegetical basis. The material involved is limited, and a great many theories and interpretations are simply handed down from one author to another. Above all, they start from presuppositions which seem utterly wrong.

The main presupposition which I intend to challenge is that mysticism is primarily a passive *experience,* something which *happens* to the mystic, a sudden illumination, an "oceanic feeling" which overwhelms him, a feeling of oneness, of undisturbed harmony, of ineffable felicity, of fusion with the universe, or with absolute Godhead. General studies of mysticism deal always with "mystical experience"; they try to describe it, to identify various types of experiences, and seek to explain their occurrence psychologically, philosophically, and theologically. This orientation determines the choice of proof-texts: time and again passages are quoted—always the same—where a mystic tells of a sudden change of mind, of an inspiration which carried him away quite unexpectedly into unbounded consciousness and infinite happiness.

It is true that mysticism texts from all religions mention mystical states which are different from ordinary consciousness. We even find technical terms and traditional definitions of such states. Consider the *hal,* the involuntary "states" of feeling and of consciousness which are one of the items of Sufi practice and experience, or of the four *jhāna* of Theravada Buddhism—neatly defined and accurately circumscribed in the canonical texts. Consider *satori* in Zen, or the various forms of *anubhāva,* of "experience," in Hindu mysticism.[1] There is no denying the fact that there is something like mystical experience. However, I maintain that the attempt to understand mysticism should not start from the experience—which is the result of the mystical quest—but from *the mystic's practice.* Mysticism is primarily a *practice,* a *way of life,* a *general worldview,* a *technique* aiming at specific results. The essential task of scientific research in mysticism consists in analyzing the practice of the mystics; philosophical or psychological investigation of the "experience" comes afterwards. This is the first methodological clarification which I shall introduce.

Why Start with Practice?

Following is the *justification* of the methodological shift I propose to make from mystical experience to mystical practice and technique.

Among those who have written about mysticism in general there is considerable *hesitation about the range of phenomena* taken into consideration. We hear of "everyday mysticism," of "mystical states" which "characterize every intense effort to create" (i.e., "creator's mysticism").[2] Authors discuss in great detail the relationship between mystical experience and psychotic states, between experiences arrived at by specifically "mystical techniques" and those which are drug-induced. Terms like possession, trance and the like are brought into discussion in order to elucidate mystical experience. The whole gamut of "Altered States of Consciousness" (ASC) comes to the fore, and finally all sorts of "peak experiences" may be considered as mysticism. This confusion about what should really be termed "mystical experience" makes it necessary first of all to narrow down the field of investigation and to *distinguish carefully between ASC in general, and those which pertain to mysticism in particular.* This means that we must focus attention on the mystic's will and avowed purpose, *on his practice.*

Most, if not all, general studies of mysticism try to isolate *various types of mystical experience.* Scholars distinguish between "sacred" mysticism and "profane" or "nature" mysticism (Zaehner), between "monistic and theistic" mysticism (also Zaehner), between "introvertive and extrovertive" mysticism (Stace), between "contemplative" and "dynamic" mysticism (Otto), and so on. Others insist that mystical experience is the same everywhere and is only variously colored by the "superstructure" of the mystic, or by his religious background. Doubtless there is a link between the general worldview (the so-called superstructure) of the mystic and the way he speaks of his "experience." However, which comes first: the experience, afterwards interpreted in terms of the general worldview, or *the worldview, through practice, determining, and producing the experience?* I maintain that *practice* and a special kind of *intention* precede the experience and that scholarly research must *start with the mystic's religious affiliation and practice,* since it determines his religious outlook.[3]

Throughout all religions, the amount of mystical literature is oceanic. Everywhere we find statements about mystical experiences. However, the bulk of the texts is not about experience—mystics do not dwell at length upon what they have felt or seen—but about *the path* one has to follow in order to obtain the experience. Mystical literature is didactic; mystics are teachers. They teach the "way", *hodos, tariga, mārga.* The "way" includes practice, effort, training of the body and of the mind. It comprises rites, moral precepts, conscious development of a certain outlook, inner and outer attunement to the goal one hopes someday to reach. The mystic does not look back on what he has already achieved. He looks ahead towards the steps he has yet to take. "No search pursued with the help of the Lord remains at a standstill," said the Sufi Ibn 'Aṭā' Allāh (d. 1309). The thousands or ten-thousands of Sufi aphorisms, the numerous manuals of Sufi practice;[4] the *sutta* of the Pali Scriptures and the great Sūtras of Mahāyāna; the countless mystical texts of Hinduism, and the works of the Christian mystics all contain teachings. They seek to instruct the inquirer, to help him along his way, to aid in overcoming obstacles, to warn of illusory experiences, and point always to the goal which lies ahead. A study of mysticism must *examine the real nature of mystical literature, starting with the mystic's practice* and its philosophical, theological, and social prerequisites. Only afterwards it may also enquire about the psychological consequences and colorings of the experience.

Mysticism and Altered States of Consciousness

We shall first consider the specific nature of mystical practice and experience within the general field of "Altered States of Consciousness" (ASC).[5] Admittedly, mystical practice induces some kind of ASC—the mystic perceives the world in a new way, understanding his own existence better or at least otherwise than he did before embarking on the mystical path. How are we to distinguish between mystical ASC and general ASC?

The distinction must be rooted in the manner in which ASC is induced. It is at this point that a somewhat arbitrary decision must be made. I propose to limit *mystical ASC to states which are induced by specifically religious practices,* by an effort which takes place within a specifically religious context. This restriction seems rather arbitrary, but it is certainly justified in view of the origin and the history of the terms "mystical" and "mysticism." Since the early Greek times, *la mystikē technē* has been understood as pertaining to religion.

This limitation of the term "mystical ASC" means that we eliminate from our study all other types of ASC, such as nonreligious drug experiences, drunkenness, psychotic states, "nature mysticism," "peak experience," "creator mysticism," and "everyday mysticism." All of these are real ASC—exceptional states of consciousness, very often wonderful and "revealing" in character—but they do not as a rule occur in a religious context.

But what is a religious context? How is it to be defined? Without entering into a discussion about the term "religion" I think that a *religious context is the context of communication with the Beyond,* with the beings and realities which are "above," usually unseen, whose presence is felt and sought after by the human community. It is *the context of communication with Other Life, with the Non-Conditioned, with Ultimate Authorities*—in short: the context of communication with "*Other Dimension.*" "Other Dimension" is identified and recognized in various ways: as ancestors, as mysterious spirits, as gods and goddesses, as an Absolute (a transcendent Absolute, of course), as God, or as *anatta* and *sūnyatā* of things, that is, as the nonsubstantiality of all phenomena. However defined, in all cases it is "Other Dimension" with which the human community tries to enter into contact. A mystical ASC is a state *induced by the practice of communication with "Other Dimension."*

Religious practice is always characterized by great complexity. It consists of a particular social organization, of rites, of specific inward attitudes (such as love and trust), and of certain mental structures called doctrines. Communication with "Other Dimension" is through all these elements. Mystical practice—that is, mystical communication with "Other Dimension"—adopts as a principle any means of religious communication. It lays special stress on inward communication, on meeting "Other Dimension" within the psychic set-up, in the "soul" and in its various layers, in the realm of human sensitivity, of affectivity, of the "Self"—whatever the terms in which the latter may be defined. That is why mystical practice, mystical communication with "Other Dimension," induces mystical ASC. Mystical practice is voluntary manipulation of the consciousness and psyche in order to internalize "Other Dimension," establishing intimate communication with it.

Mystical Techniques

We now come to mystical techniques in particular. Mystical practice leads to mystical ASC. Hence all techniques used anywhere in the world in order to produce ASC may also be found in mysticism: repetition of words, repetitive movements of the body, control of respiration, sense stimulation, music (rhythmical or nonrhythmical), dance, deprivation of sense stimulation, fasting, and in some cases also drugs. But all these techniques are integrated into the overall religious system. Thus, if repetition of certain words or formulas is used, the formula in question is part and parcel of the whole religious system: a specific Hindu or Buddhist *mantra* for the Hindu and the Buddhist, "*Allahu akbar*" or kindred formulas for the Muslim, "Lord Jesus Christ, Son of God, Have Mercy upon Me," for the Christian hesychast.

Moreover, in striving for mystical ASC, the presiding intention is of foremost importance. It makes a difference whether one intends to be possessed by a Loa (as in Haitian Voodoo), by a Zār (as in Islamic Egypt and the Sudan) or by a Pīr (i. e., a Muslim saint, as in some North Indian possession cults), or to contemplate the inner life of the Trinity and to be elevated into that inner life, or to realize the nonsubstantiality (*anatta, śūnyatā*) of things and of oneself, or to isolate *ātman* in its particular relationship of identity/nonidentity with *Brahman,* or to become Shiva and the means whereby Shiva enjoys the world.[6] The intention is manifestly dependent on the particular form of "Other Dimension" one seeks to join. Thus the technique, outwardly similar to nonmystical techniques, such as dancing, is dominated and modified by the nature of one's "Other Dimension." In Voodoo, for instance, each Loa (divine spirit) has his own personal drumming rhythm and answers to that rhythm alone.[7]

This raises the oft-debated question if mystical experience is everywhere the same, or rather, how the various types of mystical experiences are to be interpreted. The answer is given through the shift we propose from emphasis on experience to emphasis on mystical practice. Mysticism is the practice of a path; it consists in following a method, a technique of internalizing "Other Dimension." That means that the mystic is always on the way, always in progress. He never arrives at the end—it is always ahead of him. No real mystic would ever pretend to have definitely and finally reached the end of his search. He would have glimpses of it, but would again fall back into preliminary and ordinary states of mind. The end which lies before him, the goal his practice is directed to, is *"Other Dimension" such as he, in his particular religious context, understands it.* He will always be on the way, and thus his mystical experience will always be fashioned according to his particular conception of "Other Dimension."[8]

The mystic of course makes use of all the other means of communication with "Other Dimension" which his religion offers: counselling by religious authorities and competent masters, rites, prayers, and so forth. In pursuing his practice, the mystic would rarely ever consciously oppose other aspects of his religion. Moreover, rites may be internalized as part of his mystical pursuit—the Sufi's holy center of pilgrimage is *not only* the material Ka'ba but the Ka'ba in his heart—which does not mean that he would refuse to go physically on pilgrimage. The Hindu mystic accomplishes ordinary *pūjā* like all faithful Hindus, but he would also insist on the value of *antaryāga,* of internalized worship in the inner recesses of the heart. It is wrong to construe a fundamental opposition between mystical religion and ordinary religious practice.

Mysticism and the Origin of Religions

The question now arises *whether religion may be the product of mystical practice and experience.* This is a difficult and many-sided problem which cannot be adequately dealt with in the present context. Here are only some hints at the manner in which I think it should be possible to tackle it.

All religions are ultimately founded on primal religious practice as observed in tribal societies. As far back as can be traced in historical reconstruction, man has always been religious. Human communities—natural, ethnic communities—have always tried to contact and use for their benefit "Other Dimension," whatever their form of approach. Religious practice has always implied, besides outward, material means of communication, the use of inward communication. We have defined such inward communication as the essence of mystical practice. Thus we may say that mystical practice is part and parcel of all religious practice, primal religions not excepted. I refer to the various forms of communication with the Spirit Dimension which are subsumed under the term "shamanism": early and universal techniques of approaching the Spirit Dimension and entreating it to help the human community.

In the course of history—often in times of crisis—a charismatic personality or unusually gifted shaman may arise who by intense mystical practice and intuition may discover a new name or aspect of "Other Dimension." It may also happen that one particular element of "Other Dimension"—a "spirit" or "god"—may be revealed to him in a new and revolutionary way. Such a charismatic personality or gifted shaman may thus become a prophet. If his prophecy is adhered to by a sufficient number of followers, and is adequately developed into a complete system of communication containing the necessary philosophical and theological underpinning, he might even become the founder of a new religion. The experience of all the great founders of religions—the Buddha, Jesus, Muhammad, and others—followed this course. It is particularly significant that the prophecy or new insight of each of them was prepared by extended mystical practice—for years in the case of the Buddha, for days and months at least in the case of Jesus and Muhammad. There never appears a new religion without stern mystical practice.

We stated that a prophet "discovers" a new aspect or name of "Other Dimension," that impresses him as being particularly relevant. But what about the philosophical and theological problem of the nature and unity of "Other Dimension" in itself? Is there a final identity of "Other Dimension," a Reality and Being which comprises ancestors, spirits, mystical forces, gods, God, the Trinity, the

Absolute, and *śūnyatā?* Can these diverse forms of "Other Dimension" be considered as simple *names* given by men to a Reality—the final "Other Dimension"—which is beyond names and forms?

This question, the most intricate and profound a human being may ask, can receive an answer only on the basis of the mystic's total religious system. In any case the answer will be a *confession of personal conviction.* It is not a matter of debate. Some Hindus would indeed admit that all individual forms of the Beyond are only names; some Buddhists would say that everything—men, gods and Absolutes—is *śūnya,* i. e., void of proper substantiality. Muslims would almost invariably reply that Allah alone really exists, and Christians would normally refuse to bracket the Trinity. Why quarrel about these divergences? Let us admit that "Other Dimension" exists and that through mystical practice it can be approached however one chooses, in whatever form it reveals itself to the seeker. Let us never forget that the mystical quest implies strenuous work and ceaseless effort. In the long run, the mystic is happy enough to encounter an aspect of the particular form of "Other Dimension" he hopes to internalize. Inwardly he will always be convinced that his persuasion leads to the ultimate form of "Other Dimension." If other names and forms exist, they must perforce be contained in the one he is attracted to. Mystical practice is a total personal engagement, and ultimate questions can only receive ultimate—or penultimate—answers on the basis of ultimate personal involvement.

NOTES

1. Compare for instance *Nārada-Bhakti-Sūtra,* 1:6: "He becomes (*bhavati*) drunken, he *becomes* paralysed, he *becomes* one who rejoices in *ātman.*"
2. Both in Ben-Ami Scharfstein, *Mystical Experience* (Baltimore: Penguin Books, 1974).
3. See the two important methodological volumes edited by Steven T. Katz: *Mysticism and Philosophical Analysis* (London: Sheldon Press, 1978) and *Mysticism and Religious Tradition* (Oxford: Oxford University Press, 1982).
4. Like the famous and very popular *Manāzil al-sā' irīn,* by Ansāri (1006–1089).
5. Investigation of Altered States of Consciousness (ASC) is a very important field of medical and psychological research; for its introduction into the study of religious and mystical psychology, see especially the work of Charles T.

Tart, for instance, *Transpersonal Psychologies* (London: Routledge & Kegan Paul, 1975).

6. I am referring to the South Indian Shaiva-Siddhanta.

7. Gilbert Rouget, *La musique et la transe* (Paris: Gallimard, 1980), has shown that the capacity of music to induce states of trance and of possession is always culturally determined; a type of music which induces trance in one cultural context is utterly ineffective in another one. See also Sheila S. Walker, *Ceremonial Spirit Possession in Africa and Afro-America* (Leiden: Brill, 1972).

8. This means that I fully endorse the conclusions arrived at by Steven T. Katz in *Mysticism and Philosophical Analysis* and *Mysticism and Religious Tradition*.

3

The Sound of Many Waters

P. JOSEPH CAHILL

Of peculiar interest to me is the word "unification." "To make one" or "to move in the direction of unity" summarizes quite well the issues I shall deal with in this chapter. The term denotes human effort, the creation of human order, without simultaneously implying the absence of an objective basis for this undertaking. By connotation the word suggests the privation of unity as a wistful, though persistent, deficiency of the human state. It even carries the overtone that the creation of unity is a specifically human enterprise, one which fends off the classic enemies of humankind—chaos and its great ally, meaninglessness. Nor does the word "unification" necessarily imply any kind of totalitarian control in which pluralism and diversity disappear or are forcibly suppressed. Rather the verbal root proposes the possibility of what Josiah Royce long ago called "a new level of being,"[1] and what Northrop Frye portrayed as a higher integration and community of vision.[2]

In this context I will explore "Experiences of God and/or the Ultimate." These experiences are not abstractions but historical occurrences to individuals or groups as real and palpable as ourselves. The experience of God takes place in time and place and therefore always leaves a legacy of memory and hope—the remembrance, however vague, that someone experienced a hierophany; the hope, however dim, that it may recur.

One phrase summarizes the life and work of Iñigo de Loyola, mystic, psychologist, soldier, administrator, and founder of the Society of Jesus. That phrase is "to find God in all things." The injunction is intended to be universal, both extensively and intensively. It was Iñigo's belief that to find God in all things was the purpose of the truly human life.

Each individual was to find God in health, in sickness, in riches, in poverty, in honor, in dishonor, in a long life, in a short life.[3] No less was the individual to find God in plants, animals, human beings, in the elements, the entire world of nature.[4]

To the Jesuit scholastics engaged in protracted and intense study, a seemingly profane activity, he continually proposed the vision that one could as readily find God in study as in formal prayer and worship. He was engaged from the very beginning in a running battle with leading Spanish Jesuits who wished to impose long hours of prayer on Jesuit scholastics. The key to understanding the Ignation stance lies in the very first rule for scholastics in which we read: "Let our Scholastics attempt to guard a purity of spirit and a right intention in their studies, seeking nothing else in these studies than the divine glory and the fruit of souls. . . ."[5]

Three very active verbs, to intend, to try, to seek, suggest that to find God in all things is a very active process, an internal orientation demanding considerable attention, effort, awareness, and spiritual intensity.[6]

There is a peculiar force and challenge behind the charge "to find God in all things." It is not a pious wish nor a platitude of positive thinking. Rather the statement manifests the extraordinary experience of a man who actually succeeded in finding God in all things. This happened to Iñigo and therefore is within the range of human possibility.

The jejune prose of this Basque soldier cannot obscure the fact that Iñigo's life was filled with mystical experiences. The profundity and frequency of Iñigo's mystical experiences normally have not occupied either psychologists or historians of religion. There are many grounds for this omission, not the least of which is that his writings, compared to John of the Cross or Teresa de Avila, are in the words of Brodrick, like "a sparrow among nightingales."[7] This observation suggests that Iñigo knew there were more sparrows than nightingales in this world. I personally think Iñigo's reluctance to dwell on his own mystical experiences was not exclusively due to a lack of literary skill. Rather, it came from his conviction that his own experiences may have been higher in degree than those of others, but no different from those available to anyone genuinely seeking to find God in all things. If this was not the case, why would he take such enormous pains to write *The Spiritual Exercises* —his treasury of spiritual direction for leading a truly human life? Ever present was the presumption of divine favor, or grace, which is ultimately the source of the special hierophany, as genius is a gift—not an acquired characteristic. Nonetheless such a gift will dissipate without persistent human endeavor.

After an initial tribulation period comparable to that of Gautama, Iñigo paradoxically broke with a thousand years of Christian tradition, and founded a new religious order as his first major step in finding God in all things. This star gazer, who could find God in any form of nature and even behind the desk in Rome, founded an order distinguished not by clerical garb, vowed to no monastery, bound to no obligatory choral prayers, nor sequestered in religious hermitage. This order represented a complete break with all forms of past monasticism. At its heart beat the curious antiphonal relationship between freedom and obedience, innovation and tradition, conservatism, and liberalism.

Though his military metaphors preoccupied later interpreters, Iñigo's break with tradition, as well as his realization of the varied paths to God, make it clear that God is found in creative imagination and individual circumstance as much as in prescribed litanies and ascetic discipline. To those giving the *Spiritual Exercises,* Iñigo cautioned "it is necessary to consider with great care the condition and endowments of each individual. . . ."[8] He further stated, "The *Spiritual Exercises* must be adapted to the condition of the one who is to engage in them, that is, to his age, education, and talent."[9] Iñigo would not have thought twice about his concordance with John Calvin in another statement in the *Exercises:* "Granted that it be very true that no one can be saved without being predestined. . . ."[10] Nor would he have blinked at his agreement with Luther that all is due to grace,[11] though he adds a psychologically sound precaution that emphasizing grace may lead to de-emphasizing freedom and hence human responsibility.

James Brodrick, articulate, urbane, and gentlemanly scholar of early Jesuit history, humorously noted the "remarkable parallelism between the early religious development of Ignatius and of John Bunyan, though, as has been pointed out, had they met, they would have shrunk from one another in horror, unconscious of their deep kinship."[12]

Still we remain on the threshold of understanding what it means to find God in all things. From this recalling of the person who uttered and exemplified the statement, let us pursue the trail of memory to the experiential interpretations given the phrase by a few followers of Iñigo.

The notorious Bull of Boniface VIII "made the most sweeping

papal claims to temporal supremacy in all Church history. 'We declare, state and define and pronounce,' Boniface wrote, 'that it is altogether necessary to salvation for every human creature to be subject to the Roman Pontiff.'"[13] The original Latin is more vigorous: "*Porro subesse Romano Pontifici omni humanae creaturae declaramus, definimus et pronuntiamus omnino de necessitate salutis.*"[14] This document included the infelicitous theory of the two swords confided to the church. Though Boniface's reign was brief, the theory of the conjunction of church and state and the temporal supremacy of the Roman Pontiff in this unhappy alliance basically remained in effect until modern times.

Jesuit John Courtney Murray broke the stranglehold this doctrine held on Latin Christianity, and therefore on Europe, and lessened its power in widening differences between the Latin and Greek Church. The impact came first from his book, *We Hold These Truths,*[15] and then in the Document of Vatican II, "Declaration on Religious Freedom,"[16] of which he was the principal architect. Murray's discovery of God in the American separation of church and state—a new dimension within human history—led to this momentous advance. This was to find God in what seemed to be simply a political enterprise, one motivated as much by the desire to avoid the unfortunate past church-state entanglements as by any particular religious vision. While we should not forget that no one religion has a monopoly on truth, neither should we ignore the responsibilities imposed on religious historians, theologians and believers alike, to enter the delicate field of critical hermeneutical evaluations.

Here is a second instance of finding God in all things—duplex, rather like a simple fugue: Jesuit Gerard Manley Hopkins honored a lay brother Alphonsus, with a poem. For some forty years Alphonsus was the porter; his work was humble and repetitive. Hopkins found God in poetic creation; Alphonsus found God in the simple act of answering the door, presumably with the traditional thought, " *Hospes venit, Christus venit.*" "A guest comes, Christ comes."

In honour of
St. Alphonsus Rodriguez
Laybrother of the Society of Jesus

Honour is flashed off exploit, so we say;
And those strokes once that gashed flesh or galled shield
Should tongue that time now, trumphet now that field,
And, on the fighter, forge his glorious day.

On Christ they do and on the martyr may;
But be the war within, the brand we wield
Unseen, the heroic breast not outward-steeled,
Earth hears no hurtle then from fiercest fray.
Yet God (that hews mountain and continent,
Earth, all, out; who, with trickling increment,
Veins violets and tall trees makes more and more)
Could crowd career with conquest while there went
Those years and years by of world without event
That in Majorca Alfonso watched the door.[18]

A third instance of finding God in all things resembles what Hopkins called crowding "career with conquest." It is the example of Matteo Ricci who entered China's Kwangtung province four hundred years ago. His amazing ability to learn Chinese, his genuine respect for the Chinese classics, and his adoption of Mandarin dress and habit ultimately led to his acceptance in 1601 in Peking where he was court mathematician and astronomer. Here the Chinese acquired their very first notion about modern Europe, and Europe acquired its first reports about China. Ricci directed his religious efforts to finding the primordial tradition that lay behind the seemingly discrepant teachings of Confucianism and Christianity in hopes of bridging the cultural gap between the two.

At roughly the same time Roberto de Nobili (1577–1656) sailed for India in 1604. After first ministering to the untouchables, he decided his work would be more effective if he adopted the habits and customs of the Brahmans. So successful was he in this venture, this first Westerner to encounter Hinduism's sacred teachings that he aroused suspicion among ecclesiastical authorities. Although he gave a reasoned account of his work, he was subjected to an inquisition which resulted in the suspension of his work until 1623. The instances of both Ricci and de Nobili are not only pioneering forays into the history of religions—the attempts to find God present in other cultures—but are also genuinely comparative criticisms.

A final example is more complex and at the same time perhaps more pertinent—that of the famous *reducciones* in Latin America. The Paraguay reductions were founded in 1609 as a place for teaching the Indians the Spanish way of life while utilizing them as laborers. The territory then comprised large parts of present day Argentina, Paraguay, Chile, Brazil, and Bolivia. Later, the territory was directed by Jesuits.

The *conquistadores* regarded the Indians as barely above the level of animals (they compared them to orangutans). Beginning their murder and plunder in Mexico, the conquistadores were little affected by the humane admonitions of the Dominican, Las Casas, even when he advocated the human rights of all people.[18] Pope Paul III, the very Pope who had given his approbation to the Jesuits, came out with his famous Bull, "*Sublimis Deus,*" equivalently affirming the equal dignity of all human beings by virtue of creation. He condemned robbery of Indians and castigated those who deprived the Indians of freedom. What finally hindered the *conquistadores* and their patrons was an order by King Philip III stating that no white person, with the exception of the governor, could visit the settlements without the permission of the Jesuits.

Using a waterfall of the Uruguay River as a barrier against invasion, the Jesuits began their work with the Indians by singing as they travelled back and forth on the rivers and streams. This brought the shy and retiring, not to mention fearful, Indians from their hiding places. Music first established a bond between Jesuit and Indian. From music, to the imitation of figures made by the Jesuits, to the common possession of the means of production coupled with private initiative, to the creation of small states in a confederation, to the art of self-defense, to the defeat of the Spanish and Portuguese by the Indians—this is the historical progression of a group of men "finding God in all things." Yet history documents another trend—the dreary decree in 1750 that the seven protecting territories of the Indians should be given to the Portuguese. Shortly after this, in 1759, the Jesuits were suppressed in Portugal; in 1766, in Spain. Thus ended this sophisticated effort "to find God in all things," an attempt that one author has called, "*Eine Utopie im Urwald.*"[19]

Thus some two hundred years after the death of Iñigo de Loyola, his now highly institutionalized order could discover if indeed God could be found in all things. Was God present in the dissolution of the order to which many had consecrated themselves? Could God be found in the disappearance of the humane and compassionate work to which so many had contributed so much? The Jesuits were in the position of a Job with no advocate to record and perpetuate their reactions. One thing is certain: they had long been taught the statement of Ignatius when asked what he would do if his beloved Society of Jesus were dissolved. This, like dreams realized suddenly turning to ashes, was supposedly the supreme catastrophe for a man committed to his esteemed divine enterprise. His well-known answer: he asked for one-quarter of an hour of prayer to reconcile himself to the dissolution of the Society and replied he would emerge from this seeming catastrophe even happier than before.[20]

Iñigo de Loyola uncovered buried hierophanies; he sought to live deeper than the surface of experience. Amidst this temporal world Iñigo saw the arcane transactions that elevate the human spirit. His major contribution to the world is his attempt to communicate this vision, primarily through the largely forgotten *Spiritual Exercises.*

To those of us who have attempted to follow the teachings of this extraordinary individual, there is an ever-present feeling of awe and respect, and the persistent wonder at how often such people appear. It is questionable if we would recognize such prodigies today. He called himself a pilgrim. But in his case, as in the instances of all religious geniuses, he understood what this really meant.

This was brought home to me as I was writing this paper and my seven year old son walked by my desk and placed his statue of E. T. near the fireplace. Thinking I already knew the answer, I asked, "What's that?"

He replied, "That's E. T. He is a spirit that's alive. He is not real."

This *coincidentia oppositorum* accompanied me through the entire conception and composition of this journey into the past.[21]

Some have encountered Iñigo of Loyola only in the bellicose climate of reformation and counter reformation invective, or in the emotionally charged words, "Jesuitical," "casuistry," "the means justify the end." To them, I commend the man who committed himself to finding God in all things, and whose supreme contribution to the world is the little book of the *Spiritual Exercises.* Unlike many other mystics, particularly Western ones, Iñigo envisions everyone potentially capable of finding God in all things. Instead of providing us with a poetic addition to our literary universe—one that would surely have been of great interest—he left a map of spiritual growth, paths one may follow if one wants to find God in all things, a vision that can bring hope and the glory of God into the most ordinary life. It is no accident that the *Spiritual Exercises* begin with creation and a primeval disorientation and end with a contemplation to obtain divine love. These are immediately followed by the well-known three methods of prayer—methods that can be exercised by anyone under any conditions.

My own experience is that this little book, now largely unknown even within the Christian community and therefore losing its denominational origins, may extend its message of hope to a far wider audience. So may this small exercise of memory beget hope which may move us toward community and the finding of God in all things. Whatever the ramifications of seeking God in all things, one assured result is that we can thereby discover ourselves and unleash our creative powers.

NOTES

1. Josiah Royce, *The Problem of Christianity* (Chicago: University of Chicago Press, 1968), 9.
2. Northrop Frye, *The Great Code: The Bible and Literature* (New York: Harcourt Brace Jovanovich, 1982), 227–30.
3. Ignatius of Loyola, *The Spiritual Exercises of St. Ignatius,* trans. Louis J. Puhl (Westminster, Md.: The Newman Press, 1957), no. 23, p. 12.
4. Ibid., nos. 230–37, pp. 101–3.
5. *Regulae Societatis Jesu* (Rome: Curia Praepositi Generalis, 1947), 63.
6. The same injunctions may be found here and there throughout the various rules governing offices that Jesuits may hold in their work. After the "Summary of the Constitution" there follows, "Common Rules," "Rules of Modesty," "Rules of Priests," etc.
7. James Brodrick, S. J., *The Origin of the Jesuits* (London: Longmans, Green and Co., 1945), 17.
8. Loyola, *Spiritual Exercises,* no. 14, p. 6.
9. Ibid., no. 18, p. 7.
10. Ibid., no. 366, p. 160. Ignatius, in 1528, by sheer coincidence attached himself to Montaigu, a College of the University of Paris, "from which Spartan establishment John Calvin had shortly before retired." Brodrick, 34.
11. Ibid., no. 369, p. 161.
12. Brodrick, 11.
13. Sarel Eimerl and the Editors of Time-Life Books, *Giotto* (Alexandria, Va.: Time-Life Books, 1967), 104.
14. Henrici Denzinger, *Enchiridion Symbolorum,* ed. Karl Rahner (Freiburg: Herder, 1957), no. 461, p. 220. Little was said in theological manuals about Boniface's personal behavior which included appearing in imperial robes and proclaiming himself to be the Emperor, to be Caesar, as well as other unusual ways of behaving.
15. John Courtney Murray, *We Hold These Truths* (New York: Sheed and Ward, 1960).

16. *The Documents of Vatican II,* Walter Abbott, general ed. (New York: Guild Press, 1966), 675–96.
17. Gerard Manley Hopkins, *A Selection of His Poems and Prose,* ed. W. H. Gardner (London: Penguin Books, 1958), 66–67.
18. Bayard Q. Morgan & Friedrich W. Strothmann, eds., *Reading German* (New York: Ginn & Co., 1943), 68.
19. Ibid., 64.
20. Josef Stierli, "*Gottsuchen in allen Dingen,*" *Ignatius von Loyola,* (Freiburg: Walter-Verlag, 1981), 206.
21. Ignatius of Loyola, *The Autobiography of St. Ignatius Loyola,* trans. Joseph F. O'Callaghan, ed. intro. John C. Olin (New York: Harper Torchbooks, 1974). Ignatius refers to himself in the third person and as "the pilgrim."

4

Myth, Religion, and Experience on the Agenda of Theology

VIGGO MORTENSEN

A German proverb concludes about a young doctor that he's bound to have a new cemetary; about a young lawyer that he'll entangle anything into disputes; about a young theologian that he'll overcrowd hell with souls. Since they'll tend to affect things in accordance with their rules and regulations, lacking the experience which alone makes man wise. Hence they offend and make mistakes, thereby being to the detriment of both man and the matter. —Martin Luther

Myth and Religion

The New Religious Movements as Cultural Phenomena The last fifteen years have seen the upspring of a new phenomenon in Western Europe, much to the distress of established theologians, namely, the new religious movements. The phenomenon has proved viable, grown and bloomed, much to the surprise of those who initially doomed it on their foundation of dialectic theology and Marxist theory.

The number of practicing new believers may not be impressive when compared with the member figures of established churches. But their numbers are rising steadily, indicating that the movement has entered into people's cultural sphere and has found "fertile soil". This fact tells us something about our culture today—but what?

One feature stands out significantly: the interplay between our technological and religious renaissances. Simultaneously with this uprising of new religious movements, we have entered the period of the third industrial revolution—the age of technology, of information, and of the computer. This influences our understanding of life as a whole including the religious aspect. Religious life becomes technological as well. Yoga, transcendental, or similar forms of meditation do not present a world view or the meaning of life. Rather, they present a technique, a recipe for how to get beyond ourselves, how to reach a state of ecstasy, or how to merely relax from an overworked existence.

This is one point of view. Another point of view may question if the movement is merely restorative. Is the phenomenon only remaining islands in the hard stream of secularization? Is it a refuge for the person who can't cope with our modern world, marked by technology and science and who is prevented from trying to change it because of sheer lack of perspective? Or does the new religious movement simply show that man actually revolts against having to function in a technological society in which nobody cares about meaning?

To throw some light on this, we may begin by quoting the Polish writer Leszek Kolakowskij, a nondogmatic Marxist, now a philosopher at Oxford: "The legitimate need for myth face to face with the legitimate defence against the dangers of myth; this clash is the neuralgic point in our civilization." I split the quotation in order to more easily examine the individual parts. In that way we should get a closer understanding of the new religious movement as a cultural phenomenon.

The Kolakowskij quotation claims that man has a legitimate need for myth. In our time, such a claim cannot be taken for granted. We have seen so much objectivity and demythologization, so much talk about myth and ideology as being something veiling, that the myth has been subjected to hate. Kolakowskij is right in proclaiming man's need for myth. In earlier times it was a natural thing for myth to integrate and ritualize various experiences, thereby giving life shape. Such is the case in ancient Israel, described by Danish religious historian, Johannes Pedersen. In his book *Israel I–II*[1] he "provide[s] a psychological understanding of Israel's philosophy of life and the social rules in which it appears." The psychological understanding is provided through identifying more closely with the culture—a method Johannes Pedersen learned from the Danish religious historian V. Grønbech. Such an identification respects the integrity of the culture. For instance, certain words and phrases remain untranslated since a translation might give false associations. Thus, Johannes Pedersen uses the word *naephaes* rather than soul, to avoid reading a dualistic Greek body-soul interpretation into the holistic Hebraic anthropology. The word myth is not included in the subject index of Johannes Pedersen's impressive work on Israel. And yet, the book is one long description of the mythical interpretation of life by which the Israelite lived.

Any people are at any time ruled by a myth, a collective opinion, giving the people identity and solidarity and making individual activities seem meaningful. The ancient Hebraic myth centered around phenomena like "blessing" and "covenant." Is our society influenced by a myth as well?

For a number of years the myth in modern Western European societies was called the 'belief in progress'. It was apparent in many ways—as a trust in a future solution to the difficulties we face today, that is, through newly discovered technology. It was manifested as a belief in times getting better every day, or in a belief of increased future productivity.

To believe in technological progress assumes religious dimensions when one believes that scientists and experts have limitless capabilities. To believe in moral progress would readily seem more difficult but the same rule applies. Was there not a shared belief in the sixties that moral progress would be around the corner as soon as liberation was carried through? The question is, however, whether or not a belief in progress can actually accomplish what people think it can, namely, can it make our individual lives and actions meaningful?

There is nothing wrong with praising a belief in progress. We all do it in varying degrees. However, it is wrong and dangerous to think that a belief in progress can answer all our questions in the manner of a myth, giving meaningful cohesion to life. This could be called the dialectics of the belief in progress. Hence we come up against new and undiscovered fields when working to solve a problem—not by chance, but during the same line of work. It is a question of fighting for progress without believing in it.

The Myth Crisis and the Necessity of the Myth Through the sixties, Bultmann was *the* name within European continental theology. Rudolf Bultmann, professor of New Testament exegesis in Marburg through almost a generation with at least one leg firmly planted in the nineteenth century, had presented during the war a program to demythologize the New Testament. It was effectless, however, since people had other things on their mind at that time. Bultmann's basis was the fact that a person, who one moment uses electric light and listens to the radio, cannot the very next moment without further reflection enter the universe of the New Testament—a universe with a mythological world picture and dealing with supernatural interventions.

Bultmann did not intend to abolish myths like virgin birth,

ascension and others, though he was often misinterpreted in that direction. Not eliminate, but interpret, were his words. This interpretation consisted of listening to the myth's concern and expressing it in a modern nonmythic language. The myth, according to Bultmann, was almost a primitive science and carried an understanding of life. When interpreting it, it was essential to make this understanding of life transferable to modern times.

The philosophy of life carried by the myth was, according to Bultmann, similar to the views presented by existential philosophy. The demythologization was followed by an existential interpretation. That Bultmann so vehemently clung to a fixed philosophy, Heidegger's existential analysis, as the adequate analysis of modern man's life, may therefore be the decisive weakness in Bultmann's position. However, this position did have an extreme power of fascination throughout the sixties.

One of Bultmann's contemporaries, Dietrich Bonhoeffer, imprisoned and executed for opposing Hitler, in his almost visionary letters from prison, "Resistance and Devotion", drafted the idea that the Western European world was facing a period of non-religion, and one should therefore work to interpret the Biblical phrases in a nonreligious way. A second German theologian, Friedrich Gogarten, who held different views before and during World War II, developed the thesis of a positive connection between Christianity and secularization. The central Pauline and Lutheran talk of Christian freedom instigated secularization, that is, the process by which institutions, norms and conventions, formerly religious and Christ-oriented became autonomous, independent. So, if understood correctly, Christianity had to welcome secularization. It was a legitimate outcome of the preaching of the gospel. Disregarding disagreements in other areas, one point stood clear: secularization was breaking through, a non-religious period was approaching; when preaching Christianity it was therefore necessary to use measures such as demythologization.

The Kolakowskij quotation also points out the dangers associated with myth. It was precisely the eye for such dangers—for instance, false identity—which started the demythologization.

It is important when looking back on that period to realize why these positions had such an appeal. This was due mainly to a general view advocating honesty and realism. Things were to be coherent; people should not live in two different worlds. Yet the world at that time suffered a marked lack of coherence. People were only interested in the relevance of Biblical myth as it pertained to man's immediate understanding of himself. There was an intense underlying concentration on the individual, supported by both a Luther and a Kierkegaard renaissance.

Two things inevitably clashed with this theology and myth-understanding. For one thing, the message was too poor, too curtailed, too small. For another, people realized that the secular philosophy of life, which they indirectly supported, had some unfortunate effects.

The tool of this clash was a different interpretation of "myth." Taking as his basis the fact that myths often have aetiological features, Bultmann characterized the myth as a primitive science, exposed as false in the light of our knowledge, and which therefore must be conquered.

Recent myth research clarified what Bultmann also stated, namely that the myth has an incorporated understanding of existence. Interpreted so, the myth becomes a narrative of actual events which "happen again" when the myth is narrated. In this way, mythological thinking is more than primitive science. It is a feeling of dependence as well, and the feeling of being addressed. Religion can therefore make use of mythological language since it transmits a message, making the hearer part of the myth. The myth does not merely satisfy the intellectual questioning after the origin and coherence of all things. Rather, its primary function is to help us get through life. In the myth, the threatened person asks for life. The myth connected with the ritual—the narrative and the act which symbolize aspects of a cosmic order—offer an alternate interpretation of man's own experience. For the myth contains a conception of life, and present experience is interpreted in the light of the events told about in the myth. It is, therefore, a part of the sacred canopy which every society needs.[2]

Man may adapt himself within the order created by the myth. No theoretical explanation of coherence is achieved through this, but one can feel a certain power emanating from the myth—a power shaping one's conduct, inspiring one to act in accordance with the ends and values implied by the myth. The myth's social function is to shape and sanction society's moral norms, thereby becoming the cohesive force in an otherwise atomized world. Out of this, social solidarity, group identity and common harmony develop. At the individual level, the myth may contribute by dampening anxiety when the ego is threatened, since conflicts in the myth can be solved symbolically.

These explanations establishing the purpose of the myth do not include all answers. The question prevails whether or not the myth leads to comprehension. One answer may be that the myth is a useful fiction; Carl Jung has a deeper answer. He looks upon the myth as a projection of an inner psychic drama, a product of the collective unconscious. Thus the myth is looked upon as man's immediate method of experience, a collective dream presenting its elements in individual dreams. One dreams in mythological shapes and universal symbols, intuitively recognized.

That is one way of expressing that the myth leads to comprehension. The myth is not just "lies and bloody poetry." It provides recognition, knowledge about life and information about actions.

The reason for the current awakened interest in the myth and its narrative is that the myth on which Western European societies are founded, the belief in progress, is rapidly cracking. It should be evident from the preceding comments that the myth is of vital importance to both the individual and society. A new myth is therefore required. But a new, collective myth does not float about ready to be caught. Its formation is a time-consuming process—and we are right in the middle of the turn. The market is flooded with quick offers to fill the life-perspective vacuum created by the "myth crisis." These offers abound: new religious waves, meditation techniques and psycho-dynamic theories. Which shall it be? The survivor will see, since these items must prove their worth in practice. If our own tradition of narratives and myths contains an understanding of life and reflects some attitudes which must be addressed, it is essential to get them out in the open to see if they are of any value. The cultural struggle is a struggle on narratives. The Danish historian, theologian, and poet Nicolai Frederik Severin Grundtvig (1783–1872)[3] called it "the living word."

The new religious trend was therefore a symptom of what I have previously called the myth crisis. Although Marxism and dominant dialectic theology agreed that religion was the opiate of the people, religion sprang up, apparently viable and blooming. However, not all the flowers were beautiful. Like Kolakowskij said, there may be reasons for warning against the dangers of the myth, respecting its legitimate needs. This means we have to distinguish between religions.

One type of religion deserves the criticism of Marxism and dialectic theology, since it is nothing but mere escapism: escape from assuming a responsibility within society, escape from a world ruled by science and technology, escape from the future.

Yet, there is a different type of religion which has survived modern criticism and which still exists. This new type of religion confronts religious questions on a new level of experience and reflection.

According to many, the new religions which we encounter now are not "new" at all, but are variations of what has been presented to us in the past. Doubtless, this is true for many of the new religious movements. However, others really show traces of something new. If we are to understand these movements, we are bound to start reconsidering religion and what is meant by saying that Christianity is a religion. We must understand Christianity, not only from a religio-historical and religio-sociological viewpoint, but also by way of its nature as a means of religious life-interpretation.

Christianity as Religious Life-Interpretation Western European theology, to a large extent, has not been for the man in the street during the recent fifty years. People have never stopped looking upon and using Christianity as a religion. The theologians are the ones who have been fussing with the problem of the conflict between popular religion and church, between religion and gospel. The usual dialectic theological differentiation between religion and gospel has never won support in the people. To treat Christianity seriously as a religion may be done in different ways. It means having to work from a philosophical viewpoint, explicitly on the religious interpretation contained in Christianity, notably as a theologically necessary piece of work. We see in the Christian idea of creation a religious interpretation of life which can today answer man's religious questioning.

We cannot avoid talking about religion, though existential theology has universally banned it, and Marxist criticism has cursed it as creating illusion. The question is *how* to talk about religion.

Necessarily confronting the new religious movements is nothing less than a new theology starting with the concept of religion. Considering the results of modern criticism of religion one must consider what Christianity means as far as religion is understood as a mode of life-interpretation.

When encountering a phenomenon, we do not simply register it; we interpret it. We understand it, relating it to its environment and to ourselves as well. Life consists of contrasts often insoluble to us.

Our normal reaction is to try to smooth the contrasts. We prefer the unambiguous understanding of reality. But preserving ambiguity, preserving contrasts as contrasts is exactly the task of religion. Religion has its foundation where man cannot explain these contrasts, and its task is to create space, to give life meaning and shape within this reality of contrasts.

All right, people will say, this may be true for other religions, but not for Christianity. It is the brand new which contradicts all our hopes and wishes to make man free to act, whatever his position. True, but people must not be too hasty in presenting the Christian demand for exclusiveness and they must be careful not to misplace it.

If we cling to an interpretation of joy in life and of sadness in suffering and death, the question arises as to the interpretation of these phenomena. Earlier, a number of interpretation systems were available to help in understanding life and death. Our situation is difficult, because several of these interpretation systems have lost their convincing power, just like the myths.

Christian theology must now aim at creating new interpretation systems to be used by the individual and society in order to regain their identity. Such an interpretation system lies hidden in the Christian philosophy of creation. Included is a religious interpretation of life's insoluble contrasts, its glory and agony. This interpretation presents itself as a framework of understanding and as a background for future actions. The myth gives inspiration and orientation for actions. This was the myths' function during the early days of the Danish folk high school. Farmhands visited the high school, listened to the old Nordic mythological stories, and then went home and formed cooperative dairies.

Admittedly, myth and religion may have negative social consequences, but these consequences can be avoided. The danger is that it has effect only on the individual's liberation. If, however, one is aware of this danger, the danger is easy to avoid. One has to choose as a starting point man's legitimate need for myth instead of avoiding myth. The advantage of the mythic-symbolic narrative is that it preserves complexity in its description of reality. It reconciles otherwise incompatible contrasts.

Which interpretation is the best? Which mythic-symbolic narrative presents the best interpretation of life? This is the crux of the matter. It may be a choice between different myths. The criterion upon which one has to base one's choice is whether the complexity in the description of reality has been preserved.

Theology and Experience

Thinking theologically about religion in this way means putting relations between theology and religion on the agenda. The Danish philosopher and theologian Knud Ejler Løgstrup (1905–1981)[4] presented us a work within the philosophy of religion, seeing a connection between belief and experience: "The religious total interpretation of life relates to experiences, that there's nothing unusual about."[5] Too often a distinction has been made between theology and experience in order to escape from a religion of experience. Løgstrup writes about theologians' reluctance to talk about experiences, explaining it with the history that theology has undergone. It is a history which has "more than once since the break of pietism been through a Christianity of experience, and *vestigia terrent*. Just look at the narcissism in its wake.[6] The front against a religion of experience is both correct and important, but the end result should not be a total separation of belief and experience. In the words of Gerhard Ebeling: "The loss of experience . . . may be a fatal disease for theology."[7]

The connection of belief with reality is at stake in the question of relations between belief and experience. This connection is disguised if theological comments are mere claims without any base in experienced reality. Two things explain the reluctance to give experience theological significance: partly, a one-sided understanding of revelation, equating it either to a written book or a rationally understood deposit; partly, a suspicion that any application of "immediate experiences" covered for all sorts of black outs, lacking analysis of the social and historical context from which these experiences stemmed.

It is beneficial to keep in mind that to criticize religion for being based on experience is quite a modern innovation carrying some undesired effects in its wake. One such effect was that theology and the preachings of the church were pure textual readings and postulated promises of salvation, out of touch with ordinary people's experience of reality.

Two Concepts of Experience What has brought this de-emphasis of experience into theology? Among other things, the entire Western world-conquering activities have occupied the concept of experience, making it identical with empiricism and its application. However, belief and experience are connected, and one cannot do without the other. Thus we must deal with at least two concepts of experience: first, *a concept of common sense experience, the phenomenological experience;* second, *the scientifically disciplined experience,* exact because it can be constructed, *the concept of instrumental experience.*

The concept of instrumental experience developed within science. Natural science is a way to examine tangible phenomena and objects. It is based on the empiric method, which defines as real only objects which can be experienced, measured, and weighed by means of acknowledged scientific methods. Common sense or artistic experience is not considered to be true. The only value of common sense experience lies in the extent to which it can be checked and described in valueless terms.

The scientific empiricist assumes his hypotheses to be true since they can be traced back to some irrevocable basic claims. These claims are made up of sense data. Since these sense data cannot be further justified, it follows that their basic claims cannot be rationally justified.

Natural-scientific experience belongs to a special type of phenomena, starting with division. Science reduces. This is not a polemic objection to the scientific procedure, but an accurate description of the actual workings of science. This reduction may be achieved in a number of ways. One method is empiric instrumental experience, dealing only with a section of reality; another method attempts to separate the subjective element, otherwise attached to all experience. Only the exact, objective observation counts—figures, measures, and quantities. Man has invented more sophisticated sensors to broaden the observation field. Empiric observation depends on the absolute accuracy of the instruments, arguably impossible out of sheer induction. The empirist is aware of this uncertainty and calculates it in his observations.

Philosophy of science deals with making dividing lines between science and non-science. The foundation for this line-making is an empirical concept which eliminates anything as non-scientific which cannot be narrowly defined as experiencebound. The reliability of conceptual knowledge is seen as reasonable because it goes back to an empirically given epistemological base or procedure (observation and experiment). The empirical method separates natural science from Aristotelian-scholastic metaphysics. The underlying opinion is that behind all theoretical controversies, the physical phenomena themselves can solve these controversies.

Due to its force of logic, empiric science dominates and monopolizes the realm called "experience." The result is that religious experience, the experience of God, loses its coherence with world experience. Religious experience is reduced to something individually internal, and loses its focus. For when religion is submitted to empiric examination, inevitably in the shape of criticism, religious experience dissolves. Such experiences dealing with religious tradition, can only cause alienation.

It is hard to decide if this process is unavoidable. But it leads to a wide respect of secular world experience. Successful scientific experience is followed by a decline in common sense experience. The gap between them grows increasingly large and will not be reduced through popular methods. It is necessary for natural common sense experience to regain a language as a means to express its views of the world, nature, and history.

This presents a second concept of experience—that of everyday language or phenomenology. This concept is based on the unfolding of natural knowledge in common practice. This kind of experience is not unambiguous like instrumental experience, as becomes apparent when one overhears a discussion between representatives of two generations, both standing on experience. The older stands on tradition; the younger stands on new experience. Interpretation must follow once phenomenological analysis has laid open and structured all these bits of experience. Such experience *happens* to us or befalls us. Experience is linked to the subject, but on a grammatical scale "us" is passive.

In everyday language we speak of, for example, an experienced pilot, thereby indicating a person knowing his trade, that is, flying. This experience is not readily transmittable and usually is gained only through everyday life. Experience is identical with practice, confidence with certain actions. Experience is identical with life experience.

However, experience may also be something new happening to us. If we talk about experience and not just adventure, new horizons open up. By experiencing "the single," we actually experience "the whole." There is a contrast between the two concepts of experience: the everyday experience affects and influences us; the objective scientific approach isolates the experience from such subjective interaction. Both concepts are linked because both are related to life and reality. Methodically, the concept of experimental experience is superior because it helps explain phenomenological experience. Everyday experience is criticized as being inapplicable since it is not unambiguous. But it is sheer conjecture to say that experience must be unambiguous in order to make objective information possible. There are plenty of situations in which we see a different concept of experience.

This type of experience cannot be transmitted directly, like other facts can, but only indirectly, through analogous experience, containing some typically universal features.[8]

Religion and Gospel Religion must be interpreted by phenomenological analysis based on facts. Conversely, these facts demand religious interpretation. We see various aberrations on the outskirts of the religious market making distinctions between religions necessary. We cannot make such distinctions without the gospel if we wish to remain on Christian theological soil.

Man's religious longing, seen as a wish for totality and identity, is for one aspect to be continuously reformulated, but for another to be "kept in place" by encountering the words of the gospel, an encounter both in attachment and contradiction, that is, contradiction of the impression that salvation lies in religious experience.

Let me summarize and make a few statements concerning science and religion. I used the new religious movements to point out certain traits in our tradition. The new religious movements signal some lack in our revival of religious tradition. They tell us that the legitimate quest for religion must be met.

The secular myths that for a time took over could not meet the myth crisis adequately. However, the Christian message has a myth structure that fits the human experience. The situation calls for a new religious interpretation of Christianity. This is not an easy task. There are many dangers inherent in fulfilling it. The interpretation I favor, influenced by K. E. Løgstrup, tries to relate the holistic religious interpretation within Christianity to normal everyday life experience. Thus we must attend to and develop this concept of experience—quite a demanding task since empirical sciences monopolize the concept of experience.

The relationship between science and religion has digressed from *unity* to *confrontation* to *separation*. The way back to the good old days of unity is closed. The state of separation is precarious. It is not healthy for the sciences to have a monopoly on explaining the world, and theology gets too anemic when kept in a realm of its own, isolated from the reality that science deals with. When unity is gone, confrontation is unfruitful and separation is dangerous: *dialogue* is the only solution. In this dialogue one must respect that we are talking about two different approaches to reality, but they are not so different that they cannot communicate with each other. In fact it is vital for theology to keep informed of what is going on in the sciences. Preserving their independence, the two approaches are complementary to each other. The relationship between science and religion should take that direction, at least until "the post-modern science" fully takes over the scene.

NOTES

1. Johannes Pedersen, *Israel. Its Life and Culture I–II* (London: Oxford University Press, 1959).
2. Peter L. Berger, *Sacred Canopy: Elements of a Sociological Theory of Religion* (New York: Doubleday, 1969).
3. Very little has been translated by this author, who has had greater influence on the Danish church and people than Soren Kierkegaard; Nicolai Frederik Severin Grundtvig, *Selected Writings,* ed. and intro. Johannes Knudsen (Philadelphia: Fortress Press, 1976). See Kai Thaning, *Grundtvig* (Copenhagen: The Danish Society, 1972); Nicolai Frederik Severin Grundtvig, *Tradition and Renewal* (Copenhagen: The Danish Society, 1983).
4. So far only his ethical main work has been translated into English: Knud Ejler Løgstrup, *The Ethical Demand,* trans. Theodor I. Jensen, foreword by James M. Gustafson (Philadelphia: Fortress Press, 1971).
5. Knud Ejler Løgstrup, *Creation and Annihilation,* vol. 4 of *Metaphysics* (Copenhagen: Gyldendal, 1978), 171.
6. Ibid., 170.
7. Gerhard Ebeling, *Die Klage über das Erfahrungsdefizit in der Theologie als Frage nach ihrer Sache. Wort und Glaube III* (Tübingen: F. C. B. Mohr, Paul Siebeck, 1975), 3.
8. A wide theme, far from exhausted. For further reading, see for example, H. G. Gadamer, *Wahrheit und Methode* (Tübingen: F. C. B. Mohr, Paul Siebeck, 1974), esp. 329

5

Aladura Spirituality: A New Understanding of God

CHRISTOPHER OLUBUNMI OSHUN

The Aladura Communion of Churches,[1] established in the last few decades, are found principally in Nigeria with their greatest concentrations in Yorubaland and parts of West Africa. Recently, they can also be found in Britain and America.

In all probability the term "Aladura spirituality"[2] is identified with the Christian radicalism[3] that arose among the Yoruba at the turn of the century. It is also traceable to their historical, cultural, and religious roots.[4] Such radicalism in religion is not limited to the Yoruba alone.[5] Yet for the purpose of this study, the Yoruba tribe is singled out as the main index of this kind of spiritual blend of pentecostalism with a traditional posture.

Historical Foundation

Historically, the original *ēgbé-ālâdúrà* (prayer-band) in Nigeria, known also as the Precious Stone Society (PS), or the Diamond Society of the Faith Tabernacle (Philadelphia), started in Ijebu-Ode around 1918 through a series of interconnected events.[6] Not long afterwards, this group, formerly a society within the Anglican Church in the town, metamorphosed into a separate and autonomous church, the Nigerian Faith Tabernacle (NFT) in 1922.[7]

During its emergence, this group took on several names. In this study, such names can be regarded as interchangeable.

Two figures were associated with the group from the outset, and were quite influential to its early development: Senior Pastor Esinsinade (formerly Sadare) and Pastor David Odubanjo. The latter, a nephew of the former, became more influential on the group's subsequent development and course of history.[8]

Between 1922 and 1930 the Precious Stone Society or Nigerian Faith Tabernacle (NFT) was developing as an independent church.[9]

Another religious society emerged in 1925 under Moses Orimolade Tunolase in Lagos in co-operation with Miss Christianah Akinsowon.[10]

The Nigerian Faith Tabernacle was a unique holiness church[11] which emphasized personal holiness, separation from the world, reliance on dreams and visions as well as adult baptisms by immersion. In spite of its small size, its warmth of affection and group solidarity commended it to the wider society and ensured its initial spread and success.

From a tiny organization with widely dispersed pockets across the country, the Faith Tabernacle was catapulted into the limelight in 1930 through the prophetic ministry of Apostle Joseph Babalola, a roller-driver turned evangelist.[12] Likewise, his career brought the other prayer-healing churches into the public eye. This collectivity of churches, due to their great emphasis on prayer and deeper spirituality, were called Aladura, that is, prayer-people/churches/movement/person. There was no doubt that the Aladura had started a new and broader conception of God. This new God-perception was a unique contributing foundation to the Aladura experience, which, though basically Christian-pentecostal is also African. This African quality is the source of its uniqueness, and has promoted interest, fascination, and inquiry.

Traditional Base for an Understanding of God

In the traditional Yoruba understanding of God, *Olodumare,*[13] best represents their conception of deity.[14] To the Yoruba, Olodumare generates such a profound significance that his existence is not in doubt. He is conceived as an ever-present, ever-living, compelling and experienced reality.

Primarily, Olodumare is conceived as unitary and described in monotheistic terms, the presence of the divinities not-with-standing. This idea of God is fundamental to the Yoruba and derivable from deity. He is conceived also in masculine terms possibly because the Yoruba society is patriarchal. Furthermore, he is regarded as 'Source-Being', the originator and controller of life directly charged with the sustenance of his theocratic government.

By deduction, from the names given to Olodumare, his attributes and functions stand out vividly. In addition, these reflect aspects that are transcendental as well as immanent.

According to his attributes, Olodumare is known as: the Creator, the Powerful, the Immortal, the Holy, the One, Universal, the King, and the Judge.[15] Similarly, his functions depict him as: the Defender, the Healer, the Provider, and the Path-finder.[16]

External Influences

As a result of both internal and external factors, there has been a wide departure from the original Yoruba conception. On the one hand are the atrocities caused by pious-frauds and on the other, the confusion[17] caused by the conflation of new religions and ideas resulting from a conglomeration of Islam, Christianity and colonialism and the Western Victorian civilization.

Whereas Islam[18] retained the idea of the oneness of God which is also consistent with the original Yoruba conception, the various distractions caused by trade and power politics which attended its *jihads* allowed a weakening of Islamic grip on the society. It was therefore, understandable, if unexpected, that recourse was found in that idea of deity which is foundational to the Yoruba.[19]

Naturally, Christianity, coming into Yorubaland in 1841[20] after several unsuccessful attempts, was held suspect due to attitudes or interests betraying commitments to arms of colonialism.[21] While Christianity served both the spiritual and educational yearnings of the people and emphasized the universality of God, it could not unravel the mystery of witchcraft. It also could not offer solutions to the ultimate issues of life.[22] This led to a renewed understanding of deity in the traditional religion.

New Emphasis

By far, the main cause of this need to rediscover God in the pristine thought of the Yoruba, was the sheer disregard of the missionaries for the spiritual and cultural values of the Yoruba.[23] Attempts in this area progressed along two planes. The first attempt was among the newly founded African churches[24] and the second among the Aladura Churches.[25] These two sets of church organizations remained largely autonomous, self-governing, and indigenous.[26]

In the search for the original Yoruba concept of deity, the Aladura Churches come to the fore. In their preaching, worship, liturgy, and doctrines, they indicate the evocative power of the name of deity and its consequences in matters temporal and spiritual. When deity is addressed by name, attributes, and/or functions, it is believed that he properly assumes these descriptions, acts within such exalted frameworks and does even more.[27]

Concerning praying and healing, the Aladura churches, as a rule, expect instant results. Due to the fact that Jesus as Christ and Lord is paramount to Aladura faith, following the conventional Christian belief, some of the traditional conceptions of diety are transferred to Christ.[28] To this end, prayers are usually begun and ended with the phrase "In the name of Jesus." The prayer is believed to be effective due to the power imbued in the name Jesus.

Aladura Spirituality

Aladura spirituality flourishes against a background of multi-faith expressions which, consonant or conflicting, leave us with some basic characteristics of God essential to human life.

Aladura spirituality emphasizes aspects of worship, liturgy, and doctrines which constitute the life-wire of the Aladura faith as well as the Aladura Churches.

By and large, Aladura Pentecostals[29] teach the basic Christian doctrines, emphasizing the necessity of spiritual regeneration and the importance of spiritual baptism. Spiritual baptism includes the actual reception of the Holy Spirit and all its outward manifestations identifiable with emotionalism. The Aladura claim is that this experience is an extension of Pentecost.

For this reason, Aladura worship is pentecostal in nature. In worship, maximum participation, meaningful involvement, and undisturbed concentration are advocated. Every member is therefore encouraged to aspire to experience Pentecostal baptism and to acquire the accompanying gifts as well. The Aladura believe this experience is inevitable and promotes the continuing edification of the church.[30] At both the personal and corporate levels, the experience is generally viewed as a universal phenomenon. As a prerequisite to this experience, the Aladura congregations emphasize a life of holiness bordering on partial ascetism and fasting as an aid to dynamic spiritual growth.

In connection with Pentecostal baptism the Aladura tradition recognizes certain categories of adherents. Lay/Clergy, are the torch bearers of spiritual gifts, *Èbùn Èmí Mímó,* who also are bestowed with spiritual/prophetic powers/insights, *āgbárā Èmí Mímó.* They are equipped with some amount of prayer power, *āgbárā àdúrà,* varying according to their spiritual propensities. These are the charismatics, often referred to as, *ālágbárā èmí* or spiritual stalwarts, their varying and overlapping ministries not withstanding.[31]

To understand the acquisition, nurture, and demonstration of *charismata,* we must look into Aladura doctrines, which are largely biblical and Christian. The Aladura pentecostals uphold the central doctrines of the Christian faith, but extend their faith beyond Christian orthodoxy and convention in their interpretation and appropriation of the power, merit, and grace abounding in Jesus' name and blood.

They do this based on their understanding of the Christian belief that both the Father and Son are one (John 10:30; 38; 14:7, 11). They also follow the Christian teaching that the Spirit is identical with the two (John 10:16, 26). In Aladura conception, the name of Jesus is "highly enskied and sainted." Because of the merits and honors of his name, this becomes supremely evocative (Phil. 2:9–11; Rom. 10:9; Eph. 1:20–21). To this end, it is believed that whatever is done or asked in his name will be possible (Mark 9:23; cf. 10:27; John 14:13, 14). Two popular Aladura choruses follow:

Agbara mbe, agbara mbe
Agbara mbe, ninu eje Jesu.

There is power, there is power,
There is power in the blood of Jesus.
Mo l'Ore kan ti ki ndoju ti ni,
Mo l'Ore kan ti ki ntan ni je;
Agbara Re lo pin okun ni ya,
Oruko Re lo ngba ni la.

I have a Friend that does not disappoint,
I have a Friend that does not deceive;
His power divides the Sea
His name brings salvation.

The adherents believe that the authority exercised by Jesus and bequeathed to his disciples is transferable, especially due to the promise of eventual transmission of power via the Holy Spirit. (John 14:12, 16, 17; 16:7, 13–15). Consequently, the Aladura Pentecostals claim authority, following Jesus' precedence, over sin (Matt. 9:6), sickness (Matt. 8:17, 16; cf. Luke 5:24), demonic powers (Matt. 8:16), powers of darkness (Luke 10:19, 20; Col. 1:13), Satan (Mark 8:33, 34; Luke 10:18) and the world (John 1:29; 3:16; 4:42; 6:33; 16:21). In this belief, their faith and courage are reinforced in carrying out what they consider as divinely legitimate assignments:

Heal the sick, cleanse the lepers,
raise the dead, cast out devils.
(Matt. 10:8)
Go ye into all the world and
preach the Gospel to every creature . . .
And there signs shall follow them
that believe; In my name
They shall cast out devils; they shall
speak with new tongues; They shall
take up serpents; and if they
drink any deadly thing, it
shall not hurt them; they shall
lay hands on the sick, and
they shall recover.[32]

Following this, the Aladura Pentecostals, like Paul, believe that they are a victorious lot (Rom. 8:37). They seek above all, to bring out the best in the Christian faith by affirming and demonstrating their faith in the living Jesus, the man of Nazareth, who is both Lord and Christ, who holds everything in subjection to himself and who in his thought, word, and deed has guaranteed a measure of his power to men.

The life and conduct of Aladura Pentecostals is, in spite of shortcomings and extremities, a testimony to their faith in Jesus. The best place to observe the Aladura and his/her spiritual inkling is in a worship setting, the point at which the sacred permeates the secular and brings about a total transformation to life. Therefore, the worship situation can be regarded as the Aladura habitat proper.

In every worship gathering, some songs and prayers are offered either at the opening for invoking the divine presence for fellowship and direction, or at the end for ensuring a divine confirmation on what has transpired and for the benediction and accompanying blessings. In general, worship situations reflect a time of praises, devotion, prayer, supplication, and intercession.

During worship a sense of God pervades the place of worship and a worshipper is immediately transported into this profound God-consciousness. Apart from the prayer for sanctification, the Aladura believe that at the point of the Spirit's entrance into worship, the whole scenario is charged and transformed, as heaven brought down to earth, to the end that worshippers become spiritually saturated.

When viewed against this background of spiritual saturation,

Aladura liturgy takes on meaning and vitality both for faith and study. Aladura liturgy therefore includes the songs, hymns, Bible verses or psalms committed to memory, prayers, and other breviaries of worship. Add to this list the use of oil, candles, incense, water, staff, crucifixes, the Bible as a ritual symbol, and the wearing of white robes. These practices are by no means common to all Aladura communion. Some practices are predominant such as the use of water, and the Bible as "*omi-ìyè*" (water of life/holy water) and *òrò ìyè* (word of life/word of God) respectively.

Water and prayer, and their symbolic uses, are significant and integral parts of Aladura worship.

Water, when prayed over, is used for sanctification, cleansing, and healing purposes. It is also used in rites for deliverance of the soul and body from spiritually malignant forces. Water, in common Aladura practice, is viewed as symbolic of the healing graces and powers vested in Jesus, and dispensed through the much needed human agent, since in its natural content, water is free, pure, and congenial to the body.[33]

Prayer is used to promote healing or to resolve conflicts, crises or problems. Prayer is considered a viable, positive, and dynamic human resource that connects with the divine through faith in the name of Jesus, and the word(s) uttered or addressed to God through Christ.[34] The utterances of Amen, *Amin,* or *àsē* (so let it be/may it be done) indicate the finality of God's intervention in human affairs, beyond which no human can appeal.

Claims and Objections of Aladura Spirituality

From the onset, Aladura spirituality became a radical element within Christianity calling attention to possible reviews and reforms of the entire Christian faith. It is both a challenge and an illumination to the more orthodox churches. It is perhaps a strange visitor or friend within Christendom. Furthermore, it serves a dual purpose in the world. On the one hand, it holds out a mirror to obvious weaknesses in the Christian faith, on the other, it seeks to break the myth of secularism or humanism.

By far, the highest yet the least common factor of all Christian confessions is the Holy Spirit. It is the source of inspiration to the church universal and the factor of continuity of the accomplishments of Christ.[35] Yet, it also forms the dividing line and the bone of contention within Christendom.[36] Both Protestants and Catholics agree that the Holy Spirit is alive and active in the church. Their disagreement hinges on the question of traditions—which the Catholics regard as complementary to Scripture and which Protestants regard as the transmitter of the Holy Spirit.

Yet the Pentecostals[37] look in vain into both confessions for the dynamism and reality of the Holy Spirit. To them it is not a gift granted in a distant past already dwelling in us. Rather, it is a gift in the fashion of a promissory note, continually bestowed upon man and capable of being withdrawn or renewed, according to the measure of faith and appropriation. The Spirit indwells and actuates us to the extent that we reflect the personality of God and Christ in us.

In spite of these bold claims of Aladura Pentecostals to spiritual gifts and graces, some objections are raised against their beliefs and practices. Apart from the challenges of Aladura spirituality, controversies arise in consequence of an increasing number of charlatans and the misconduct attached to their activities.

For instance, during Aladura Revivals[38] of the 1930s, indiscriminate witch hunts prevailed, running counter to contemporary government orders against them. Due to the revivals, a class of prophets emerged. Included among them were secondary prophets. Certain prophecies circulated, highly sarcastic of the colonial government and tending towards sedition.[39] Many prophets openly defied both traditional customs and formal courtesies, collecting icons for burning and disparaging other religions. Such was their impatient method to fulfill their master's behest and evangelize the world.

In more recent times, the Aladura prophets came under suspicion and mockery for a variety of reasons. Cases of false prophets were not uncommon. Some Aladura prophets were accused of immoral practices including adultery and fraud. Some allegedly blended traditional magic rituals with Christian rites and sacraments. The persistence of these malpractices could be due to the proliferation of Aladura churches and, hence, prophets or vice versa.

Despite the controversy surrounding the Aladura, there is sanity and sincerity in their midst. A majority are devoted to Christian service and dedicated to the Aladura cause. The major Aladura churches have their own form of church administration and government and have won recognition as Christian groups. Since they do have their names and reputation to keep, the various church authorities always try to protect the image of their churches by enforcing discipline and discouraging flagrant contravention of their rules and regulations.

Five additional objections are frequently leveled against the Aladura. These are: prolonged services, extortion and commercialism, syncretism, and ecstatic tendencies.[40]

The Aladura view these objections, except where their practices could be proven unbiblical, as a gross misconception of spiritual faith and practice.

Regarding noise-making, the Aladura might respond that God should be praised with one's whole being amidst noises and shouts, clapping of hands, dances, and musical instruments including drums and cymbals (Pss. 34:1; 47:1; 81:1; 95:1; 149:1–3; 150:3–5). The Psalms are replete with instances of this.[41] Aladura music varies in tempo, volume, and mood—all according to how the Spirit moves them.[42]

As to prolonged services, the Aladura believe worship is an unending offering to God. The duration of worship services or prayer meetings does not usually exceed three hours. However, on special occasions the time could be extended. To the Aladura, worship is an offering to God—praises and time alike—and so is done at the receiver's pleasure.

The charge of extortion and commercialism—is another matter. In some Aladura congregations the holy water and oil are retailed. There are professional ascetics who will fast for a fee, charging their Aladura clients for the service.

Other commercial enterprises include the sale of records and tapes of Christian music. Proceeds from such ventures may be ploughed back into the church or evangelical works, but this does not seem to remove suspicion completely.

On the question of syncretism,[43] people were already influenced by the traditional milieu before becoming Christians of Aladura. The Christian faith has always assimilated the various cultures it has come in contact with.[44] In spite of this legitimate overlap, there are still Simon Maguses in the world who would hybridize the "new" and the "old" in religion. Jesus cautioned against this unwarranted approach (Matt. 9:16, 17).[45] Syncretism, for whatever reason, makes a mockery of the Christian faith and the case for spirituality. The danger begins at the point of an overemphasis of rituals or symbols in religion.

Syncretism is worse in some groups than in others. Just as there are cases of deliberate syncretism, there are also cases of superficial syncretism resulting from an unconscious or conscious adaptation of forms and practices that seem common to the new faith.[46] Beyond a certain point, any further merging of the religions might reduce Christian faith to a level of magic and medicine—which it is not, and must not be made to resemble.

On the issue of ecstatic tendencies, it is often the case that appearance is taken for reality. The gyrations of the body during prayer and worship are outward manifestations of the influence of the Holy Spirit. There is a poem which I find apposite: "Who has seen the wind, Neither you nor I; But when the trees bow down their heads, The wind is passing by."[47]

The difference between a past inheritance of the Holy Spirit and a direct spiritual baptism as an individual experience is that there is a direct transmission to, and continuous impact upon, the recipient (Acts 2 is normative). This encounter may include a feeling of awe, shuddering, bewilderment, or appreciation to the point of being "lost in wonder, love and praise".[48] It is not only the physical movements that are charismatic, unusual, or unconventional and therefore controversial; the whole set of spiritual experiences, including the gifts and graces, are a point of blessing and controversy.

To the individual, once the Spirit takes over the drama of service or worship, one is wholly under his direct influence and control, and any subsequent action on the part of the individual is far from being induced remotely or directly. In the general opinion of the Aladura, man is regarded as a tool in the hands of God to be used at will (Ps. 8:4–6; Prov. 33:12; Jer. 10:23). This is why the *ruach,* or Spirit of God, could possess the Old Testament prophets (1 Sam. 10:5, 6, 10, 11),[49] transport them (2 Kings 2:16), give them utterances (2 Kings 3:15–19), or open their vision (2 Kings 6:17, 16). As well, the *pneuma* or Spirit of God in the New Testament was dynamic and multi-functional in the way it guided and used the disciples. Acts remains for us a classic document of early apostolic ministry in this regard. In all, the Aladura claim subsists precisely on these biblical precedents in accordance with God's will to employ human agents in the accomplishment of his tasks.

From another perspective we will consider the Aladura opinion of secularism, humanism, and godlessness. To the Aladura as well as to most Nigerians, the concept of godlessness would be foreign, since the existence of God is never in serious doubt, and has never been a point of controversy or debate. Moreover, it is not easy to come by confirmed atheists, humanists, or secularists in this part of the world. Nigerians generally believe in a being or Being, god(s), goddess(es) or God, realities or the Ultimate Reality. Everyone starts with a measure of faith in something. While in a crisis of life one tends to lose faith in that something, it is common practice to change beliefs, or resign to fate, but not to deny completely the existence of a god too many. However, as a consequence of Western education and acculturation, we can see traces of secularism—if not atheism (and there are some celebrated ones).[50] To these individuals the Aladura holds out a warning: "The fool hath said in his heart, There is no God."[51]

On the contrary, what the Aladura faith teaches is that no man can completely deny or avoid God (Ps. 139:7, 8; note also Ps. 139:9–16; 1 Kings 18:21, 39; Jon. 1:6). The Aladura believe that God can find an inroad into individual lives at his own pleasure according to his eternal plan, since he is the controller of all flesh (Num. 16:22; 27:16; John 17:2; Acts 17:24–28a). They also believe that since nothing is impossible for God (Luke 1:27–35; 18:27), he will meet each individual in an encounter at his own time.

On the whole, the Aladura faith appears largely consistent with Christian faith, validly based on scriptures and the major cornerstones of Christianity, fired regularly by the Holy Spirit as its life.

Conclusion

If the Aladura experience is anything to go by, it either means that new grounds in spirituality are being broken, or, (and this would seem more likely), that lost grounds (following the Old Testament prophets and the New Testament apostles) are being retrieved or rediscovered.

The process of this Aladura retrieval or rediscovery of God presents a striking spirituality which is both meaningful and relevant to man's predicament and his environment, while it is equally indicative of a very significant contribution to man's understanding of, relationship with, and witness of God.

In spite of imperfections, objections and obstacles, the Aladura experience, bewildering as it appears, is largely, genuinely Christian based on a firm biblical foundation.

Perhaps, the Aladura spirituality is, in fact, a reexamination of the Christian faith, vis-à-vis the nature of the divine personalities that are revered in Christianity: God, the Father, Jesus Christ, his Son, and the Holy Spirit. The Aladura experience observes the intimacy among the three persons of the Godhead and the relevance of this for a dynamic living faith. This fact is borne out in the typical Aladura exercise of faith, ardent affirmation, and immense praises accorded God and his Christ. In this way, the Aladura seek to preserve for us, especially in their liturgy, prayer, and songs, the livingness, activeness, and greatness of God, and the significance of these attributes for the health of man.

Undoubtedly, the Aladura exhibit an all-important factor, the Holy Spirit, as both the anchor and source of their spirituality. This, if infused into Christianity and the Church Universal alike, could produce positive and dynamic tranformation, enrichment, restoration, and revitalization in the faith, conduct, and destiny of believers.

While on the one hand, the Aladura incursion into Nigerian society is going on unabated, on the other hand, world attention is being focused on Africa and her spiritual churches. It is expected these kindred churches which have been causing consternation on the African continent, will continue to play a significant role in the revivification of Christianity and Christendom. Already they are fast becoming influential in the Third World and the West. One might soon expect a global "*All-Souls*" Pentecostal explosion (Acts 1:8).

In summation, the Aladura spirituality as another approach to conceiving God, is one of the many contributions to the endless discussions about God.

NOTES

1. For an elucidation of the term *aladura* = prayer-person/group/churches, see, Chris O. Oshun, "Christ Apostolic Church of Nigeria: A suggested Pentecostal consideration of its historical, organizational and theological developments, 1918–1975" (Ph.D. diss., Exeter, 1981), later cited as "CAC of Nigeria." On the growth and expansion of Aladura churches in Nigeria and West Africa, see Harold W. Turner, *African Independent Churches,* 2 vols. (Oxford: Clarendon Press, 1967), which discusses the Church of the Lord (COL); J. D. Y. Peel, *Aladura: A Religious Movement Among the Yoruba* (London: Oxford University Press, 1968), which discusses the Christ Apostolic Church (CAC) and the Cherubim and Seraphim (C&S) Movement from a sociological viewpoint; R. C. Mitchell, "The Babalola Revival: A Non-Arrested Prophet Movement" (unpublished paper, Vanderbilt University,

Nashville, Tenn., 1965), which discusses the Aladura movement under the aegis of Babalola from a sociological viewpoint; Akin Omoyajowo, "The Cherubim and Seraphim Movement in Nigeria," (Ph.D. diss., Ibadan, Nigeria, 1970); idem, *Cherubim and Seraphim: The History of an African Independent Church* (New York/Ibadan: NOK Publishers, 1983), which is a study in African church history; C. R. Gerloff, in "Religion in the Birmingham Area" ed. A. Bryman (Birmingham University, Department of Theology, 1975); J. Highet, "Aladura Hits Britain," *Skypower,* The inflight magazine of Nigeria Airways, June, 1983. Cf. Hollenweger, "Handbuch der Pfingstbewegung," 10 vols. (Th. D. diss., Zurich, 1965–67, and Yale University Divinity School, New Haven, Conn.); idem., *The Pentecostals* (London: SCM, 1976), 187, 195 n. 68. It is worth mentioning that an outcrop of the *Aladura* church, the Celestial Church of Christ (CCC), which originated in Dahomey c. 1947 under its Pastor Founder J. S. Oschoffa and recently shifted base to Lagos, is fast gaining ground in Nigeria.

2. This is a term I have coined for use in this paper to refer to the Pentecostal or spiritual nature of the *Aladura*.
3. See, Chris O. Oshun, "Original Concept of Deity: Unity or Plurality? With special reference to the Yoruba Context" (M.A. diss., Birmingham University, Birmingham, Eng., 1976), 39f., later cited as "Concept of Deity."
4. Ibid., 38f.
5. Otherwise, we should be running the risk of particularism or ethnocentric pride.
6. See, "CAC of Nigeria," 9f.
7. Ibid., 12.
8. Ibid.
9. The use of terms such as "separatist" or "independent" though popular among scholars remain largely debated insofar as the churches themselves are concerned. See, for instance, Harold W. Turner, "A Typology for African Religious Movements," *Journal of Religion in Africa* (*JRA*) 1, no. 1 (1966): 13ff.
10. See Omoyajowo; idem., "The Cherubim and Seraphim Movement," *ORITA: Ibadan, Journal of Religious Studies* 4, no. 2 (1979): 128.
11. "CAC of Nigeria," 10ff., 25ff.
12. Ibid., chap. 2.
13. See discussion on this in my "Concept of Deity."
14. Ibid., 12.
15. Ibid., 28–33.
16. Ibid., 34–37.
17. Ibid., 38f.
18. Ibid., 39.
19. Ibid.
20. Ibid.; see also, "CAC of Nigeria," 1.
21. Ibid.; see also, "CAC of Nigeria," 2.

22. Ibid., see also, "CAC of Nigeria," 6.

23. Ibid., see also, "CAC of Nigeria," 5.

24. Ibid., 40; see also, "CAC of Nigeria," 7ff.

25. Ibid.

26. Peel, *Aladura,* 5ff.; E. B. Idowu, *Towards An Indigenous Church* (Ibadan: Oxford University Press, 1967), 4f.

27. See Oshun, "Concept of Deity", 15. Cf. O. O. Olatunji, "The Power of the Spoken Word: Its Articulation in Yoruba Literature" (paper presented at the 2nd Conference of the Linguistic Association of Nigeria, Kano, July 26–29, 1981).

28. See "CAC of Nigeria," 372–75.

29. This is a term I have coined for the adherents of Aladura churches. See "CAC of Nigeria," 73 n. 1.

30. Ibid., 331.

31. Ibid., 423 nn. 209–210.

32. Objections to the validity of these verses are on the grounds that they could not have been said by Jesus since they were conspicuously absent from some other ancient manuscripts. Nonetheless, these passages would seem consistent both in tone and content with a type of command Jesus would have issued.

33. Cf. Turner's treatment in his, "Pagan Features in West African Independent Churches," *Practical Anthropology* 12, no. 4 (July-August 1965).

35. Some petitions might remain unspoken, yet they constitute the soul's sincere desires. The prayer of Hannah at Shiloh is a good example (1 Sam. 1:12–14).

35. See R. M. Brown, *The Spirit of Protestantism* (New York: Oxford University Press, 1961).

36. Ibid.

37. Ibid., 214ff. I include in this category those of the evangelical, Pentecostal, and charismatic persuasions.

38. See "CAC of Nigeria," chap. 2.

39. Ibid., 158f.

40. In this connection, some other terms such as, "emotionalism," "charismatic," "spirit-possession," "pentecostal-baptism," "speaking in tongues," or "prophesying" are both crucial and related. Any of these may imply or include dancing, clapping, jumping, rolling, or frenzied moods.

41. For instance, Pss. 146–50.

42. See "CAC of Nigeria," 366ff. See also Highet, "Aladura Hits Britain," 6.

43. Turner, "Pagan Features . . .,"; idem., "Pentecostal Movements in Nigeria," *ORITA;* idem., "They hold a mirror to our weaknesses," *The Outlook,* Christ Church, New Zealand, no. 19 (Sept. 1964): 6f.; idem., "The New Tribal Religious Movements," *Encyclopedia Britannica,* 1974 ed., 18: 697, 699, 704. See also E. A. Ayandele, "A Legitimate Branch of the Church Universal," *ORITA*

4, no. 1 (June 1970); idem., "The Aladura Among the Yoruba," *The Nigerian Christian* 3, nos. 7–9: 14ff.

44. See Chris O. Oshun, "Nigeria's Pentecostalism: Dynamics and Adaptability," forthcoming.

45. The clash between Judaism and Jesus' new teaching is apparent, but inspite of the common religious traditions between the two, it was better to keep both separate until the new, yielding better insights, would fully transform the old.

46. For instance, the practice of ablution in Islam has found its way somehow into the C&S. Other examples are the burning of incense in the C&S (Islam) and the Aladura churches (Catholic), excepting the CAC and the Apostolic Church (TAC); the Corpus Christi feast in the C&S (Catholic); water for santification and healing in the Aladura churches (traditional belief for purification); divining, prophecy, and other visionary gifts in the Aladura churches (traditional religion, Islam); the love feast (or *ipese,* offering of fruits feast) in the C&S, the COL, and the CCC (Methodist).

47. Christina Rossetti, in "SingSong," *The Penguin-Dictionary of Quotations* (New York: Penguin, 1960), 360. The outpouring of the Holy Spirit is seen as a wind-like operation (Acts 2:2) in which the wind acts as the driving force behind the experience as it does the windmill, trees, or the modern pneumatic equipment for drilling. Also, it brings in its wake electric-like waves, currents, shocks, or signals which are affectations and intelligible and sometimes decipherable prophecies, dreams, and visions. The experience is not only for the infilling, but also for energizing sustenance and the envisioning of those who experience it. See also Highet, 6. On the comparison of the Holy Spirit to the wind see the following expressions: (1) "as impatient as the wind," in William Wordsworth, "Surprised by Joy," *Oxford Dictionary of Quotations* (New York: Oxford University Press, 1979), 247; hereafter *ODQ;* cf. Matt. 2:7b. (2) "Loose as the Wind," in Lord Herbert, "The Collar," *ODQ* (1981), 73. (3) "Not I, not I but the wind that blows through me!" in David Herbert Lawrence, "Song of a man who has come through," *ODQ* (1981), 311; cf. Gal. 2:20. (4) "And the spirits of those who were homing Passed on, rushingly like the Pentecost Wind" in Thomas Hardy, "Souls of the Slain," *ODQ* (1966), 236. (5) "Come; and strong within us, Stir the Vikings' blood Bracing brain and sinew Blow, Thou wind of God" in Charles Kingsley, "Ode to the North East Wind," *ODQ* (1966), 293.

48. *Ancient & Modern* (AM) (1981) no. 177:1, cf. no. 161, no. 167:6, no. 169, no. 184:1, no. 185:4, no. 258, no. 372, no. 373.

49. The popular question, "Is Saul also among the prophets?" is very indicative of the experience, life-style, and esteem of the prophets as very ecstatic people.

50. Names of such die-hards as Dr. Tai Solarin and Mr. John Clinton will quickly spring to mind, but men of this caliber are few and far between in talking of Nigeria.

51. Ps. 14:1.

6

Hume's "Voice From the Clouds"

MICHAEL SMITHURST

> Suppose, therefore, that an articulate voice were heard in the clouds, much louder and more melodious than any which human art could ever reach; suppose that this voice were extended in the same instant all over nations and spoke to each nation in its own language and dialect; suppose that the words delivered not only contain a just sense and meaning, but convey some instruction altogether worthy of a benevolent Being superior to mankind—would you possibly hesitate a moment concerning the cause of this voice, and must you not instantly ascribe it to some design or purpose?[1]

There is no speaker in the *Dialogues Concerning Natural Religion* who enunciates directly the opinions of Hume the philosopher. He has no personal mouthpiece, as does Berkeley in his *Dialogues,* where Philonous speaks the philosophy of the author and Hylas the objections set up for rebuttal. Hume's *Dialogues* are dialectically more complex; in part they are a counter to the "experimental theism" of Berkeley, and from them emerges an attenuation to the vanishing point of the claims of natural religion. Natural religion is the enterprise of establishing certain theological propositions by the use of reason and empirical evidences, unaided by revelation. In the eighteenth century its most accomplished construction was the argument from design, and in the final dialogue Hume files this down to what he calls the ambiguous and undefined proposition that "the cause or causes of order in the universe probably bear some remote analogy to human intelligence."[2]

Natural religion reaches its conclusions by "empirical" arguments, inferring the existence and nature of God through reasonings in the sphere of what, for want of a more apt characterization, I shall call science and common sense. (I make the pairing with trepidation, referring to an area where many beliefs are uncontroversial and where, if difference exists, common agreement is thought possible.) Inferring on empirical evidences that there is a God is no different from inferring on empirical grounds the existence of a tenth planet. The existence of God is an hypothesis susceptible of confirmation. The proponents of natural religion see it as an extension of natural knowledge. A man acquainted with the evidences and reasoning rightly extends his science.

In the quotation above Cleanthes makes the claim that there could be a decisive event that for a reasonable man would settle affirmatively and immediately the question of God's existence. He describes a stereotypical idea of perceptual confrontation with the deity. It is not one man's experience, like Moses hearing the voice from the burning bush, but a world-wide event. The voice is heard addressing all nations in all languages (simultaneously!), the sentiments expressed are worthy of a divine being. Who, if that happened, could hesitate to credit the existence of ('God' may take too much for granted at this point so I will use Cleanthes' term) a Superior Being?

Cleanthes is aware that philosophical objections can be made to the cogency of this inference that he claims would be made unhesitatingly. In particular, the Pyrrhonian skeptic will imagine that he could resist the inference and sustain his doubt. Hume's attitude to Pyrrhonism is that while one may affect it as a position in philosophy, one cannot actually hold to the belief that nothing is to be believed. Hume gives reasons that make it sound as if he regarded Pyrrhonian suspense of judgment as simply psychologically impossible. "Nature breaks the force of all skeptical arguments in time, and keeps them from having any considerable influence on the understanding."[3] This suggests that someone might actually be a Pyrrhonian skeptic if, for some reason, he were lacking the natural inferential propensities that always overcome skepticism. One can also argue the impossibility of skepticism by maintaining that there is no way in which universal doubt can manifest itself in behavior. A man's actions may show that he doubts this or that particular thing, but what behavior would warrant us saying that there is nothing he believes? Such an argument against the impossibility of skepticism may not be unacceptable to Hume, since a recurring theme of his is the idea that truly held beliefs are those that manifest themselves in deportment.

Cleanthes' description of the circumstances of the irresistible inference is made in response to certain observations of Philo, which Cleanthes stigmatizes as extravagantly skeptical. Philo is, indeed, often the skeptical voice of the *Dialogues,* but the arguments to which Cleanthes is responding come from the principles of Hume's academic skepticism, the parent of probabilistic scientific empiricism. It is not Pyrrhonian to argue, as Philo does, that only experience furnishes us with grounds for hypotheses about the causes of phenomena; that when we reason analogically any dissimilarity subtracts from the probability of an analogous; that inference from the nature of parts cannot prove the character of a whole, particularly so, where the part is anything you select and the whole so questionable a composite as "the universe." Philo maintains that experiential arguments are made *within* experience, that is, from what is met with in experience to what can be met with in experience:

> When two *species* of objects have always been observed to be conjoined together, I can *infer,* by custom the existence of one whenever I *see* the existence of the other; and this I shall call an argument from experience. But how the argument can have place when the objects, as in the present case, are single, individual, without parallel or specific resemblance, may be difficult to explain. And will any man tell me with a serious countenance that an orderly universe must arise from some thought and art like the human because we have experience of it? To ascertain this reasoning it were requisite that we had experience of the origin of worlds; and it is not sufficient, surely, that we have seen ships and cities arise from human art and contrivance. . . .[4]

This is the familiar Humean contention that causality cannot be *sui generis,* but requires a general law relating kinds of phenomena. The thought that experimental arguments must be interior to experience I shall expand on later. Cleanthes' response to such claims is that there could be circumstances in which inferences beyond possible experience would be natural. I will now briefly examine the place of the "natural" in Hume's philosophy.

Hume is an originator of major skeptical arguments, subversive of all belief and reasoning. There is his skeptical argument concerning inductive reasoning, which undermines common sense expectations as well as scientific reasoning. There are his skeptical doubts concerning the understanding, which call into question the efficacy of any chain of reasoning, including the *a priori* reasonings of mathematics and metaphysics. There is his skepticism regarding the senses, giving a particular twist to the old theme of doubting the existence of external bodies. Finally, he raises the question whether one has a coherent concept of the self. In spite of these intricate contributions to the literature of skepticism, Hume is not a Pyrrhonist, but what he calls a moderate or mitigated skeptic. "Just philosophy," which he contrasts with superstition, "can present us only with mild and moderate sentiments."[5] A true skeptic will be diffident of his philosophical doubts as well as of his philosophical conviction. Skepticism is moderated by "nature" because no one can assent to skeptical conclusions for any length of time. Philosophical opinion seldom interrupts "the course of our natural propensities," Hume says. The picture he gives of the triumph of nature over reason is as follows. In philosophizing one engages in some sequence of reasoning which, as it appears to the fallible monitoring process with which reason surveys itself, is rationally impeccable. Thus reasoning, one comes to conclusions with which the mind cannot long maintain accordance, such as: that there is no reason to believe that there are external independent bodies, or that there is no simple, continuous self, or that no inference from experience is more warranted than another. For such time as it can sustain the studious gloom of philosophizing, the mind credits these conclusions, but the beliefs are then swept away. Natural mechanisms of belief-formation operate again, and estimate certain future contingent statements as more probable than others. Belief in external bodies, etc., reassert themselves.

This contrast between momentary skeptical beliefs and overmastering natural ones, parallels the setting up of epistemological problems found in Russell's *Problems of Philosophy* and numerous introductory texts. Philosophical problems arise when an apparently sound chain of reasoning leads to a conclusion that one does not and cannot believe. Philosophizing yields conclusions at odds with common sense and the methodically established propositions of science. Skeptical conclusions are not really believed because belief in the head is opposed by belief in the bones. A man's life and actions cannot manifest a disbelief in his surroundings, i. e., that there are no tables, no other people, etc. This is not quite Hume's position. For him, all beliefs are beliefs in the head, though some of them cannot last long in a healthily constituted head. A skeptical conclusion may possess the power of thought that constitutes belief, but by the grace of nature and backgammon its power will soon decay. "Nature is always too strong for principle."[6]

Philosophizing leading to Pyrrhonian doubts can only momentarily usurp the beliefs that Hume calls "common life." Reason is impotent to resolve such unreal doubts (unreal because unconnected to action). Philosophical reasonings are equally impotent to shake the beliefs of common life. Correct philosophy shows the "narrow capacity of human understanding" and leads us to limit our enquiries to such subjects as are best adapted to it. A correct judgment avoids "all distant and high enquiries, confines itself to common life, and to such subjects as fall under daily practice and experience; leaving the more sublime topics to the embellishment of poets and orators, or to the arts of priests and politicians. To bring us to so salutary a determination, nothing can be more serviceable, than to be once thoroughly convinced of the force of the Pyrrhonian doubt, and of the impossibility, that anything, but the strong power of natural instinct, could free us from it . . . philosophical decisions are nothing but the reflections of common life, methodized and corrected. But (philosophers) will never be tempted to go beyond common life, so long as they consider the imperfection of those faculties which they employ, their narrow reach, and their inaccurate operations."[7] Reason has no power of justifying itself. The right use of reason in philosophy brings us to an understanding of reason's limitations.

Hume's distinction of natural and unnatural reasonings cuts across the distinction of sound and unsound reasoning. To Hume's concept of inference, the centrality of experimental or inductive reasoning makes his account so remorselessly psychological. He distinguishes principles which are "permanent, irresistible and universal, such as the customary transition from causes to effects" and which are "the foundation of all our thoughts and actions, so that upon their removal human nature must immediately perish."[8] He notes others which are "changeable weak and irregular." Sound and unsound reasonings are both natural, but the latter, says Hume, are natural as disease is natural:

> One who concludes somebody to be near him when he hears an articulate voice in the dark, reasons justly and naturally; tho' that conclusion be derived from nothing but custom, which enfixes and enlivens the idea of a human creature, on account of his usual conjunction with the present impressions. But one, who is tormented he knows not why, with the apprehension of spectres in the dark, may, perhaps, be said to reason, and to reason naturally too: But then it must be in the same sense that a malady is said to be natural. . . .[9]

Which reasonings then are unnatural? Should Hume not say, like the Marquis de Sade, that everything is natural because everything is of nature? The answer must be philosophical reasonings unconnected with the course of common life are unnatural. These are not necessarily fallacious reasonings (remember Hume's reference to the salutary effect of appreciating the force of Pyrrhonism) but are unnatural because they are powerless to affect action and the principles that guide it.

This gives an answer to the question of how a natural phenomenon, certain principles or habits or reasoning, can constitute a standard of rationality. The test of sound principles is suitability to "common practice and experience."[10] Hume would regard as idle the question, "Given that certain habits of reasoning are natural, what makes them justified?" There is no escaping the modes of reasoning that nature has given. An argument conceived to be justificatory, or a sense of dismay, at the lack of it, would be both equally unconnected with active life, where the phenomenon of real belief is to be found. If the lack does cause dismay that is just a bit of natural history about the philosophical temperament. The dismay cannot prompt us to renounce the modes of reasoning in question: "These principles may flourish and triumph in the schools, where it is, indeed, difficult, if not impossible, to refute them. But as soon as they leave the shade, and by the presence of real objects, which actuate our passions and sentiments, are put in opposition to the more powerful principles of our nature, they vanish like smoke, and leave the most determined skeptic in the same condition as other mortals." One might also attribute to Hume a justification of natural reasoning founded in natural reasoning itself (and so useless in placating the skeptic). He observes that the permanent principles of natural reason enable the anticipations of "common life" and facilitate our dealings with the "real objects which activate our passions and sentiments." Inductive reasoning, imposed on us by nature, fits the course of nature. It is adaptive.[11]

In the light of this naturalistic system, how should one assess Cleanthes' claim about the voice from the clouds, his claim that the inference to a Superior Being would be both immediate and justified? Does Cleanthes' opinion on the voice fit with Hume's naturalism and mitigated skepticism? We have already noted that the mitigated skeptic confines his judgments to "such subjects as fall under daily practice and experience." In one sense, a voice from the clouds is not an object of daily practice and experience. But in another sense, the one Hume most likely intended, it is: that is, it is perceptual in character and a relation of impressions is described. However, if the natural inference is the existence of God, then it leads outside perceptual experience, assuming the absurdity of taking God to be an object of potential empirical investigation. Cleanthes forestalls Philo by himself bringing objections to the inference:

Might you not say that all conclusions concerning fact were founded on experience; that, when we hear an articulate voice in the dark and thence infer a man, it is only the resemblance of the effects which leads us to conclude that there is a like resemblance in the cause; but that this extraordinary voice, by its loudness, extent, and flexibility to all languages, bears so little analogy to any human voice that we have no reason to suppose any analogy in their causes; and, consequently, that a rational, wise, coherent speech proceeded, you know not whence, from some accidental whistling of the winds, not from any divine reason or intelligence?"[12]

Cleanthes then dismisses these considerations as strained and excessively skeptical. In fact, these objections are not Pyrrhonistically skeptical. It would be frivolous to suppose the voice arising from the accidental whistling of the winds, but to judge the cause unknown pending further investigation is surely what one would expect of an empiricist.

The topic is the argument from design, and Cleanthes' strategy is to find natural analogies for an attribution of intelligent production. He will then maintain the inference to divine production from the marks of order and design in the world as it is. He now leaves the voice and switches to another analogy, the vegetable library. He supposes that "there is a natural, universal, invariable language, common to every individual of human race, and that books are natural productions which perpetuate themselves in the same manner with animals and vegetables, by descent and propagation."[13] The argument then runs:

Suppose, therefore, that you enter into your library thus peopled by natural volumes containing the most refined reason and most exquisite beauty; could you possibly open one of them and doubt that its original cause bore the strongest analogy to mind and intelligence? When it reasons and discourses; when it expostulates, argues, and enforces its views and topics; when it applies sometimes to the pure intellect, sometimes to the affections; when it collects, disposes, and adorns every consideration suited to the subject; could you persist in asserting that all this, at the bottom, had really no meaning, and that the first formation of this volume in the loins of its original parent proceeded not from thought and design? Your obstinacy, I know, reaches not that degree of firmness; even your skeptical play and wantonness would be abashed at so glaring an absurdity.[14]

Philo is represented as confounded by this comparison, and the third participant of the *Dialogues,* Demea, intervenes "to save his countenance."

Although Cleanthes' claim about the voice and the library is reminiscent of the appeals to natural inference that Hume makes in the *Treatise* and the *Enquiries,* there is this great difference: we are required to draw a conclusion about what it would be natural to infer given the occurence of events altogether at odds with well-established beliefs about the order of nature. A world containing the vegetable library would be so disconsonant with present theories that it suggests we may be wrong about just anything. The grounds of probable inference are altogether removed. Empirical inference is made against a background of other, unquestioned scientific and common sense beliefs. Cleanthes' proposed discovery calls everything into question at once. As to what anyone might infer in such circumstances, who can judge? Cleanthes' conclusion holds only if we arbitrarily assume that the psychology of inference remains the same in this world turned upside down.

Contrast Cleanthes' position with Hume's opinions on miracles.[15] Hume questions whether a rational man could ever be justified in believing, on the evidence of testimony, that a miracle had occurred. He argues that the testimonies will always be countered by a vastly stronger weight of evidence showing that the order of nature is such that statues do not bleed or weep, men cannot walk on water, etc. The evidence in favor of a regular order ("laws of nature"), taken with certain generalizations about the probability of error, deception, self-deception, and delusion, lead him to say that "we may establish it as a maxim that no human testimony can have such force as to prove a miracle."[16] Hume is sometimes read as arguing that testimony provides some evidence for the occurrence of a miraculous event, but that the evidence favoring scientific theories implying an exceptionless order is invariably greater. There are two sets of probabilities, but one set always outweighs the other. However, I believe his actual position to be that testimony of supernatural events has no weight, and we are entitled to disregard it altogether. He states that "it appears that no testimony of any kind of miracle has ever amounted to a probability, much less to a proof."[17] The Cardinal de Retz heard from a number of witnesses of good character that an amputee had regrown his legs. Hume praises the Cardinal's reception of these claims because the Cardinal concluded "like a just reasoner, that such an evidence carried falsehood upon the very face of it, and that a miracle, supported by human testimony, was more properly a subject of derision than of argument".[18] It has been argued against Hume that he makes a dogmatic presumption in favor of existing science. Scientific theories are sometimes overthrown, and falsification requires that we admit evidence of the occurrence of particular events contradicting the universal claims of a theory.

Hume's position on miracles and his absolute rejection, if such it is, of testimony tending to establish the occurrence of supernatural events can be defended. First, his assumption that there is a natural order need not rest on a belief that contemporary science is true and permanent. There are facts of common observation that any theory would have to accommodate. Supernatural events are so described as to contradict those common regularities. No new science will comprehend and explain as part of its natural phenomena, say, bleeding statues. With the advance of biological science it is possible that men may be made to regrow severed limbs, but, even so, the phenomenon would not be of a kind with the ear restored in Gethsemane.

Second, Hume's position is helped if one substitutes a more sophisticated philosophy of science for his inductive, causality-centered one. Scientific theories are not falsified instantly or *in vacuo*. Under certain circumstances events are admitted as *prima facie* counterinstances to a theory without being recognized as falsifying. To begin with, they are treated as, in T. S. Kuhn's term, anomalies.[19] Anomalous events are only received as falsifying instances where there is a competing theory that has approximately the explanatory successes of the existing theory, and has the added advantage of incorporating within its explanatory scheme the phenomena that the presently accepted theory deems anomalous. On this view, scientific theories are not falsified by one-off counter-events, or even by regularly reproducible incompatible phenomena, but only by advance to new theories.

Third, unlike scientific claims, supernatural ones are only accessible through historical evidence; hence the centrality of testimony in the debate over miracles. Scientific evidence is not historical in that way. Physics would be unshaken if it were discovered that Galileo performed none of the experiments attributed to him. Science is supported not by a testimonially based chronicle of past events, but by its capacity to provide a backing for present claims. Science deals in reproducible kinds of events; hence, skeptics need not be invited to peruse the records.

Fourth, testimony itself, as Hume was aware, is a natural phenomenon to be assessed by empirical methods. One factor entering into estimation of it is consonance with the belief of a natural order. Mere say-so, taken in isolation, is not evidence at all. If it did constitute a degree of evidence, then the claims on our attention would become unmanageable. "Does a man of sense run after every silly tale of witches or hobgoblins or fairies and canvass particularly the evidence?" asks Hume.[20]

If this adaptation of Hume's position is correct then so is the general trend of Hume's thought on miracles. Whatever the probity and sincerity of the witnesses, there is no route from the scientific worldview to the truth of claims of one-off supernatural or miraculous happenings. Canvassing the evidence in the particular case really is irrelevant. This result will be surprising to anyone who still holds to the idea that empirical science has an ultimate foundation in eyewitness reports of particular events.

It could be argued that there is knowledge that comes from a knowledge of another, bringing with it an unquestioning confidence in his word. In certain circumstances one can know that someone is innocent of a charge even though he is altogether unable to prove it. But questions of the sanity of a witness, or whether he is imposed on, will always arise when he testifies to the supernatural. Who could absolutely answer for another in a concentration camp, in battle, under the greatest temptation and provocation? Whatever the terms of the knowlege that comes from a just confidence in another, it is certainly not a transitive relation. I cannot be absolutely convinced of another's veracity because you are. There is no road this way from individual experience to the domain of public knowledge.

Should one say that although a scientific rationality will never accept the testimony of the voice from the clouds or the vegetable library, nevertheless, both are possible? What can one make of the claim that such things are possible?[21] Encouraged by Hume, discussion of scientific theories gives a central place to the metaphor of 'regularity', to which it is useful to add that of 'density'. To say that a book may grow on a tree merely invites us to juxtapose images. There is no account of plant genetics here, no effort to accommodate the numerous constraints imposed by biology's detailed account of generation, no postulated tie-up with evolutionary theory. It is a surreal painting, not a worked-out thought about trees. It is a suggestion at odds with established science at literally thousands of points. Compare the miracle at Fatima where crowds witnessed "the sun dancing in the sky." Had the sun moved as claimed, no one would be here to tell about it unless numerous other physical consequences are imagined suspended as well. For this reason even the most devout consider such happenings as holy apparitions, not perturbations of the solar system. Miraculous events, whether large scale or not, are incomplete objects[22] in the sense that, like characters in fiction, the story told leaves them indeterminate at many points. *Pickwick Papers* tells us nothing of Mr. Pickwick's parentage, or the state of his teeth. Richard Rorty,[23] considering how one might try to complete the fictional specification of Sherlock Holmes by providing arbitrary answers to the questions about him on which the Holmes stories are silent, says "we shall never construct an object which can be fitted into a complete story of nineteenth-century London (all the space-time intervals being, alas, already full of other objects)." Something similar holds for historical claims of miraculous occurrences. The scientific picture of the world is regular and dense. What in detail is predicted and retrodicted will vary with the science of the time, but some facts will be retrodicted by any theory (for instance, that, though no one looked in, Caesar had a brain in his skull). A miraculous story cannot fit with the fine detail of the scientific narrative, any more than fictional characters can fit with that of the historical one. Science fills up our picture of the world. The less science a culture has, and the less integrated and cross-referenced the branches of its science, the more conceptual room for the wonderful.

"But what if it really happens, what will you think then?"[24] As I have indicated, I don't grasp how one is to fill out the phrase "really happen" here. Take for comparison something that Descartes postulates,[25] that the people around one are really cunningly constructed pieces of machinery. Of course, I can imagine something like the following: I am with a friend who crosses the road suddenly, and is knocked over by a car—a shocking event. I run across and look down. The vehicle has split his skin like a bag, and, spilling out are wheels, springs, and all sorts of clockwork, or, to accord with the times, lots of microchips and some very small batteries. Cleanthes would ask what would one naturally infer in these circumstances? Well, I might infer that the person I knew was a machine. But I would also be as much, or as little, entitled to infer that ten seconds before he was hit by the car his innards transubstantiated themselves into clockwork. The grounds of judgment are removed. The only question accordant with existing scientific rationality is why do these things seem to be happening? Why am I having these experiences?

Does not Cleanthes ask how one would respond to a certain *public* happening? The voice is heard by others, it is commented on everywhere, and these surprising events are continuous with the rest of my world. But it is not obvious that one can relinquish questions about one's own mental state here and move to unperturbed belief of a public event. Extended systematic delusion getting worse and more elaborated might be expected in some circumstances. Perhaps I have a brain tumor. As for the events fitting the rest of my world, so it is sometimes with schizophrenia. Delusions can be harmonized with veridical perception. A person with a grossly disordered belief-system may still address himself to objects and the actions and words of others in a relatively normal way. In so far as Descartes was tempted to represent the mad as solipsistically sealed-off, he was applying, for most cases, a wrong picture.

I conclude then that scientific method does indeed create a closed circle that excludes certain claims from ever being established by empirical evidences. Its impenetrability to supernaturalist claims arises from its particular manner of admitting theory-contradicting facts (that is, only when they are comprehended under a new, wider ranging, theory), from the integrated and integumental character of science, and from the induction of "common life" that the world has a natural order (even though the best opinions about that order must always be the science of the moment). One persisting in following scientific rationalism, in the face of highly recalcitrant experiences, may despair of the method. Or he may conclude that his own condition is such that he is cut off from the world in which scientific rationality is applicable.

This argument is not subversive of religious belief but of natural religion, which takes the existence of God to be a probabilistic theory. To make religion into a series of hypotheses supposedly continuous with science is rightly to be stigmatized as superstition.[26] Attacking religion as if it were a set of queer postulates based on flimsy empirical evidence is one way of not really looking at it. I can understand that someone might think that in the matters I have considered here no important question of religious belief has yet been addressed. Hume's well-known references to faith and revelation as a foundation of belief stronger than mere fallible human reason were unquestionably ironic.[27] Nevertheless, there is no intrinsic reason why a rejection of natural religion should be seen as unfriendly to religious enquiry. Arguments such as Hume's, or this adaptation of it, can fit equally well with the words of the Leveller Winstanley:

> Whether there were such outward things or no; it matters not much. . . . The whole Scriptures are but a report of spiritual mysteries, held forth to the eye of flesh in words, but to be seen in the substantial matter of them by the eye of the spirit.[28]

NOTES

1. David Hume, *Dialogues Concerning Natural Religion* ed. Nelson Pike (New York: Bobbs-Merrill, 1970), 34.
2. Hume, *Dialogues,* 122.
3. Hume, *A Treatise of Human Nature,* ed. L. A. Selby-Bigge (New York: Oxford University Press, 1978), 187
4. Hume, *Dialogues,* 30.
5. Hume, *Treatise,* 272.
6. Hume, *Enquiries Concerning Human Understanding and Concerning the Principles of Morals,* ed. L. A. Selby-Bigge (New York: Oxford University Press, 1980), 160.
7. Hume, *Enquiries,* 162.
8. Hume, *Treatise,* 225.
9. Hume, *Treatise,* 225–26.
10. Hume, *Treatise,* 272.
11. Quine invokes Darwinian evolutionary theory and gives a similar answer to the problems of induction. Willard V. Quine, "Natural Kinds," in *Ontological Relativity and Other Essays* (New York: Columbia University Press, 1969).
12. Hume, *Dialogues.*
13. Ibid., 34–35.

14. Ibid.

15. Hume, *Enquiries,* sec. 10.

16. Hume, *Enquiries,* 127.

17. Hume, *Enquiries,* 127. The "obvious" and "common sense" position against which Hume is arguing is well characterized by what Sherlock says of a miraculous event: "I do allow that this case and others of like nature, require more evidence to give them credit than ordinary cases do. You may therefore require more evidence in these than in other cases: but it is absurd to say that such cases admit to no evidence, when the things in question are manifestly objects of sense." Thomas Sherlock, *The Trial of the Witnesses of the Resurrection of Jesus Christ* (New York: Garland, 1979).

18. Hume, *Enquiries,* 124.

19. Thomas S. Kuhn, *The Structure of Scientific Revolutions* (Chicago: University of Chicago Press, 1962).

20. Hume, *Letters,* 1: 350.

21. I discuss this at greater length in "Hume on Existence and Possibility," *Proceedings of the Aristotelian Society,* vol. 71, 1980–81.

22. I do not want to endorse the ontological theory that goes with it, but I borrow the expression from Terence Parsons, "A Prolegomenon to Meinongian Semantics," *Journal of Philosophy* 71 (1974).

23. Richard Rorty, "Is there a Problem About Fictional Discourse?", in *Consequences of Pragmatism* (Santa Cruz, Calif.: Harvester Press, 1982).

24. Richard Swinburne, *The Concept of Miracle* (New York: Macmillan, 1970), 35, puts the question: "What, one wonders, would Hume say, if he himself apparently saw a man walk on water?"

25. Descartes, *Meditations,* Meditation 1.

26. Ludwig Wittgenstein, *Lectures and Conversations on Aesthetics, Psychology and Religious Belief* (Boston: Blackwells, 1966), 59.

27. See for example, Hume, *Enquiries,* 131.

28. *The Works of Gerard Winstanley,* ed. G. H. Sabine (Ithaca, N. Y.: Cornell University Press, 1941), quoted by Christopher Hill in *The World Turned Upside Down* (New York: Penguin, 1975) chap. 7.

7

Experience of the Divine, Experience of God

ANTOINE VERGOTE

The Ambiguous Quest for Religious Experience

In the twentieth century *religious experience* has become a major topic of interest in the religious sciences as well as in the personal search for religious fulfillment. It should come as no surprise, then, that the idea of religious experience bears with it the ambiguities of the cultural and religious context out of which that interest arose. We simply have no reasonable grasp of the topic without considering the shifts in culture and religion which came about through focusing religion on experience. In the Gospels one never finds such an expression, and as the cultural anthropologist Needham[1] convincingly demonstrates, the so-called primitive religions ignore it as well.

The sciences of religion coined the expression *religious experience* as the keystone of religion. If we are not to be caught in the snares of this topic, we must consider the scope of these religious sciences and take a stand on them. The new religious sciences reversed the traditional concept that religion comes from above: from divine beings, through the mediation of the original ancestors, of inspired prophetical figures or, in Christianity, of Jesus, believed to be the Son of God. In the strict historical sense of the word, religion is revealed. Human sciences have tried in various ways to elaborate theories explaining how man created religion, evaluating it as superstition, as illusion or as truth and cultural value. Applying the principle of a genealogical explanation, scientists of religion have sought the elementary data from which complex religions supposedly originated. The most important elementary factor proposed is that of experience. The following represent major schools that endeavored to reconstruct the constituents of religion on the basis of the elementary religious experience: the empiricist psychology of James,[2] the sociology of Durkheim,[3] and the Kantian philosophy of Otto.[4] The failure of all these attemps to explain the origin of religion has been stressed by recent cultural anthropology [E. E. Evans-Pritchard,[5] R. Needham, C. Geertz.[6]] A critical inquiry into the works of James, Durkheim and Otto reveals the vicious interpretive circles wherein those theoretical reconstructions evolve. I will point out some ideas drawn from critical examination of these theories, stressing similarities between their guiding principles and the motives of some of today's nostalgia for religious experience. By so doing, I hope to prepare a correct conception of religious experience.

Proponents of religious experience view it as replacing or at least producing the former belief-assent. All evidence suggests that the shift toward experience is an attempt to find a new and personal ground for religion for writers at odds with Christian doctrines and with the church-institution. The factors which caused the crisis or decline of Christian faith are known. Secularization made religion, at least in the Western world, less socially relevant and oriented religion to the private sphere of personal, interior life. The progress of science, technology, and critical philosophy brought about a skepticism of the belief in the workings of supernatural forces within the world. The widespread distrust of institutions and truths taken over from the past shook the conventional dogmatic authority of the churches. One is acutely conscious of the historical contingency of the Christian religion within the spectrum of living or dead religions.

In this critical situation of Christian faith, the claim of religious experience gives the assurance of a religious dimension to mankind, and, for many, frees religion from its past authoritarian and institutionalized structures. People became more disposed to give credence to religious experience because this reinterpretation corresponded with the major tendencies of the modern mind. Indeed, one of religious experience's primary characteristics is subjectivism. Inner feelings are considered more authentic than the acceptance of a coherent body of doctrines or the practice of historically transmitted and institutionally proposed rituals. Belief as such is a major problem for the subjectively oriented mind, for belief evokes distance and estrangement. Language creates the distance. People want to suppress this distance from experience, for experience means direct contact.

The idea of experience corresponds to a second characteristic of modern mind: empiricism. Nothing is more certain than what our senses convey. For religion that means our inner senses. This trend underlies many inquiries concerning occurences of religious experiences. As expressed in the titles of some studies, we search for so-called ecstatic or paranormal experiences of supernatural forces lifting us out of ourselves. This empiricist conception follows the empiricist introspective psychology of W. James, and the apologetic preoccupation is manifest. We wish to ground a religious certitude on a direct experience. I would like to characterize these essays somewhat ironically as the search for supernatural telepathy. The most crude and naïve expression of such a 'belief' in experience without belief has been the attempt to awaken religious experiences with drugs among people without any religious convictions whatsoever.

A third characteristic of the modern mind is preoccupation with a universal ecumenism that effaces the frontiers between distinctive religious doctrines and practices. If all religions are derived from an original element, represented in different formulas and symbols, then the skepticism regarding the varieties of religions should be surmounted by recognition of the basic religion-forming capacity, supposedly innate to the mind. In the former metaphysical proposition, the concept of the natural desire for God was the basis for the conviction of man's religious nature. Now, the theme of religious experience gives a new foundation to the thesis that man, by his very essence, is *homo religiosus*. Paradoxically, this theory is also used to explain the undeniable decline of religion in the Western world. Hence it is argued that the functional and technological culture destroys or at least reduces the inborn propensity to experience supernatural reality.

I do not hold the theory which proposes that religions developed out of an original experience. Religions are complex systems of symbols, language games, and ritual behaviors. If there is religious experience, it occurs within the framework of the symbolic religious systems which present the supernatural being with such suggestive power that it acquires the quality of supreme reality.

If my criticism of the emotionalist theories of religion and my interpretation of the conceptual origin of religious experience are correct, then a model of religious experience that accounts for the positive values of this religious interest and is critical of the confines of a subjective and empirical mind should be elaborated. My analysis and research is limited to Christian religion. As my critical introduction suggests, experience occurs within specific religious references, deriving its peculiar meaning from them. Another reason for this choice is that the problem of experiences arose specifically within the Christian culture. This is not a chance occurrence. Christianity's original key term, belief, determined the peculiar tension between itself and experience. It probably also thoroughly influenced the philosophical and scientific criticism of religious belief which developed within the Western Christian culture. Consequently, I deliberately refrain from an ecumenical preoccupation in this chapter. The terms of ecumenism are well thought out only if one addresses the central issues of the distinct religions taking form and shape within the culture, transcending it and creating a fundamental and universal bond of fellowship.

The Modalities of Religious Experience

The expression *religious experience* is a far-reaching abstraction. It suggests the idea of knowledge through immediate contact. However, the evidence of seeing or touching something is not yet an experience of the object, but only the experience of self-awareness of seeing and touching. One can speak of experience only when sense perception delivers the qualities of the object, that is, when immediate contact supports understanding and when knowledge enlightens contact.

Although a person may read many valuable studies on a foreign country, he has not actually experienced it. Tourists knowing nothing of a country's history, economy, language, or religion—have a limited and possibly distorted experience of it, projecting their own prejudices onto what they imagine as firsthand observations. Thus my definition of experience is restricted to evidence resulting from an integration of documentary knowledge or testimony and direct personal contact, of language conveying the ideas and perception of reality itself. Experience occurs only within an interpretive framework.

To illustrate the complexity of religious experience with another analogy, consider the scientific experience in the natural sciences. Only the highly trained theorist is capable of carrying out and accurately interpreting a scientific experience. Reflecting on the concept of experience makes it clear that we should ask the following questions:

1. What is the relationship between experience and belief? Is there

a religious experience without belief? What does experience add to belief or belief to experience?

2. What is the function of emotion in a religious experience? This question involves a psychology of emotions.

3. Is religious experience paranormal?

These questions are interconnected. To answer them without getting lost in the labyrinth of interconnections, we must turn towards the religious experiences as they occur, describing them, analyzing their structure, and interpreting their apparently enigmatic aspects with the theories of normal psychology.

We will first investigate the visual/perceptual types of religious experience. The following are criteria for distinguishing the psychological organization of these experiences.

1. There is religious experience resting upon perceptual data. Some experience God in nature or through sacred music. Others under the same circumstances experience a sacred reality but not God. Although we can further analyze these differences both are perceptual experiences.

2. Some experience God's presence without any external perception. Such an experience is exceptional, strongly emotional, and characteristically causes an abrupt change of perspective. It always produces a conversion experience.

3. There is the religious experience resulting from the ensemble of religiously pursued life-experiences. It is comparable to the love persons have after years of togetherness, sustained through joys and sorrows. In religion, this experience implies the purified consciousness that God is in Isaiah's words, the God oft hidden. Characteristic of this experience is an understanding mediated by religious life itself.

4. There is the mystical experience. The term mystical is confined to the experience of classical mysticism. The experience characteristically results from an ongoing process of systematic prayer and meditation, marked by different stages of development. The resulting ecstasies are unique momentary occurrences which, according to Christian mystics, are not the full consummation of their union with God.

Doubtless, one could widen the concept of experience. In prayer a religious man can intuit God. He might vividly apprehend God and be lifted out of his ordinary perceptions of himself, the world, and others. There is no denying this experiential quality which evolves into an awareness of God's presence. Thomas Aquinas states belief by intuition does not address ideas, but that ideas mediate the access to divine reality and that belief goes to God himself. A believer does not say "I believe in the concept of God," or "I believe in God's existence"; these are not religious but theoretical utterances. The believer says "I believe in God," expressing an I-Thou relationship. In that sense every prayer, as traditionally formulated, is a contact or commerce with God. However, if questioned, people will not call their prayer an experience of God, except in the first three types of experience I mentioned: when prayer makes them perceive God's manifestation in worldly signs, or when it is (rarely) an affective and illuminating event, or when after long years of prayer and meditation, one acquires retrospective and prospective wisdom of God. There is today a pervading religious rhetoric about experiences. The consequences of this rhetoric are more disturbing than enlightening.

The processes in these four distinctive types of religious experience are obviously different. But all four experiences occur within Christianity. Consequently, we note that different forms of experience do not bring about different religions. I doubt whether every religion produces these four types of experience. The perceptual experience is probably the most common to all religions. However, the consciousness experience requires a mental attitude particular to certain civilizations and religions fostering awareness.

The Religious Experience as Perception of Divine Manifestation

The occurrence and meaning of religious experience should first be considered an object of empirical research, not of philosophy or of theology. Bracketing all theories, I did some research on this subject among others, with a projective test consisting of photographs depicting various normal life situations. People imagined themselves in possible settings of their religious experiences, recalling them and talking about them. I will mention the main results which I will then interpret.

Death is a negative experience stirring intense emotion. It is not the locus of a religious experience, but of questioning, revolt and, among believers, of surpassing their protest against God in confidence and prayer.

Sexual love is intensely experienced, but is in itself too fully positive an experience to become the locus of religious experience.

The experience of nature, on the contrary, awakens less intense emotions but is the most likely locus of religious experience. This observation goes against the conception of William James, to whom religious experience is exceptionally emotional, or psychopathic, as he calls it.[7] These findings also contradict the idea of some sociologists who think that nature has been desecrated by modern technological civilization.[8] It would be worthwhile to examine the preconceptions which lie behind these theoretical constructions of psychologists and sociologists.

There is a complication which is instructive rather than disturbing. Among the people who said they had a religious experience, some said it was an experience of a mysterious power in the living world, of an infinite might, or of a mystery within our deepest self, or of a sacred reality but by no means an experience of God. The term *the ultimate* I never heard. Obviously, this is a philosophical term belonging to the field of movement and desire and is therefore not convenient to indicate the object of an experience. We experience the *here and now,* whereas the ultimate, by its very essence, is the *not yet present* reality we seek.

In other descriptions, people said they experienced God. Still others denied having any religious experience whatsoever. The perceptual religious experience is apparently ambiguous. However, this ambiguity exists only for the observer taking an exterior neutral vantage point and comparing different subjects. From these differences one cannot draw an objection against the value and reality of the religious experience. On the contrary, they reveal its dynamic structure which I shall now analyze.

The following experience results from a dynamic process, in which three factors operate together.

1. There is the perception of positive qualities of nature: the grandeur and infinity of the mountains, the beauty of the flowering spring, the fecundity of the earth in summer, the quasi-eternity of the sky, etc.

2. This perception is subjective. To appreciate this experience, we must have a correct conception of emotion. Feelings are not only inner states of mind but are also a dynamic investment of definite qualities of the world or of persons. Emotions are the awareness that qualities respond to one's desires or contradict them. As phenomenology insists, affectivity is a mode of evaluative knowledge fulfilling perception. Personal affective capacities or defects enlarge or restrict, respectively, man's cognitive powers. With the aid of the

clinical Rorschach test, we observed that different personality structures condition different perceptions of the qualities of nature. There is a significant correlation between the introvert personality and the accentuation of feminine or motherly qualities in nature and in God. There is a converse correlation between the extrovert personality and the more complex perception of masculine or fatherly and motherly qualities, in nature and in God. The perceptual experience is both subjective and objective.

Another interesting observation was made. Among a masculine population, the two situations which produced the highest rate of religious experience, were photographs of the ascent of a mountain and that of the first man on the moon. There man experiences his own greatness in his triumph over nature and himself. At the same time, he is the most impressed by the grandeur and the beauty of the universe. We observe an intense dialectical tension between self affirmation and admiration. At the climax of his own mastery, man inverses his self-centeredness in a contemplative perception of God's majesty and glory. Clearly, religious perceptual experiences are neither romantic emotionalism nor an artifically triggered emotional rapture.

3. When accompanied by religious belief, these subjective perceptions of nature's qualities are the perceptions of a divine manifestation. Without a religious reference, there is no religious experience. However, it would be a misconception to think that these people "interpret" nature as a divine manifestation. They see it, but in the same way as they see objective forms and later fulfill them with affective qualities. The explanation of such perception with the concept of projection is as false as the explanation of movement as the mere organization of the neuromuscular mechanism. Only a symbolic logic gives an account of these perceptive experiences.

Consequently, this religious experience consists of the interaction of three factors: perception of forms, affective and selective investment by emotion and desire, and religious language. The experience is the integration of belief and affective perception. This integration results from the crossing of two movements. The ascending movement goes from the perceived and affectively invested world to the invisible divine reality proposed by religious language upon visible qualities, endowing them with a supplementary signification. This dynamic process is comparable to that of metaphorical language. Metaphors are created by the interaction between two language-chains.[9] Metaphors are not comparisons, for the mediating element of a comparison fails. Therefore metaphors do not prove a reality; they bring about a real and new understanding.[10] Religious perceptive experience entails a metaphorization, and expresses itself in metaphors. The experience, however, is more than metaphorization. The metaphors do not express a device for a religious outlook on the world; they state the perceived manifestation.

Such an experience brings about a unity of the world and of God, a unity which maintains their essential difference. God is not absorbed within the world, but is manifested within it. Outside of it he manifests as the identified personal presence to whom people address themselves in a personal relationship. This experience effectuates an integration which gives a living content to the religious words about God: source, living water, generosity, glory, majesty, infiniteness. On the other hand, the qualities of the world are transformed into tokens of a concealed and disclosed divine presence.

This integration is accomplished in varying degrees. It is situated on a continuum, starting from the threshold of a minimal experience and moving toward the perfect integration found in some mystics at the end of their journey, or in Christ's perception of the world reflecting God's qualities. Thus we understand the ambiguity of this kind of religious experience. If some people do not really believe in God but are searching for him, or are doubting their former belief, they will perceive only a vague mystery, an infinite creative power. The concept of an anonymous sacred power as an object of experience is a cultural derivation from religion among persons who either deny God's existence or who suspend their belief-assent. They vacillate between merely rationalistic denial of religion and a belief-conviction. The sacred thus becomes a transitional and mediating object of experience between the pure world-immanence and God. Believers recognize in this transitional sphere the manifestation of God. I propose the following as a general psychological law: when a person wishes to ascertain belief in God by experiencing him in the world, the experience will be minimal; when the person has a firm belief in God, the integration will be more perfect and the experience will be given along with his belief. In other words, the search for an experience giving a guarantee and a criterion of the truth of religion hinders the experience itself. The desire for religious experience is natural and legitimate. Experience is enjoyment. God is not really the God of mankind when he does not give mankind a deep peace and spiritual enjoyment. God would also remain strange and far away from man's existence if man could not experience God in his world. But there is manifestly a psychological problem with the search for experience in opposition to belief. Mankind wants to suppress the distance which religious language creates. But language means a possible presence accompanying the alternative distance. Thus a normal experience of God is an integrated process of hearing the revelation through religious language and perceiving the positive qualities of the world one enjoys. Religious experience has the same dynamic structure of all experience—of love, esthetic, or scientific experience. Consequently religious experience is no more elusive than other experiences and it is no less naturally given. It also supposes an education of perception, of affectivity, and of religious attention. The study of religious experience requires a genuine phenomenology of perception, a psychology of affectivity, a philosophy of the revealing power of language, and a logic of the metaphorization.

The Direct Experience of God Without Mediating Perception

There is obviously a special problem with the direct experience of God without mediating perception. God seems to be beyond the normal domain of immediate experience. Because some people claim to have had it, one may be easily led to look for a particular ecstatic and paranormal capacity in the depth of the human psyche. The cases of mystical ecstatics supposedly confirm this view. Based on this, some have tried to awaken or intensify this occult capacity by means of drugs. However, we shall be in a better position for interpreting these data if we do not mix them with an abstraction, but focus on the distinctive features, conditions and processes of each type. Only rigorous case studies can settle this subject.

Such experiences occur within particular cult settings—in Baptist churches or in Pentecostal groups. In these settings psycho-social laws of conformity with the expected behavior and identification with models partly explain these experiences, together with personal affective dispositions and a desire for belief-certainty. I do not contest the supernatural efficacy of these events, but as a theologian I maintain that God works throughout the psycho-social and the inner-psychological processes. I resist belief in an extraordinary visible supernatural happening. Due to the psychological conditions of these events, such a belief appears to have a self-verifying tendency.

Private direct experiences of God's presence can be even more easily misinterpreted. A striking feature of such cases is that people often forget the events preceding the experience: the prayer of the unbelieving or doubting person "God, if you exist, make yourself known to me;" some religious statements one has heard and which impressed the person; times of tormented preoccupation, etc. The overwhelming experience of God's living presence pushes away the foregoing events, making the experience stand out as a quasi-miraculous event. The preceding determining events returned slowly to memory when I encouraged the persons to remember concretely the location, content, and accompanying representations of the experience. These elements have precisely the character of rendering a causal account of the experience.

A conscious desire to have an experience of God is an important factor. Does it produce the experience? Is this a case of the illusion of desire? Yet desire is not born of a void. It is awakened by someone who offered a token and who was seduced. The word *God* circulates and is charged with emotional connotations. It contains a message and a promise which desire transforms into experience. How can we understand this? The experience of God is obviously a transportive leap beyond the distance separating the person from God. This leap is not so enigmatic from the perspective of emotional psychology. The emotion in the experience is the feeling, *as a result of the belief assent,* that the existential link with God is accomplished. For the full experience follows an inner struggle between the "yes" and the "no" to the untrained idea of God. The experience occurs after the decision to say "yes," that is, to make a believing assent. A deep counter-desire previously conflicted with the religious desire. This sometimes is still observable in the compulsive "no" flashed by at the last moment. The breakthrough of the ultimate surrender gives these experiences their particular intensity. The intensity of emotion is correlative with the strength of the resistances the belief triumphed over. This intensity explains in part the vivid impression of God's localized presence here and now. Often, at the moment of the experience, human figures—the mother, the grandmother, the father—are seen in a dreamlike quasi-perception, and their quasi-physical presence mediates the feeling of God's localized presence.

The unconsciousness of the dynamic belief processes, in tension with the resisting unbelieving tendencies, creates the impression of a distinct supernatural event. Such unconscious interweavings of memory and desire lead some psychologists or sociologists to term this sort of experience as paranormal. Still others, adopting the reductionistic Freudian interpretation, presume that such experiences are derivations of the past. These psychologists are aware of the unconscious processes preparing and provoking the experience, but do not take into account the belief-conflict and the psychological work of the belief-assent.

As to whether such an experience is an illusion, I offer three meanings of the word. First, one can consider as an illusion the impression of God's quasi-miraculous observable intervention. A psychological account dispells this illusion. Second, God's presence and revelation in this experience does not have to be considered as an illusion. For a believer, God is present and works through people as well as psychological processes. When a person assents to God's presence, he is effectively present. Third, the person can have the illusion of having worked through his or her emotional resistances in the surrender of the experience-moment. This is often the case. After a period of intense happiness, they may enter a cold wintertime where they no longer experience God's presence. Then they must sustain and restructure their belief-assent which initiated the experience. Otherwise, they will afterwards look upon their experiences as on an illusion of the emotion.

Conclusion

The following four propositions summarize the lessons which my analysis of religious experience illustrates.

1. From the vantage point of human sciences: the experience of God occurs within a given symbolic system of religious references which have a guiding and structuring influence on the neophyte. All experiences can be explained by normal psychological processes operating within the culturally given references, but cannot be explained as having their origin in an extraordinary experience.

2. From the point of view of theology: God's work, the "supernatural grace," should not be separated from human factors. Theology involves an anthropology and a psychology as its constitutive elements.

3. From the point of view of philosophy and of theology: the occurrences and contents of religious experiences point to human

religious capacities, but they do not sustain the assertion that mankind is by its very nature religious (*homo religiosus*). I concur with Saint Augustine that man is capable of God. I do not concur with a religious finality in human nature, nor do I subscribe to the view that people who are not religious in the proper sense of the word, produce a so-called substitute-religion, be it an ideology, art, sex-fascination or nationalism. Religious language has the symbolic efficacy of actualizing latent spiritual capacities, but mankind must achieve belief-assent in working through deep existential conflicts: the tension between acceptance of the dependence upon God and human striving for autonomy; the tension between fear of religious illusion and confidence in the desired presence of God; the tension between utopic desires, stirring revolt and resentment, and the recognition of the enjoyable qualities of the world. God is not merely an answer to human desires but is likewise a challenge for us and our most personal human adventure.

4. From the point of view of religious life and development: religious experiences will be forthcoming and will support the basic belief-conviction, depending on the development of emotion and on the progress of belief-assent. Experience is a moment of integration between the human potentialities and the claim of the religious message. Focusing religion on experience alone is not to recognize the multi-dimensional structure and the dynamic processes of religion. The question whether God, the divine, the sacred ("the ultimate") is the real object of religious experience, can only be settled within this view.

NOTES

1. Rodney Needham, *Belief, Language and Experience* (Oxford: Basil Blackwell, 1972).
2. William James, *The Varieties of Religious Experience* (New York: Longmans & Green, 1902).
3. Emile Durkheim, *Les formes élémentaires de la vie religieuse* (Paris: Alcan, 1912).
4. Rudolf Otto, *Das Heilige* (Munich: C. H. Beck, 1917).
5. E. E. Evans-Pritchard, *Theories of Primitive Religion* (Oxford: Clarendon Press, 1965).
6. Clifford Geertz, *The Interpretation of Cultures* (New York: Basic Books, 1973), 87–125.

7. James, chap. 2.
8. For example, S. S. Acquaviva, *L'ecclisi del sacro nella civilta industriale* (Milano: Communitā, 1961); Harvey Cox, *The Secular City* (London: S. C. M., 1965).
9. Max Black, *Models and Metaphors: Studies in Language and Philosophy* (New York: Cornell University Press, 1962), 25–47.
10. Andrew Ortony, ed., *Metaphor and Thought* (Cambridge: Cambridge University Press, 1979), 40–41.

Part Two
SYSTEMATIC HISTORICAL

8

Varieties of Spiritual Experience

ARABINDA BASU

Spirit by definition must be self-existent. Anything derived from another thing is part of phenomenon and not spirit as such. The whole world of phenomenon is shown to be contingent and therefore not necessary or self-existent. Within the phenomenal world an entity is the manifestation of something relatively more fundamental, but the world of mutation as a whole is considered self-existent. Whether a relation exists between immutable self-existent spirit and phenomenal change is an important question. We will touch upon it later in this chapter.

Is there any empirical evidence of a self-existent reality? The answer depends on our idea of experience, which is closely related to the nature and personality of man. We must consider whether man is just personality and nature. If we probe deeply enough into ourselves, we arrive at something which can only be described as pure consciousness or awareness—which may or may not be conscious or aware of anything. This is such an overwhelming experience that ordinarily man does not wish to encounter it. A bare awareness that is not aware of anything may undermine our normal personality and activities. We are so accustomed to identifying ourselves with our mind, life, and body that anything even vaguely suggesting that we are not any of these constituents of our personality, or a complex of them, is a threat to our existence.

The truth of something other than what we know, deal with, and enjoy may not be part of our common experience, but that is no reason for denying its existence. This brings in the question of the complexity of man and his psychological constitution. There is a light which illuminates everything but needs nothing other than itself for its illumination. This is awareness or consciousness. To question the truth of its existence or its nature presupposes its reality. Any experience of this self-existent reality is spiritual experience.

The self-existent reality must be one. This fact of unity of the ultimate reality may lead, or rather mislead us to imagine that there can be only one kind of experience of this one fundamental fact. But this is not the case. There is a great variety of spiritual experiences. The spirit, being, awareness, consciousness can and does have an incredible plethora of aspects. Men of different temperament and capacity experience this one reality diversely.

Is there anything common among these experiences which are so varied and yet can be described as spiritual? One definite answer is that a genuine spiritual experience will dissolve man's predilection for putting himself in the center of the universe. A man who has a spiritual experience knows unity to be the basic fact. Multiplicity is either a manifestation of unity, or created by it, or in certain cases, imposed on it by the human consciousness. This last experience has as a corollary the feeling that the world is not real. Nevertheless, as long as the world of multiplicity is experienced as something objectively given, though not real, it is based on the unitary Reality. Taken further, this experience is formulated as that of Nihil, Shunya, Nirvana. The Nihil is not non-existent but non-being. It is perceived as such because the human mind cannot conceive of only modal existence. To be is to be something, and Shunya or Nirvana is not anything. Thus 'being' is also an inadequate description. Note through this experience man overcomes that which misleads him to separate himself from reality. This is why this experience can be described as spiritual.

If the world is not truly real, but imposed on the bare ground of spiritual reality, the latter experience would be static and devoid of the power of self-manifestation or creation. This is not the only possibility. Great mystics and yogis experienced this reality as dynamic. If it is existence of existent, it is also conscious-force. The force is conscious because the reality is consciousness. Before addressing the aspect of manifestation, we must look at another aspect of the matter. The expression consciousness should read also as self-luminous. The term self-luminous can mean either or both of two things. First, awareness is fundamentally self-luminous because it is self-manifesting. Second, consciousness is self-revealing, i. e., it reveals itself to itself. Put the matter in this form: does spiritual reality know itself? Shankara, one of the greatest philosophers and a yogi of high caliber, gave a negative answer. Brahma has no knowledge of itself; pure consciousness cannot split itself into subject and object. Aristotle, another great philosopher, speaking of God, said that thought itself is bliss. Both philosophers are right and both experiences are confirmed in various mystics' direct knowledge of the reality. We speak of consciousness moving towards itself and discovering itself as self-conscious existence and self-existent consciousness. This self-discovery by the spiritual reality is delight or bliss, causeless and independent of objects. It is the third aspect of the ultimate reality.

A study of Plotinus will show that he has both these ideas of reality in his system. Nous is God's knowledge of himself. But the 'One' beyond Nous cannot be said to know itself. Nevertheless, the 'One' has life, or dynamism by which it moves and manifests itself as the world by descending to different levels of its own being. This descent is followed by an ascent back to the reality, to the 'One'. Plotinus makes it quite clear that this ascent cannot be affected by mere intellectual conception of the nature of reality, but by a spiritual and living experience of it.

The idea that reality knows itself without losing its status as pure consciousness is closely connected with the concept that consciousness is also will. Thus consciousness becomes knowledge-will. How does reality know itself? As existence, consciousness and bliss, as complete knowledge and infallible will, and as full of potentialities waiting to be actualized. The world is nothing but the actualization of these potentialities. Knowledge comprehends all potentialities as reality waiting to be made objective. The will realizes this objectivization as reality manifested as the world. Many mystics believe that everything is the same reality variously manifested as the world of multiplicity. This is a reflection in human consciousness of the truth that the knowledge-will of conscious and self-existent reality projects itself as the world.

Here are two experiences which encounter reality in two extremely different ways. In the first, reality is static, without features, attributes, qualities, relations, and creative power. Consequently, in the light of the experience of the spirit, the world is reduced to illusion. In the second experience, reality is static in its basic aspect but dynamic in its movement of consciousness, knowing itself as the seed of the world and willing it to grow as the Tree of Life. This latter experience knows reality as Person while the former pronounces it Impersonal. Actually the second experience finely balances status and dynamism, personality and impersonality.

Those who accept the world as a manifestation or a creation of God will also acknowledge that God is both transcendent of and immanent in the world. This immanent aspect of God gives many mystics the living sense that everything is the Lord's dwelling. Seeing the universe in a flower and eternity in an hour harmonizes the universal and the individual manifestations of the transcendent reality. This reality is neither individual nor universal exclusively but both simultaneously.

We have not yet mentioned the relationship between man and God, that is, the 'Absolute' revealed by spiritual experience. People who experience this reality as a transcendent absolute, static and impersonal, will realize pure identity of the being within it. In other words, the spiritual self in man and the Absolute Self are experienced as identical. This means that the individual self is not truly real. This presents many philosophical difficulties but there is no doubt that the experience is genuine. This may not be a complete experience according to some mystics and yogis, but it is found in many mystical traditions belonging to different world religions. Pseudo-Dionysius, Eckhart, and others can be cited in this connection within the Christian tradition. Unlike Shankara in the Hindu tradition, they also believe in the personal God and the reality of the individual soul. But they admit in their experience and formulation of the nature of reality, there is a status of reality transcending its personal aspect.

In the Hindu tradition there are three main formulations of the relation between the spiritual self in man and God, or the supreme Self: first, pure identity rendering the individual self unreal; second, unity in distinction with stress put on the side of unity; third, unity in distinction but with emphasis on distinction. The Bhagavad Gita characterizes the individual self of the living being as an eternal 'portion' of the supreme Divine (portion being interpreted as partial manifestation). In some experiences, such as the one Ramanuja tries to substantiate philosophically in his various writings, the individual self is not a manifestation of God, but an eternal reality existent with God but real only within and dependent on his being. The individual self is to be controlled and supported by God in willing and devoted servitude, man's highest spiritual status. This relationship between the liberated self and God is described in the school of Chaitanya as that between the Lover and the Beloved. According to this great mystic, acknowledged by many as an incarnation of God, reality is non-dual consciousness endowed with inherent conscious-force, best displayed in the enjoyment of love. The liberated individual self is a lover loving the Divine, the Beloved, for the sake of loving with utter self-abandon and complete surrender. God exalts in sharing his love with these devotees. This relationship is reminiscent of St. John of the Cross and also of St. Theresa in some phases of their spiritual development.

Another great experience vouched to man in his spiritual quest is that of God as Lord and Master of cosmic nature and the world. Some seekers are volitionally oriented and look upon all life and its activities as a sacrifice to the Lord of all works. Giving up all desires for the fruits of works, viewing the Lord's cosmic energy, not themselves, as the real doer, they arrive at a stage where they can offer themselves as instruments of God for fulfillment of his purpose in this world. This spiritual gospel of spiritual works synthesizes knowledge and devotion with works. The seeker must know the nature of the true self. Otherwise, the seeker cannot be detached from egoistic clinging to the fruits of works, running counter to the spirit of sacrifice. If one has no personal desire for anything transitory and is bent upon realization of the supreme value—union with God—one will become an instrument of God due to one's love and devotion for God. There is no other motive. This is the synthetic yoga of the Bhagavad Gita. As Sri Aurobindo puts it, "The first step is Karmayoga, the selfless sacrifice of works, and here the Gita's insistence is on action. The second is Jnanayoga, the self-realization and knowledge of the true nature of the self and the world, and here the insistence is on knowledge; but the sacrifice of works continues and the path of works becomes one with but does not disappear into the path of knowledge. The last step is Bhaktiyoga, adoration and seeking of the supreme Self as the Divine Being, and here the insistence is on devotion; but the knowledge is not subordinated, only raised, vitalized and fulfilled, and still the sacrifice of works continues; the double path becomes the triune way of knowledge, works, and devotion. And the fruit of the sacrifice, the one fruit still placed before the seeker, is obtained, union with the Divine Being, and oneness with the supreme Nature."[1]

Regarding the relation between the spiritual self and the ultimate reality, Sri Aurobindo says it is possible to have a comprehensive and integral experience in which pure identity—union in distinction with emphasis on union, and distinction in union with stress put on distinction—can simultaneously be enjoyed. This is possible because the Divine has different aspects and these above-mentioned different experiences reflect these different sides of God.

The Divine is indescribable. Spiritual experience reveals God as pure identity which nevertheless is a multiple unity. Multiplicity in this context does not mean the many things of the world but the community of individual spiritual selves, manifestations of the supreme self, the personal-impersonal Divine Lord. Hence, the individual self can realize identity with the Absolute—union with God with its own distinctions subordinated, and distinction from God with its own self-identity emphasized. God knows himself in all of these three different ways and therefore the individual self can do likewise because he is fundamentally one with the Supreme.

If the world is deemed as the manifestation of God through his inherent conscious force, what does a complete, comprehensive and integral experience indicate about humankind's destiny? We find an answer in the non-dualistic, realistic philosophies based on the scriptures of Tantra. The Divine limits himself by his own free will and appears as the world and the individual soul in it. This is described as a descent of the conscious force, the last limit of which is matter. God, dormant in matter, ascends by stages back to his original status as the free divine spirit. This is looked upon as a game—*kṛda*. It is difficult to see why this tremendous drama should be played unless there is a purpose of God in the world itself and not merely beyond it. Sri Aurobindo in his basic metaphysics arrives at a similar conclusion but on the foundation of the Vedanta, that is, the Upanishads, and ultimately their source, the Veda. He unequivocally admits that God limits himself freely to become the world and the individual self and evolving soul in it. But he adds that this descent of the Divine into the world is to make the world divine. "God having become Nature, Nature seeks to be God."[2] Needless to say, the soul must first realize its true and highest Self—God in all its aspects. The soul must also realize that the Divine is not only manifested as individual self but also as soul, mind, life and body through stress of his own conscious force—Supermind, the integral Knowledge-Will, in Sri Aurobindo's terminology—and though veiled is present and involved in the world. The liberated soul's spiritual mission is not to realize God beyond the world but to unveil and manifest him in this world, transforming mind, life and body divinely. Thus they do not remain masks veiling their indwelling spiritual reality but become molds manifesting their inherent divine truth.

For this experience to be possible man must evolve a new consciousness, a new instrument of knowledge, will, and enjoyment. This is the Supermind which in reference to the Divine, is "God's own knowledge of himself and his own inherent power of acting." The integral supramental realization of God effectuates the radical transformation not only of the spiritual soul but also of his now-unspiritual, mental, vital and physical nature. In the inspiring words of Sri Aurobindo, "To know, possess and be the divine being in an animal and egoistic consciousness, to convert our twilight or obscure physical mentality into the plenary supramental illumination, to build peace and a self-existent bliss where there is only a stress of transitory satisfactions besieged by physical pain and emotional suffering, to establish an infinite freedom in a world which presents itself as a group of mechanical necessities, to discover and realise the immortal life in a body subjected to death and constant mutation,—this is offered to us as the manifestation of God in Matter and the goal of Nature in her terrestrial evolution."[3]

The divine life on earth is the ultimate fruit of the spiritual quest of humankind.

NOTES

1. *Essays on the Gita, the Core of the Teaching* (New York: Sri Aurobindo Library, Inc., 1950), 35.
2. Sri Aurobindo, *The Divine Life* (New York: Sri Aurobindo Library, Inc., 1949), 45.
3. Sri Aurobindo, *The Life Divine* (New York: Sri Aurobindo Library, Inc., 1949), 2.

9

Luther's Trinitarian Experience of God and the Spirituality of Advaita Vedānta

MICHAEL VON BRÜCK

Luther is only occasionally concerned with speculation about the nature of God. He did not develop a systematic doctrine of God as such. His whole concern is of a soteriological nature. That is why he emphasizes our actual encounter with God as the origin of all theological knowledge. Through Christ, God can be experienced and felt as one's closest friend. He is present every moment and everywhere. He is a comforting as well as frightening presence, *fascinosum et tremendum* in Rudolf Otto's terms.[1]

The Christian understanding of God is based on the experience of the triune God. In order to investigate Luther's experience, we must consider all the aspects appearing on this background of God's triune nature. Thus, we must approach the subject from different points of Luther's theological argumentation in order to come closer to the core of his experience of, or with, God.

Without giving a systematic outline of Luther's concept of God, we will finally compare the core of his experience with some basic trends in the spirituality of Advaita Vedānta. We presuppose the knowledge about this Indian system and explain only a few basic features which are of utmost importance for our cross-cultural attempt.

I

Luther took the doctrine of the Trinity from the scholastic tradition basically without adding new points of view. He considered this doctrine scripturally founded, and felt he had to uphold it.[2] Luther's concept of the doctrine of the Trinity should not be underestimated. It is noteworthy that for a Protestant theology indebted to Luther "the difference of the general and christologically mediated talk about God and man is inbuilt according to the distinction of law and gospel: *Aliud enim est, de Deo incarnatio vel homine deificato loqui, et aliud de Deo vel homine simpliciter.*"[3]

There is no single text of Luther's comprehensively dealing with the doctrine of the Trinity. Among Luther's earlier works, the Christmas sermon of 1514[4] and the sermon on the Sunday of the Trinity[5] reflect this doctrinal stance. However, most important are Luther's later works: *Die letz en Worte Davids,*[6] as well as some of his disputations.[7] There is a remarkable continuity to Luther's thinking on this problem.[8] Luther's Trinitarian conception of God can be best understood in the larger context of some of his central theological ideas. Luther's whole theology of the cross and justification are recognizably rooted in this Trinitarian concept.

In his Christmas sermon in 1514 Luther contributes new analogies to the understanding of the Trinity. He goes beyond Augustine in taking his analogies from the whole of created reality, as well as from the field of the human soul. On the one hand, this suggests that Luther rejected Augustine's position giving the soul a special place as *imago Dei.* On the other hand, he related God equally to the whole creation. Luther used these analogies more than just occasionally[9] in his sermons.[10]

If Luther had any reservations concerning the classical analogies, it was because he rejected the idea that some parts of human beings were "less sinful" than others. In Tauler, the *Seelengrund* was understood as an image for the Trinity.[11] This transcends the immediate psychological analogies of Augustine. For the mystics the *Seelengrund* is not a phenomenal realm of the human psyche controlled by the will. It is the transcendent experience in and beyond the psychic realm. Luther's ideas and images from the mystics must be understood in this transcendental sense.

Another reservation concerning the analogies—and even the idea of *relationes*—was that Luther was afraid to spoil man's search and betray that God is inaccessible by any accidental means. The Godhead of God cannot be sought and expressed, but only adored and worshipped. Luther uses the term *relationes* for lack of any better name or solution to the problem.[12]

God is one and the same in all his actions. He is discernible as creator, redeemer, and faith-creating Spirit.[13] He is triune, and there is a relationship between the *personalis pluritas* and the *unitas naturae et essentiae.*[14] God is not known to us as he is known to himself. We know him only through his revelation. To know God through his revelation commences with the economical Trinity. Luther considers the consequences of his economical concept of the immanent Trinity much less than Augustine. Thus, Luther understands the Father as the real absolute God. At the same time he stresses the total and essential equality between the three persons.[15]

To know God *extra revelationem* would be human hubris and sin; it implies man is equal to God. Human beings could never obtain such a clear understanding. They would find only an image of God reflecting their own desires and wishes (*applicuerunt pro votis et desideriis suis*). Each would subordinate the knowledge to his interest (*quisque studio suo subsumere voluit*).[16] Man alone can know only his projection of God, a product of his own ego.

In revelation, God limits himself to human capacity. He is recognizable as the Trinitarian God through his threefold manifestation. We can actually experience his revelation. We do not know him in himself, but *pro nobis.* Thus we can be assured of salvation.

He reveals himself in Christ as the loving one who gives freely out of grace, yet his is still the omnipotent and predestining God.[17] Man adheres to the *deus revelatus* because God as *deus incarnatus* promises the salvation of man.[18]

All actions of God are acts of the whole Trinity. Thus, the creation is understood in a Trinitarian way: God as Father is the source of creation, as Son he is the word which calls creation from non-being into being, and as Spirit he is the protecting divine love by which the creator takes the creation into his heart, giving being and permanence to the word.[19] The appropriations of creating, speaking, and blessing do not abolish the unity of the one act in three persons.[20]

As the whole Trinity works in creation, so redemption is also the action of the triune God. The Father is the source of the word, calling back those lost in sin. Renewed in the Spirit, these lost ones are taken to the son.[21] Since Father, Son, and Spirit work together in creation as well as redemption, creation and redemption are only two moments in the one process of salvation history. In the Word, that is, in the Son, God gives himself and sustains everything by the Spirit (*id est spiritus sanctus, qui omnia vivificat, tenet, conservat*).[22] God as Spirit is the "link" keeping all creatures together.[23] God in himself is one. Therefore, he is unified in all actions. That is why discriminations such as creation, redemption, sanctification, etc., are meaningless *sub specie Dei.*

God is knowable only in his revelation, but Luther stresses this is qualified by the humanity of Jesus Christ. God gives himself to us in the man Jesus. Hence, we can know and grasp him.[24] The desire to know him in any other way is merely pride.[25] When one knows and follows the man Jesus, Christ himself will add the knowledge of his Godhead. Thus, one is removed from oneself and led towards God by the man Jesus, "*quod prior sit Christus homo, quam deus apprehendendus, prior humantas eius crux, quam divinitatis eius gloria pretenda. Christus homo habitus Christum Deum sponte sua adducet.*"[26]

Knowing Jesus as man means knowing his suffering and crucifixion in which he totally united his will with the will of the Father. This is the *sacramentum incarnationis.* In this the *crux Christi* becomes knowable. Knowing him in the cross removes us from our sinful egocentricity into unity of the will with God and into community with him.[27] The cross is the center of the *huminitas Christi* and the center of Luther's theology. It leads to the self-knowledge of man as sinner[28] and prepares for the *fides sola gratia: crux sola est nostra theologia.*[29]

There are two ways of speaking about God: the *theologia gloriae* and the *theologia crucis.*[30] *Theologia gloriae* means to know God from his deeds (*ea, quae facta sunt*), but the problem is that they are actually invisible. Human beings misuse the knowledge of the *maiestas Dei* for their own glorification. That is why God is hidden behind the cross. Therefore *theologia crucis* is the only proper theology. The cross and suffering, the humanity of Jesus are the only visible manifestations by which God wants to be known. The suffering and cross refer to the suffering of Christ as well as to the suffering of the Christians. The knowledge of the hidden God *sub contrario* can be attained only in faith which excludes human pride. "The attempt of man to be justified by his own deeds, and the other one, to know God by his own speculation and thinking in his glory and majesty are closely interconnected. Both of them have their root in the will which is natural to man, to give himself the glory and deprive God of it whom fear is due to, anyway."[31]

Luther's insight is taken from his experience of justification, namely, that God reveals his grace through the contrary, into the whole relationship between God and man. The *theologia crucis,* the knowledge of the triune God in the humanity of Christ, the understanding of the two ways of speaking about God, the doctrine of law, and gospel, the notion of the *opus proprium et opus alienum Dei,* etc., are only variations of this same experience and topic.

This distinction of law and gospel leads to the center of Luther's understanding of God. It signifies the double aspect of the encounter with God leading towards life on the one hand and towards death on the other. On one side there is the grace of God and on the other side there is his wrath. By means of the law God brings man to the end of his pride and egocentricity (*usus theologicus legis*). By means of the gospel, the desperate man experiences that God alone controls all, and grants life and grace.[32] In order to express the unity of wrath and grace, law, and gospel, etc., Luther coins the formula of the *opus alienum* and *opus proprium Dei.*[33] The law is the *opus alienum* through which the grace of the gospel works unseen. The gospel is the *opus proprium.* These *opera* are not equally valid; "God in the deepest and most essential way is love."[34] In our human experience, law and gospel remain always in tension overcome only *sub specie Dei* or eschatologically.

God is the one free and absolute will, necessarily determining everything.[35] Luther has been misinterpreted as teaching absolute determinism,[36] especially since this statement accompanies others on predestination (stating that God can condemn innocent beings since they have no free will to do good).[37] This certainly does not have a biblical background.

Luther's point is actually quite different. In *De servo arbitrio* (1525) he wants only to emphasize God's omnipotence,[38] which excludes the sinner's free and cooperative will regarding the problem of salvation. Man cannot do anything without God's grace, which is *bonum* or *iustum coram Deo.*[39] This does not imply metaphysical determinism which Luther neither affirmed nor negated. It simply was not his concern.[40] Even the doctrine of the *deus absconditus* does not deal with the problem of a theoretical knowledge of God. It points out the way in which God works man's salvation, namely *sub contrario.* Man must come *sub contrario* because of his pride and ego-delusion. This is the key for a proper understanding of the whole argument. A direct knowledge would only boost our ego and pride; thus we would fall deeper into the trap of sin.[41] Luther's notion of the *deus absconditus* means God is not object but *subject* of the knowledge of God.

Luther starts with the *deus revelatus* because God revealed himself in his word, Jesus Christ.[42] Here God is totally knowable,[43] but hidden behind the cross in the unpretending reality of the child. That is why Luther stresses the *word* in revelation. The word for him is the simile for spiritual self-communication exemplifying that the life in the word is the most powerful thing on earth.[44]

Christ is the word of God which becomes present by mediation of the Spirit. This is the Trinitarian key to Luther's understanding of the word. It is the creative power. By the word we exist. By the word God transforms us into what he is himself: "*qua deus iustus est, ut eadem iustitia Deus et nos iusti simus, sicut eodem verbo deus facit et nost summus, quod ipse est, ut in ipso simus, et suum esse nostrum esse sit.* "[45] We partake of God by his word. The sacrament is only one way of God's utterance of the word.[46] The sacrament is also "word." For Luther, there is no basis for any intellectual misunderstanding of the reality of God's word.

Christ is the word, but that is not all. It is necessary to distinguish the different dimensions in Luther's understanding of the word.[47] God does and creates everything by means of the word. That is why all creatures are words of God.[48] By the word God addresses man and works salvation.

Luther distinguishes between the internal and the external word of God. God addresses man first in the external word, basically in the incarnation of Jesus Christ. Human speech and its foundation in scriptures are also means which God uses to speak to the external word.[49] The inner word is and remains in God. Through his power and wisdom God speaks to himself. The inner word is Christ, according to the divine and eternal nature; thus the Son is one with the Father in the inner-trinitarian encounter.[50] The inner word is the true word of God given without any mediation into the heart of man by the power of the Spirit. It is divine, enlightening presence; "The Holy Spirit, therefore, belongs essentially to the inner word."[51] Yet, normally the external word mediates the internal word. The external word exists for the sake of the internal one.[52] Hearing and listening to the word works faith—a kind of transformation of man: "God becomes man so that man becomes God."[53] The external word (for instance a sermon) penetrates man only up to the ears. The transformation of the heart is the work of the inner word.

Without any difficulty we can discover four states of the word in Luther's understanding:

1. The inner word which is in God, described by *inner-trinitarian* relationships.

2. The external word in the revelation of the incarnation of *Jesus Christ.*

3. Derived from (2); the mediation of the external word Jesus Christ through the *scripture.*

4. The external word of the third state, expressed in spoken language, in the *viva vox evangelii.*

The important cut is between state (1) and states (2) through (4). The first state describes the immanent Trinity, whereas states two through four deal with "forms of manifestation" of the word in the realm of the economical Trinity.[54]

II

Luther's deepest experiences and thoughts are connected with what he calls "temptation" (*Anfechtung*). God acts *sub contrario* in wrath through the law, the cross, and the despair of man. The *usus theologicus legis* forces man to abolish his egocentric desire against God. The ego has to die repeatedly so that the renewed man can be resurrected with Christ.[55] Wrath, *mortificatio,* the *usus theologicus legis* and the whole hardship of temptation must be understood as the *opus alienum Dei* by which God prepares the ground for granting grace, *vivification,* and the gospel. The experience of temptation, therefore, belongs already to God's work of grace.[57] Hence, Luther can call the wrath of God *benignitatis ira.*[58] The temptations are in reality "embracements of God."[59] The *opus proprium Dei* is experienced after the *opus alienum.* God creates or sends temptations in order to break the pride of the sinner. They are preparations to make him suitable (*aptus*) for the grace of God.[60] Temptation means to experience existentially the loss of security in a self-centered and ego-projected salvation. It is painful because it is experienced as the absence of God.[61] God is actually very near, despite this feeling of his absence. But due to the egocentric striving of man, God's nearness is hidden until the egocentricity *coram Deo* is broken.[62] This tension lasts until the death of man. It is solved only eschatologically.[63] Man remains centered on his ego, that is, he remains a sinner (*peccator*) even if he is already justified (*iustus*) due to the grace of God—*simul iustus et peccator.* Life in faith is life in transition; it is balancing between the two poles.

In view of the omnipresent God, man becomes aware of his *nihileitas.*[64] The *ira Dei,* the accusing power of the law and the cross, are the places where man experiences God as absent (*deus absconditus*). Thus, the experience of temptation is a total end, a complete break and a radical death of the "old Adam." Luther describes this with terms like *descensus ad inferos,*[65] *resignatio ad infernum*[66] or—the strongest term—*excessus in nihilum.*[67]

An unconditional surrender to the will of God is required to eradicate the sinful egoistic will. The will of God then becomes the will of man. The powerful concepts make one shudder to contemplate the depth of Luther's experience of temptation.

The man in temptation experiences nothingness (*nihileitas*). In faith one experiences the nothingness of one's own egocentric striving, without despairing of it. Despair is the greatest sin against the first commandment. God reveals himself in the experience of nothingness. The no-thing of man *coram Deo* means in the truest sense God *is* and *acts*. The one who returns to the nothing returns to God, for he gives up a wrong identity: "*Quo enim perveniat, qui sperat in deum, nisi in sui nihilum? Quo autem habeat, qui habit in nihilum, nisi eo, unde venit? Venit autem ex deo et suo nihilo, quare in deum redit, qui redit in nihilum.*"[68]

The death of the ego is a total break. Hence, the experience of grace in temptation is a totally new beginning. The creation of the new man is as underivable as the *creatio ex nihilo* in the beginning of the world.[69] The nothingness of the human ego goes through temptation until faith opens up a new dimension of being, where man receives his being and identity from God *sola gratia*. Faith is not at all mere *fides historica*, but through faith in Christ man has hope in the midst of temptation. This hope is the work of the Spirit. It enables man to wait and be receptive for the *transfiguring grace* of God.[70] This does not contradict Luther's emphasis on the doctrine of justification. Rather, justification should be seen in the light of real transformation.[71] It is much more than rational acceptance of a *iustitia imputata*, though this line of thinking occurs also in Luther's writings. In other words: the imputation is a transforming process.

Luther's thinking concerning temptation is rather similar to the understanding of *mortificatio* and *vivificatio* in other mystics. But Luther's main point is to maintain that *mortificatio* comes from God alone. It is his *opus alienum*. God appears, but he appears *sub contrario*. This appearance under the opposite does not mean that it is not God. It is not man's work, but a gift of grace through the realization of the Spirit. We know this and can have trust because God has appeared as *deus revelatus*. He shows a way out of nothingness—the new life, the new creation. Man can now trust in the *deus revelatus* in order to cope with the spiritual process of dying known as temptation. Only then will he be able to gain new life in communion with God.[72]

The Trinitarian God works both the temptation as well as the new creation. God reveals himself as redeemer in Jesus Christ; the Spirit mediates the redeeming presence of Christ. As *Spiritus creator* he works steadily on the growing reality of man.[73] The more the ego has been abandoned by temptation, the more God's grace can renew man, "*quando maxime deserit, tunc maximo suscipit. Et cum damnat, maxime salvat.*"[74]

In this renewal, man experiences his real personhood. Man, once free of his ego and determined by God is a real person. He is free to relate to any other being. Such a God-centered personhood will be accomplished only eschatologically, but it starts as a continuous process. Man becomes increasingly free to do the will of God and is less and less bound by the egocentricity which drives him away from God.[75] Only in this sense is man free. To say that a man under sin and the slavery of his desires could have a *liberum arbitrium* would be to call slavery freedom.[76]

Note that a certain dualism is found throughout Luther's thinking, as seen already in the contradictions of *opus proprium* and *opus alienum,* law and gospel. The ongoing struggle between Christ and the power of darkness, or Satan, is mirrored here. God uses even these powers—as in the case of the *usus theologicus legis*-for the establishment of grace.[77] His understanding of the fight between Christ and Satan signifies a real struggle between two powers[78] linked with each other; they are both God's creation.[79] Through them God brings about final salvation. The same holds true for wrath and death. They are not two equal and lasting principles, they are a means of experience for a person realizing within himself the action of the Trinitarian God.[80]

Through temptation, man is led to integrate with the will of God. As Christ coped with the anger of God on the cross and unified his will perfectly with the will of God, man should immerse himself into perfect discipleship with Christ. Luther expressed this with the term *conformitas.*

God became man and entered human conformity in the incarnation. Therefore, there is now the possibility that man can enter into conformity with God. When man recognizes himself as sinful—acknowledging his *nihileitas coram Deo*—he conforms with the will and judgment of God.[81] This is the cardinal step. It is the reality of the cross. Only under this presupposition is it right to speak of *conformitas.* Luther speaks about a "*Christum mortuum in se transformare atque conformare*";[82] and elsewhere: "*Qui enim credit Christum esse suum, esse sibi datum tulisse suum peccatum vicisse suam mortem, ita in Christi spiritum transferentur, ut omnia mala, omnem concupiscentiam, omnem quoque impatientiam vincat.*"[83]

However, the *conformitas Christi* comprehends also the *vivificatio* of man *per fidem Christi,* because we share also in Christ's passing over from death to resurrection. The death and resurrection of Christ are "present reality in the conformity with Christ which are given for man in the efficacy of the Spirit."[84] The rescue from temptation and the new reality of a life built on God alone is conformity with the resurrection of Christ.[85]

There is a strong realism in Luther's understanding of conformity. The Spirit really creates a new man through the communion with Christ.

> *Fides Christi* means for Luther the life in and from the redeeming reality of the presence of Christ. In faith the Christian is so much one with Christ, that faith possesses the redemption through Christ as an immediate reality. By faith in Christ we possess the reality of his redemption as our own reality. His victory is our victory. And this sentence does not want to be understood metaphorically but literally . . . The *fides Christi* is the real unification with the living Christ as redeeming reality.[86]

How can this "real unification" be understood? In line with our former findings we have to conclude that *conformitas Christi* means a new identity, that is, personhood in the sense described above. In the *unum cum eo fieri,* man reaches the perfection of his life. By conforming with God, the right knowledge of God is given. Under the *sapientia carnis* man projected only an idol on the basis of the desires of the ego and his petty interests.[87] Due to the death of the old ego, the enlightenment of the Spirit is granted. Man becomes grounded in God. He has overcome the ego and lives by the spirit. Thus, he knows according to the *sapientia spiritus.* His natural *sensus* has been transformed: "*Et sic odisse animam suam et belle contra proprium velle, sapere contra suum sapere, peccatum concedere contra suam Iustitiam, Stultitiam audire contra sapientiam suam, hoc est 'crucem accipere' et 'Christi discipulum fieri' et 'transformari nouitate sensus'.*"[88]

Conformity with Christ or God does not mean a total identity.[89] The *fides Christi* is not our own piety nor our own work. It is God's action alone.[90] It is not an active *imitatio Christi* by the carnal man. It is a being lifted into the saving action of the Trinitarian God who creates, redeems in Christ, and transforms us by the Spirit into a new being. We are given a new identity—not of the ego but of God. This is what Luther calls *conformitas Christi.*

III

Conformity with Christ, according to Luther, is the new being granted *sola gratia* overcoming his temptation. This combines with his understanding of justification. Luther's doctrine of justification is well known, but so much needs to be clarified. This doctrine has its roots in the above described experiences and motivations. Its summary is paradoxical: *simul iustus et peccator.* It describes one who has passed temptation and awakened to a new life and new identity through the action of the Trinitarian God.

In all described relations, God is a living, acting, and above all a saving presence, that is, he is Trinitarian. The soteriological concern is the starting point for Luther's understanding of God. His doctrine of the Trinity is basically shaped according to the experience of grace and salvation which is offered in Christ *sub contrario.*

The Father is especially linked with creation, the Son with redemption and the Spirit with sanctification.[91] But the whole of the Trinity is at work in all these actions. The three works are explications of the one divine work of grace. Yet, Luther sometimes sees the Father as the true source of the Godhead.[92]

The difference of the three persons is derived from the appropriations, that is, economically.

> Der Vater gibt sich uns mit hymel und erden sampt allen creaturen, das sie dienen und nütze sein müssen. Aber solche gabe ist durch Adams fall verfinstert und unütze wordem, darum hat darnach der son sich selbs auch uns gegeben, alle sein werck, leiden, weisheit und gerechtickeit geschenckt und uns dem Vater versunet, damit wir widder lebendig und gerecht, auch den Vater mit seinen gaven erkennen und haben moechten. Weil aber solche gnade niemand nütze were, wo sie so heymlich bergorgen bliebe und zu uns nicht komen künete, so kompt der heilige geist und gibt sich auch uns gantz und gar, der leret uns solche wolthat Christi, uns erzeigt, erkennen, hilfft sie empfahen und behalten, nützlich brauchen und austeilen, mehren und foddern. Und thut dasselbige beide, ynnerlich und eusserlich: ynnerlich durch den glauben und ander geistlich gaben, eusserlich aber durchs Euangelion, durch die tauffe und sacrament des altars.[93]

The Father is the "original source," the Son is the "ruling form principle," and the Spirit is the "life giving empowering activity."[94] As Luther appositely analogizes: Christ is the door to the Father; the Spirit is the doorkeeper opening the door and giving certainty that man is allowed to enter.[95] "All actions of the one God" are experienced in the variety of his Trinitarian works.[96] The inner-trinitarian relationships are to be concluded. And Luther does so, indeed.[97] His interest is to maintain the personhood of the Spirit, too. The Spirit is really God.[98]

The realization of salvation depends on the work of the Spirit, appearing as *consolator* and *interpolator* in the process of temptation, and acting as both the *accusatio sui* and the *iustificatio Dei.*[99] He is given as *donum gratiae* particularly and especially in the church.[100] The Spirit mediates Christ and the church's integrity is preserved as long as this mediation takes place. The means used are word and sacrament. To understand this properly we must refer to Luther's concept of the word. The Spirit creates the realm of renewal in man, in *consolatio* and *illuminatio.*[101] Due to the Spirit's action, the presence of God in man is real. Man, driven by the Spirit of God, is called to cooperate with God[102] in the history of salvation. Here, too, the subject of man's actions, is definitely not the ego but the Spirit.

For us people, the saving action of God appears as a process with varying moments of creation, redemption, and sanctification. Thus there is a historical or temporal differentiation experienced and expressed in anthropocentric ways. For God, however, this historical process is eternal presence. The history of salvation, the whole process of creation, actually, is one simultaneous occurrence to him. Creation, redemption, etc., cannot be separated. They are in a similar relationship to each other as the three relations of the Trinity. Everything appearing as historical contingency is actually perfect action already present in the inner-trinitarian process of God's omnipotence and omniscience. Everything follows from the love of God with inner necessity, because this love has completed its work already. For God, said Luther, the day of judgment is already present. From our perspective the perfection is still to come.[103] Thus, there are two ways of knowing things, either from the perspective of God or from the perspective of man. Both of them lead necessarily to a different kind of understanding. From the human point of view all things are highly changeable: *Deus est mutabilis quam maxime.* God appears as one perceives him, that is, who and what man is forms his experience of God: *si iustus, iustus; si mundus, mundus. . . .* However, this is only an external changeability of God, seen only in the eyes of man (*verum hoc mutatio extrinsecus est*). In reality God remains one and the same.[104] Change would mean that God was subjected to time. Luther conceives of

God as a being beyond space and time. Only his actions appear to us in temporal categories.[105]

Luther explains the relationship of God and the world in his doctrine of the real presence of Christ in the Holy Supper. As creator and sustaining reality, God is present everywhere and in all of reality. He is the omnipotent power "which is at the same time nowhere yet everywhere."[106] He is in all creation, even in the devil.[107] Luther agrees with Cusanus' idea of the *coincidentia oppositorum* in order to demonstrate that the omnipresence of God cannot be conceived of in our temporal and spacial categories of experience.[108] God is present in both the innermost essence of every creature as well as in the outermost essence.[109] He can be there "deeper, more internal, more present than the creature is for itself, that he certainly comprises everything, but nothing comprises him and is in him."[110]

This means that God is in everything, but at the same time he is also "beyond and above all creatures."[111] God is present and totally transcendent. He is the innermost principle and the essence of the unity of the world. Yet he is transcendent and of a different nature than the world; he is creator, the world is creature. Luther speaks about God in such a way, that "the common alternative of transcendence and immanence is overcome as a totally irrelevant question." This enables him to clearly and precisely stress the *extra nos* of God's action.[112]

God is present in a hidden way. He is present everywhere, yet is not perceptible everywhere. He is free, unlimited, and unconditioned.[113] That is why he wants to be known where he has made himself known, namely, in his revelation, in his word, in Jesus Christ.[114] The revelation is a light shining on us so we become aware of the omnipresence of God in creation. Thus, we realize that the God of revelation in Christ is everywhere. This is a basic experience which the faithful enjoy.

For Luther, all reflection on the essence of God and also on the Trinitarian problem is connected soteriologically. The triune God works creation, redemption, and sanctification as one. The result of this process is that man is brought back into unity with God. There is a continuous growth in sanctification, but this is the work of the Holy Spirit. It is not due to man, who has overcome his attitude in the process of temptation, justification, and renewal. [115] This happens through faith, the real acceptance of Christ as *donum Dei* in us through the work of the Spirit. Faith is no longer determined by the ego, but by God. Faith is the work of the Trinitarian God. In faith we participate in God with full awareness. This participation transforms, conforms, and unifies the whole of life.[116]

Luther's theology is intrinsically connected with his personality, his experiences, and his striving for a God of grace on the one hand and with the historical situation on the other. That is why comparisons between Luther's thinking and other theologies must be carried out extremely carefully. Since Luther's entire theology is permeated by his spiritual experience, we can look for parallel experiences as bases of comparison.

Everything concerning the problem of temptation and justification—*mortificatio* and *vivificatio,* the radical and dialectical negation of the egocentric striving of man—climaxes in the reformatorian *solus: solus deus, sola gratia, solus Christus, sola fides.* Only God is; the egocentric isolation of man (sin) is overcome by God's action in the Spirit.

IV

The following section contains some preliminary remarks of justification, indicating both the theological as well as the methodological problem of cross-cultural studies.

This chapter's title speaks about the spirituality of Advaita Vedānta in comparison with Luther's experience. This chapter will not attempt to deal with the dogmatic systems on both sides nor with other dimensions of the religious reality. It will focus on the spiritual experience of a Western man and a type of Eastern spiritual experience. These experiences are necessarily expressed in words and terms which are to be understood in the original context.

Taking this clarification into consideration it is easier to dare the attempt. Spirituality is not identical with religion, but is its underlying ground, expressed in the differing dimensions of religion. Though it is hardly possible to separate a universal spirituality from a concrete and historical religion, it is obvious that certain types of experience, and certain patterns of expression as well, occur in different situations. They are, therefore, translatable. This makes cross-cultural studies possible. There is no universal language—but there is man's universal experience of his encounter with God, expressed in different languages, symbols, and other modes. The universality of this reality enables us to translate these experiences cross-culturally.

Luther's case supports this observation. Once liberated from a purely rationalistic misinterpretation, Luther's mystical personality shines through. This is clear when we see him on the background of Tauler, Seuso and the Theologia Germanica. We hope to shed more light on Luther by comparing some of his insights with Eastern mysticism. Our understanding of Luther should benefit from this rather unusual enterprise.

Advaita Vedānta is based on a specific spiritual experience: the experience of the non-duality, *advaita,* of experiencing subject and experienced object, of reality and consciousness, matter and spirit, world and God. Transcendence and immanence merge into one point of unified awareness beyond the contents of consciousness mediated by perception of the senses.

Reality is one. This oneness is experienced by discovering the real 'Self' (*ātman*) beyond all the different roles and activities of the human being. Ātman is finally not different from the one reality, *Brahman.* This is the basic intuition of Vedānta. Brahman is changeless, eternal, and, self-existing, *svayambhū.* It is the one-without-a-second, *advitīya,* truly being, *sat,* pure consciousness, *cit,* and perfect bliss, *ānanda.* Hence, the macrocosmic and the microcosmic realities are one. They are dimensions of consciousness separated only in the illusory subject-object perceptions of man.

There are two ways of looking at reality: from the absolute point of view, that is, in unified awareness, *pāramārthika,* and from a relative point of view, that is, on the basis of the knowledge derived from diverse sense-perceptions, *vyāvahārika.*

The non-duality of being is the very essence of the advaitic experience.[117] Peace, *śanti,* is the result of this transrational experience. Its opposite, pain and restlessness, are a result of our illusion of being separated from the One, of existing independently. This illusion causes fear and anger and is the basis for evil. That is why the experience of the One is directly connected with salvation or liberation, *mokṣa.* In reality we are one with *moksa,* but are unaware of it due to our ego-illusion which creates dualities. There is nothing to be attained which is not already there; the real and universal presence of the One remains to be realized.[118]

Brahman is all and in all. He who realizes this unifies with Brahman and becomes also all in all. This knowledge is not intellectual knowledge, but life transforming insight. The One is beyond all the masks which make up phenomenological reality, but at the same time, it is *in* all these masks also.[119]

It is important to understand that Brahman is not to be conceived of as the creative or material cause of the world. Rather, Brahman appears only *vyāvahārika* as world. The separation of the two is upheld only because man is caught up in his illusion. The Brahman, however, is not at all affected by its appearance as world. Thus, Brahman is not the cause of the world but is the cause of the cause, *yataḥ,* that is, it is the transcendent ground. This ground, however, does not differ from what is grounded in it.

Thus, Brahman is totally immanent and totally transcendent simultaneously. How I perceive it depends on my point of view. It is *immanent transcendence* and *transcendent immanence.*

Brahman ātman is the true subject. It is not the ego-illusion which is the core of man's physico-psychic-spiritual actions, but it is the ātman. Ātman is the internal ruler, *antaryāmin,* in all cosmic as well as human processes.[121] It is the seer in the process of seeing, the hearer in the act of hearing, the thinker in the activity of thinking. Because this subject is inaccessible to sense perceptions (which are derived and therefore unable to comprehend the final subject), it is called the "unseen seer, the unheard hearer, the unthought thinker, the unknown knower."[122] Man can think, but he cannot think thinking.[123] Thinking requires an objectified content, thus always creating a dualistic split inherently separating the perceived subject from the thoughts perceiving it.

Hence, the proper *pramāna* (means of knowledge) is a direct spiritual experience, *anubhava,* based on and guided by the scriptures, namely, the advices of the *rsi's.* The transcendent experience goes beyond ordinary states of consciousness. Consciousness experiences itself as the One reality.

The eternal is not extrinsic but intrinsic to the temporal. We can speak of a *tempiternal* (R. Panikkar) oneness. The creative power, *māyā,* is responsible for spacio-temporal differentiation in the process of the one consciousness. The monistic relationship between Brahman and māyā, however, cannot be clarified. It is simply indeterminable, *anirvacanīya.* Yet, if we look at this differentiation (the historical reality) only as on isolated beings and events, we are caught up in illusion, *avidyā.* We do not realize the eternal *in* the temporal and the temporal *in* the eternal. Temporal existence is illusory only when we regard it as absolute reality—something which it is not. In the proper perspective, however, the world must be seen as dependent existence, actually different than the One, *ekam.* The One *is* the relative, and the relative *is* the One. They are not two sides of a coin but different levels of consciousness. Thus, *advaita* is the experience of the eternal presence or the present eternal.

Advaita should not be misunderstood as subjectivism, because it teaches what transcends subject and object:[124] the One which, in spite of the movement of māyā, remains as the homogenous pure intelligence, transcendent of change or any other qualification.[125]

The *advaitin* as *jnānin* (knower) tries to penetrate into this pure transcendence. He aims at a totally unconditioned vision of God, beyond the danger of revering finite values. He has surpassed the egoistic attachment to one's own thoughts and images. It is an act of participation (or merging) in the One. Some schools stress either the participatory or the dynamic aspect, others insist on a perfect merging.

Therefore, in spite of the radical apophatism of the Upanishads concerning the *nirguna Brahman,* it is possible to adore the Highest Self (*paramātman, Brahman*) in a more hymnic than logical formula: *saccidānanda.*

Saccidānanda is the very "being" of the One. This understanding is connected with the experience of power, *śakti.*[126] Brahman is the actuality fully united with its potential to produce the forms or levels of appearance. Saccidānanda means that reality is perfect being, perfect consciousness and perfect bliss. This includes the notion of perfect energy or power expressed in the threefold dynamism of *sat-cit-ānanda.*

Sat as 'Being' is the imperishable. It is also truth, *satya,* the unchangeable. No modifications whatsoever can affect Brahman.

Cit is perfect awareness or pure consciousness. It means that sat is self-reflected. The point is that Brahman does not merely possess consciousness, but *is* consciousness itself. Cit is not a qualification on sat, but is the self-expressing awareness of the One.

Ānanda is the ecstasy of being, perfect bliss. Again, it is not a modification. Rather, the very being of the One is bliss in self-awareness.

Participation in this one mystery of saccidānanda is mokṣa, liberation, the goal of life. Actually, saccidānanda is our very being, but we are ignorant of it because of the ego-delusion which deprives us of real being.

Thus, realization is the need. The man who has overcome his illusory ego realizes the ātman, the true self. The realized jnānin, however, is not perfect within or due to himself, but due to the new man born in and from the ātman.[127]

Thus, the *mahāvākya: ahām brahmāsmi* (I am Brahman.) could be and is often misinterpreted. It is not the "I" which speaks, but the ātman. Hence, the ātman brahmāsti remains. It is uttered by the man who has realized his true identity.

V

The previous explanation of Advaita Vedānta is sufficient to shed some light on Luther's experience. The same parallels can be drawn with other Western mystics such as John of the Cross, Teresa de Avila, Tauler, and Seuso. However, our topic concerns Luther.

For Luther, faith is a total transformation of man by the indwelling Christ. Faith is *conformitas Christi.* The "old Adam" disappears, and Christ becomes the center of life or the real subject (Gal. 2:20). There is a process of identification, participation, and merging.

Justification is an event, an outside occurrence. It enters man's life to be repeatedly realized in faith. Justification by faith means also a surrender into the trans-individual power of the Spirit. He is—in Eckhart's words—our *isness.*

The Holy Spirit is the indwelling God, creating and renewing life in every aspect and at any time. The Spirit actually is the subject of everything. Hence, Luther speaks about the *spiritus creator.* It is either the Spirit or the ego who rules man. Genuine life, prayer, and meditation always have the *Spirit* as subject. Thus, God is the subject leading man's life in faith.

Without going into details we see clearly an affinity to the pattern of spirituality in Advaita Vedānta. There is the ātman, the center and ground of the personality. Here it is the Spirit. To find the true identity is to surrender into the reality of God/Brahman. The human ego is not the subject. In both cases man must overcome the illusion of an independent center of subjectivity.

It is the task of man to be silent and to listen, to internalize the "point of view of God" and to become transformed. Faith is similar to the Eastern participation in the One and realization of the ātman. It is unification with the eternal presence, that is, the absolute standpoint in Advaita Vedānta.

God is the subject in the process of salvation or liberation. Similarly, the ātman is the subject of knowledge, the subject of everything. But we realize it only if we look at reality, *pāramārthika,* or from the standpoint of God,—we judge out of faith. *Vyāvahārika* there are all differentiations, spacio-temporal discernments, etc. But pāramārthika or *sub specie Dei* there is no difference, no time and the "day of judgement is already here," as Luther says.

The underlying experience leading to those similar views and patterns of thinking must also be similar.

However, in contradiction to the *donum Dei* in Luther's understanding, the ātman is not given by a personal God who gives free will. Thus, ātman is not contingent in any regard, but true reality appears in the ātman. The ātman is the very being of things. Nothing is real except the ātman.

But perhaps this argument would not be totally strange to Luther, because he perceives the unity of creation, redemption, and sanctification as the unity of the Trinitarian God who is universal and eternal presence.

The opposite of the Spirit is the flesh, or the egocentricity of man *coram Deo* reflected in the physical as well as the psychic levels of the human being. Paul's understanding that human pride and self-glory (*kauchēsis*—Rom. 3:27, 15:17; 1 Cor. 15:31) are to be overcome by the being in Christ, *en Christo,* is the center of Christian self-understanding due to Martin Luther's doctrine of justification.

In Advaita Vedānta a similar experience and its reflection in the Bhagavad Gita is very central: one who pretends to be righteous, *dambha,* and wants to be something on the basis of his ego and selfish action instead of being totally in God or the Spirit, ātman, is demonic in nature and called hypocritical, *dharma-dhvajitva.*[128]

One has to realize the nothingness of ego first in order to be prepared for the advaitic experience. Expressed in the words of Luther, man must go first through the experience of temptation where he realizes his *nihileitas.* Then he will attain communion with God or conformity with Christ by the experience of justification. He realizes that only God really is and acts. Probably a very similar spiritual experience is at the root of both of these understandings. They differ, of course, in other aspects.

According to Luther, man can regard everything as *donum* or *proprium.* It depends on the point of view of man whether his piety and desire for salvation, that is, his religion, are seen under the hope of resurrection or under the curse of death.

Man's relative standpoint must be distinguished from the absolute standpoint of God. This is especially evident concerning the question of a *liberum arbitrium*: man has relative freedom concerning worldly things, whereas *coram Deo* he is totally unfree.

For both Luther as well as Shankara (the greatest philosopher of

Advaita Vedānta, ca. A.D. 800) freedom, or, the personality of man, is not based in any quality found or developed in the ordinary empirical human being, but only in God or the ātman/Brahman.

A similarity between Luther and the *pāramārthika-vyāvahārika*—discrimination can again not be overlooked. What to man is a temporal process consisting of his own decision and action is in reality—*sub specie Dei*—supratemporal unity, divine will, and gift of the Spirit.

The presence of God in the world is described advaitically by Luther. God in the world is the driving force and essence of all. Yet, he is not identical with the world. He is, as described in the understanding of the real presence of Christ in the Holy Supper, beyond the differentiation of transcendence and immanence, beyond subject and object as well. He is both and not both at the same time. Transcendent immanence and immanent transcendence expresses well the experience of both Luther and the Vedāntin.

Luther said God can be known only in his revelation. Revelation is God's very essence, not an accidental act which Luther explained in Trinitarian terms. In India the same idea is expressed by the terms *nirguna* and *saguna Brahman* which are also non-dualistic. The revelation is experienced in and through the word; Luther speaks about four dimensions of the word corresponding to the advaitic understanding that the Brahman manifests itself in three steps, each more actual and concrete than the previous step. They are states of revelation (*īśvara-hiranyagarbha-virāj*).

Such parallels continue: the selected *theologoumena* were chosen only because we sought to investigate the actual experience of God and some of its implications. However, Luther stands in a totally different tradition than Śankara. Both are representatives of unique historical developments which can be related retrospectively without negating their uniqueness. We now focus attention on two significant points of difference selected because they represent a typical difference.

First, for Luther the revelation of God is experienced in Jesus Christ. He is not only an example or preacher, but the bearer of the revelation of the love of God. This is Luther's paradigm. This is his most important foundation for the understanding of God. The Spirit makes this unique historical figure present; faith is everything else but *fides historica*. The historical figure of Jesus Christ, the *logos* who took upon himself the weak human conditions and shone in them, mediates the human, relative, weak, unworthy elements with the divine, absolute, strong true being. For Luther, overcoming is integration.

This is different in Advaita Vedānta, at least concerning the evaluation of historical reality. The world of māyā is not. It simply disappears when truth is realized. It is not integrated. However, there is also a certain integrative tendency in the advaitic vision. The consequence of the advaitic experience can only be universal integration. Since it lacks the integration of incarnation, there is always an inferiority of the historical reality causing a negative and disintegrating understanding of history.

The second point of difference is of equal importance. For Luther the tension between law and gospel, wrath and grace of God, *mortificatio* and *vivificatio,* temptation and overcoming of temptation, old man and new being, remains until the death of man. Due to the power of the Spirit there is a growth in the Spirit and in the conformity with Christ, i.e., in faith. Man can realize more and more his true identity in and from God, overcoming his egocentricity and isolation. But the tension remains. Fulfillment is never accomplished: *simul iustus et peccator.*

In Advaita Vedānta (and nearly all kinds of Indian spirituality) the ideal of the *jīvanmukta* (the one who is liberated totally already during this life) suggests a perfection under the conditions of temporal existence.[129] Man lives still in the body, but in the Spirit he is already perfect with no danger of falling back under the rule of ego and ignorance. One wonders whether this differentiation of the physical and spiritual existence would not introduce again a certain kind of dualism. The ideal of *jīvanmukta* describes man's spiritual path undialectically and—according to a Lutheran understanding of the power of sin—unrealistically.

According to Luther the existence in the Spirit of God is a simultaneous one, a non-duality of God and man: the antiphony of unity and tension.

According to Advaita Vedānta, one who has realized the non-duality of ātman and Brahman lives in the awareness of the ātman free from any tension. Human conditioning is overcome and illusion unmasked. Thus, the *jnānin* abides in perfect non-duality of God and man, because empirical man has disappeared.

NOTES

1. It is not by chance that Rudolf Otto's first major work was on Luther's understanding of the Holy Spirit, greatly influencing his later book, *The Holy*. Cf. Rudolf Otto, *Die Anschauung vom Heiligen Geiste bei Luther*(Göttingen: Vandenhoeck & Ruprecht, 1898); Michael von Brück, *Möglichkeiten und Grenzen einer Theologie der Religionen* (Berlin: Evangelishe Verlagsanstalt, 1979), 71ff. B. R. Hoffman, *Luther and the Mystics* (Minneapolis: Augsburg, 1976), 131ff.
2. Regin Prenter, *Spiritus Creator. Studien zur Theologie Luthers* (Munich: C. Kaiser, 1954), 177. The fact that Luther and the following reformatorian tradition had difficulties to find a biblical foundation of the doctrine of the Trinity has been stated recently again by Eberhard Jüngel, *Gott als Geheimnis der Welt* (Tübingen: Mohr, 1977), 476.
3. J. Baur, "*Die Trinitätslehre als summe des Evangeliums,*" in *Kerygma und Dogma* (Göttingen: Vandenhoeck & Ruprecht, 1976), 124, quoting Luther, *D. Martin Luthers Werke: Kritische Gesammtausgabe,* Weimarer Ausgabe (Weimar: H. Bohlau, 1883–present), 8, 126, 27ff., hereafter referred to as WA.
4. WA 1, 20, 1ff.
5. WA 12, 58ff., (probably 1523).
6. WA 54, 28ff.
7. WA 39/2, esp. 1ff., 92ff., 122ff., 284ff.
8. Reinhold Seeberg, *Dogmengeschichte IV,* 1. Die Lehre Luthers (Leipzig: A. Deichert, 1933), 173.
9. Reiner Jansen, *Studien zu Luthers Trinitätslehre* (Frankfurt: Peter Lang, 1976), 218.
10. This is referred to by Eberhard Jüngel, *Gottes Sein is im Werden* (Tübingen: Mohr, 1965), 16, ref. 12, cf. Prenter, 178.
11. Prenter, 355., ref. 12.
12. Seeberg, 232f.
13. Ibid., 235.
14. WA 42, 17, 2f.; 167, 7ff.
15. Jansen, 215ff. However, it cannot be concluded generally that Luther had thought in a subordinative way.
16. WA 56, 177, 9f.
17. Seeberg, 179ff, where many quotations and locations are listed. Cf. also Prenter, 179.
18. WA 18, 684ff.
19. WA 10/1, 1, 182–87; WA 42, 27, 1ff.
20. Jansen, 208f.
21. Prenter, 197.

22. WA 14, 101, 24; cf. WA 24, 30.20–29.
23. WA 12, 250, 7ff; cf. R. Weier, "*Das Thema vom verborgenen Gott von Nikolaus von Kues zu Martin Luther*" (theological diss., Mainz, 1965), 85ff.
24. Seeberg, 223f; WA 34/1, 147.
25. WA 57, 99.
26. WA 5, 129, 9ff.
27. WA 5, 128f.
28. WA 2, 138, 15ff. Cf. Frederik Gogarten, *Luthers Theologie (*Tübingen: Mohr, 1967), 91.
29. WA 5, 176, 32f.
30. WA 1, 350ff. (Heidelberg Disp. 1518, esp. thesis 19ff).
31. WA 1, 358, 4ff., according to Gogarten's translation into German, 35.
32. WA 39/1, 455; Cf. Theodosius Harnack, *Luthers Theologie,* (Munich: C. Kaiser, 1927), 1:70ff., 444ff.
33. WA 3, 246, 19f.; 4, 87, 22ff.; 4, 332, 16. Here Luther uses the terms "*opus alienum*" and "*opus suum.*"
34. Weier, 205.
35. Seeberg, 174.
36. Ibid., 178.
27. WA 18, 633, 15ff. Cf. for this problem the excellent study by H. J. McSorley, *Luthers Lehre vom unfreien Willen* (Munich: n.p., 1967), esp. 317ff.
38. WA 18, 661, 28. Cf. Hellmut Bendt, *Luthers Lehre vom verborgenen Gott* (Berlin: Evangelische Verlagsanstalt, 1958), 117.
39. WA 18, 753, 36ff.
40. McSorley, 278ff.
41. WA 42, 11, 11ff.; cf. Weier, 176ff.
42. Harnack, 84.
43. That is why Luther warns of the *via negativa* of Dionysius the Areopagite, see Seeberg, 174, and Bandt, 43, because God has become flesh and is hidden in a very different sense than that of speculative philosophy.
44. Heinrich Bornkamm, *Luthers geistige Welt* (Gütersloh: Gütersloher Verlagshaus, 1953), 86.
45. WA 5, 144, 19ff.
46. Gogarten, 127.
47. For the following explanations see Helmar Junghans, "*Das Wort Gottes bei Luther während seiner ersten Psalmenvorlesung,*" in *Theologische Literaturzeitung* 3 (1975), col. 161–74, Cf. D. R. Reinke, "Martin Luther: Language and Devotional Consciousness," *The Spirituality of Western Christendom,* ed. E. R. Elder (Kalamazoo, Mich.: Cistercian Publications, 1976), 152ff.
48. WA 3, 561, 1ff.; 1, 28, 2ff.
49. Junghans, col. 164f.

50. WA 1, 21–24; Junghans, col. 166.

51. Junghans, col. 166ff., says that there is also an inner word of Satan and therefore man can be under temptation.

52. Luther's theology is founded in this experience of the inner word which hints at a kind of transrational experience. See Hoffman, 133. The rationalization of Luther's understanding of the word is a later misinterpretation.

53. Junghans, col. 171, ref. to WA 1, 28, 35.

54. This cannot be found in Luther *verbis expressis,* but it can help to structuralize his thought correctly. It is interesting that Luther speaks about a direct inner word not mediated by any action of the external word (at least in his earlier writings). Since the Spirit goes out also from the Father, there is another transition from the immanent to the economical Trinity which, however, would interfere with the scheme if understood in a strong consecutive sense.

55. WA 30/1, 191, 17ff.

56. Horst Beintker, *Die Oberwindung der Anfechtung bei Luther* (Berlin: Evangelische Verlagsanstalt, 1954), 170.

57. Prenter, 220ff.

58. WA 56, 300, 11.

59. WA 40/2, 585, 5.

60. WA 5, 111, 35; 207, 7ff.; 387, 9f.: *tamen in media tentatione non apparet inimicus, sed solus deus omnia facere.*

61. Prenter, 39ff.

62. WA 5, 411, 40d.; 5, 297, 30ff.

63. WA 10/3, 11ff.

64. WA 3, 283, 5.

65. WA 5, 604, 8; 5, 176, 24.

66. WA 56, 388, 11; 391, 10.

67. WA 5, 168, 1.

68. WA 5, 168, 1–4.

69. WA 40/3, 154, 11ff. Cf. Gogarten, 145f.

70. Cf. esp. Prenter, 207ff. That Luther's understanding of faith has to be seen in connection with such mystical terms as *raptus* and *translatio* has been clearly demonstrated again recently by Hoffman, 141, 156ff., 174ff.

71. Cf. WA 40/3, 738, 6ff.; WA 57/3, 144, 10.

72. In the mystics, too, *mortificatio* is understood not only as an exercise in *Gelassenheit* which man carries out himself. For John of the Cross the experiences of temptation come from God alone. Thus, Luther stands on a long tradition (against Beintker, 88).

73. Prenter, 242ff.

74. WA 4, 87, 22f.

75. Gogarten, 167f.

76. McSorley, 278ff. The true free will is according to Luther the "theonomous" will. WA 2, 104, 1f.

77. WA 40/1, 488, lff. (Rörer 1531): *ad hoc iusta humiliatio, contritio, contusio per ferreum malleum servit, ut gratia ad te veniat. Sic lex est praeparator ad gratiam.* Prenter, 222f. Cf. also WA 5, 179, 31; 183, 21; 7, 556, 30.

78. WA 18, 782, 30ff.

79. Gogarten, 61ff; Beintker, 41f.

80. WA 40/3, 517 Cf. Gogarten, 51ff.

81. Gogarten, 39; with reference to the problem of the *communicatio idiomatum* (cf. Hoffman, 174ff.) "Christ becoming me and I becoming Christ" is the formula (WA 17/1, 187, 9). The one in faith can say: "I am Christ." (WA 40/1, 285, 5).

82. WA 1, 125, 24.

83. WA 4, 703, 36f.

84. Prenter, 41.

85. Ibid., 43.

86. Ibid., 44, who brings a lot of references for this kind of realism, WA 1, 593, 1ff.; *per fidem Christi efficitur Christianus unus spiritus et unum cum Christo*; WA 2, 146, 14f.; *qui credit in Christo, haeret in Christo estque unum cum Christo*; WA 2, 535, 24: *Credere enim in Christum est eum induere. unum cum eo fieri.*

87. WA 56, 250, 18ff.; 359, 27ff.: *Spiritus enim occidit, prudentiam carnis et vivificavit hominem inferiorem facitque mortem contemni et vitam prodigi ac Deum solum omnia diligi.*

88. WA 56, 450, 2ff.

89. Cf. Harnack, 1: 76ff.

90. Prenter, 41; 185ff.

91. WA 30/1, 183, 8ff.

92. Wa 54, 64, 4.

93. WA 25, 505f., quote also in Seeberg, 234.

94. Seeberg, 234.

95. WA 10/1, 16, 14f.

96. WA 52, 344, 11.

97. Seeberg, 233.

98. WA 50, 274; 46, 536.

99. WA 56, 360, 2ff.; 343, 16ff., where man is regarded as *spiritualis et carnalis, iustus et peccator* on the basis of the efficacy of the Spirit.

100. Seeberg, 231.

101. Prenter, 188.

102. Seeberg, 112f.

103. WA 45, 175, 18ff. (Rörer 1537): *Qui baptisatus, est renatus coram deo nach seiner rechnung, er hats angefangen. Ideo coram eius oculis schon geschehen, der jungst tag*

sthet in fur oculis und in der thur. Coram oculis nostris nondum sic. Sed sua misericordia schon gerechnet, quando plenus, quasi effusus opulente etc. modo halten fast an dem anfang. Cf. also Prenter, 230ff. Other references are WA 24, 158; 18, 203 and 205.

104. WA 56, 234, 7ff.

105. Cf. Seeberg, 173ff.

106. WA 23, 234, 7ff.

107. WA 17, 2, 192, 28; WA 18, 709, 22; WA 19, 219, 31, etc. Cf. Hoffman, 142f.

108. WA 26, 339, 39ff.: "*Nichts ist so klein, Gott is noch kleiner. Nichts ist so grass, Gott ist noch grösser. Nichts ist so kurtz, Gott ist noch kürtzer . . . Ists ein ausussprechlich wesen uberund ausser allem, des man nennen odder dencken kan.*"

109. WA 23, 135, 3ff.

110. WA 23, 137, 33f.

111. WA 23, 135, 35ff. Cf. Bandt, 108ff.

112. WA 23, 133, 26; 151, 4. The problem of necessity and freedom, determinism and contingency in Luther's notion of God cannot be explicated here. Cf. Seeberg, 177ff., 194ff. and McSorley, 242ff. The hidden presence concerns not only the realm of nature, but also human history which is expressed in the doctrine of the "masks" of God. Cf. Seeberg, 192f.

113. Gerhard Ebeling, *Luther. Einführung in sein Denken* (Tübingen: Mohr, 1964), 305, cf. 301. Cf. also Hoffman, 131ff.

114. Bandt, 109ff.

115. Prenter, 225f. and 77: "Regarded as *proprium* our real piety is flesh, belonging therefore to the old man and is under the ira Dei. Regarded as *donum* it is spirit, belonging to the new man and is sub gratia Dei."

116. Hoffman, 177.

117. Bṛhadāranyaka Upanishad (*BU*), 2, 5: 1ff.

118. Śankara's commentary on Taittiriya Upanishad (*TU*), 2, 6: 1.

119. Cf. Heinrich Zimmer, *Philosophie und Religion Indiens* (Frankfurt: Verlag Suhrkamp, 1976), 366.

120. Brahma Sūtra (*BS*), 1, 1:2.

121. Ibid., 3, 7: 4023.

122. *BU* 3, 7: 20.

123. *BU* 3, 7: 5.

124. *BU* 2, 4:14; T. M. P. Mahadevan, *Guadapāda. A Study in Early Advāita* (Madras: n. p., 1975), 108.

125. *BU* 5, 1: 1; cf. *BS* 2, 1: 27 and Śankara's commentary on it.

126. Cf. Paul Deussen, *Das System des Vedānta* (Leipzig, 1883), 244ff.

127. For a detailed discussion of this issue, cf. von Brück, "Advaita and Trinity.

Indian and Christian Experience of God," in *Dialogue of Religions* (unpublished thesis in German, University of Rostock, Rostock, 1980), 315ff.

128. *Bhagavad Gītā* (*BG*), 16: 4; 13: 7 and Śankara's Commentary.

129. An excellent study of the ideal of *jīvanmukta* is to be found in "Chacko Valiaveetil, Liberated Life. Ideal of *jīvanmukti*" in *Indian Religions,* esp. in Śaiva Siddhānta (Madurai/Madras: Arul Anandar College, 1980).

10

The God Concept Among Muslims

MARCIA HERMANSEN

The purpose of this chapter is to explore, in a preliminary way, issues raised by the consideration of the God-concept presented in Islam, and how the form and manner in which this concept is presented influence the relationship of the Muslim individual with Allah. The paper consists of two sections: the first is an overview of the God-concept in Islam and the second discusses the potential significance of research on the personal religious experience of Muslims in their relationship with God.

God in the Quran and Islamic Theology

It is not appropriate to speak of a God-"image" among Muslims since Allah is characterized as being unlike anything else—"*laisa-ka mithlihi shai*" (Quran 42:11). At the same time, the Quran says many things about Allah's activities as creator of the world and judge of the actions of men and nations in history. The Muslim knows about Allah through the revelation received by his prophet, Muhammad, and through the work of God, embodied in his creation, said by the Quran to be replete with signs of its maker. In the Arabic language the word for signs, *ayāt,* is the same word used for the verses of the Quran. The statements which the Quran makes about Allah were readily understood and accepted by Muhammad and his followers in the early generations. As time went on, however, and Islamic intellectual life became influenced by Greek rationalism, the early theologians began to scrutinize the Quranic assertions concerning Allah. One issue which was raised was the interpretation of the seemingly anthropomorphic statements in the Quran which speak of the hand of Allah, or his seeing, or sitting upon his throne. While one group, the people of the Hadith, insisted that these be taken literally, the Mu'tazilites, who favored rational interpretation, saw these as being metaphorical. The mainstream view in Sunni Islam is that of the theologian al-Ash'arī (d. 935) and his followers who stated that these verses should be accepted as they are, "without knowing how," *bi-lā kaifa,* they should be understood.

The Quranic view of Allah is that He does not have personal relations of a human type, and one of the greatest sins in Islam is *shirk,* associating anything or anyone else with Allah or his prerogatives. This prohibition in Islam is so strong that even a metaphorical reference to God as a father would be forbidden and utterly inappropriate. The denial of family relationships for God or anything resembling them in Islam is confirmed in the Quranic chapter *Ikhlās.* "He does not beget nor was He begotten, and there is none equal to Him." (Quran 102) This was a rejection of the pagan Arab notion that God had daughters who were worshipped in the form of idols, but also is understood as extending to Christian notions of sonship or being children of God. Another early theological issue involved the vision of God promised to those Muslims rewarded by paradise in the next life. Again the rationalists contended that this could not be meant literally as God was not a material entity to be seen with human eyes. The literalists accepted this vision as fact, although they did not know how it would be possible. As if in anticipation of these later controversies, there is a Hadith report of the prophet which states, "Ponder the creation of God but do not think excessively about the Divine essence or you will perish." Thus, Muslims are directed to contemplate the fantastic order and complexity of the universe around them as a proof of the existence of the maker, rather than questioning the details of what sort of being he might be.

God's Names and Attributes

If God's essence is beyond scrutiny, Muslims have a clear Quranic basis for knowledge of His attributes, *sifāt,* and names. The Quran often uses these attributes to refer to God, and there are said to be ninety-nine names by which Allah can be named. The guiding principle in selecting the ninety-nine names, known as the "Beautiful Names," *al-asmā al-husnā,* was to affirm no attribute not expressly indicated in the Quran. An active quality expressed verbally in the Quran could be nominalized. While these names are not listed in any rank order, some of the more prominent ones are:

"Your God is One" (Wāḥid 37:4), or the Unique (Aḥad);
"The Living, the Self-Subsisting" (Al-Ḥayy, Al-Qayyum 20:3);
"Exalted be Allah, the Real, the Sovereign" (Al-Ḥaqq 20:14);
"The Sublime" (Al-'Aẓīm 69:33);
"Light Upon Light," (Nūr 'alā Nūr 24:35) "Allah guides to His Light whom He will."
"The Wise" (Al-Ḥakīm 76:30)
"He is the Hearer, the Seer." "He is the Omniscient," (Al-Samī', al-Baṣīr, al 'Alīm 42:11–12)
"Allah is the Witness of all things" the Witness (Al-Shahīd 85:9);
"The Bountiful" (Al-Wahhāb 51:58);
"The Forgiver," "Seek the forgiveness of Allah; indeed Allah is "Forgiving, Merciful" (Al-Ghafūr, Al-Raḥīm).

God is often invoked by one of His names and the vocative particle "Yā" - "O." For example, "Yā Laṭīf," "O Kind One, O Subtle One" is an exclamation of surprise or dismay in the Middle East. Muslims do not believe that Allah has only these ninety-nine names, but rather feel it is properly respectful to apply to Allah only those names which he uses for himself in the Quran.[1]

In addition to the ninety-nine "Beautiful Names," Allah is known by Muslims to have attributes and qualities. These attributes and their relationship to God were also controversial among early Muslim theologians. The main issues concerned whether the divine attributes were part of Allah's essence or additional to it, and whether they were co-eternal to God. Later scholars classified these as:

1. The attribute of essence—God's existence which is a necessary part of his essence.
2. Attributes which are essential (dhātī or nafsī), such as his eternity.
3. Attributes of "qualification" (Ma'ānī), which add a concept to the essence.
4. Attributes of action (Af'ālī) not intrinsic qualities but possibilities for God, namely, creation, command, consent.[2]

Mainstream Sunni opinion is that Allah has certain attributes which from all eternity subsist in His essence. They are not he nor are they other than he.[3] There are seven such essential attributes: power, will, life, knowing, hearing, seeing, and speech. In addition, Allah may be described by things which he is not, the privative attributes.

The Islamic mystics took a great interest in the divine attributes. Ibn 'Arabī (d. 1240) made them a prominent feature of his description of the emanation of the world. According to his description, God cognized his own attributes, which then emanated down through various stages to form the world of multiplicity, which reflects the attributes of its creator. According to Ibn'Arabī, each human being consists of a combination of these various attributes. The Sufi practice of repeating various names of God, "dhikr Allah" or "remembrance of God," seeks to reunite the mystic with his divine origin. For the Muslim, these names and attributes are one way of relating to Allah and may be discussed since they can be related to human experience. In the words of the Egyptian modernist, Muhammad Abduh (d. 1905): "Thus the Quran and the earlier scriptures confine themselves to directing attention to the Creator's existence and to His perfect attributes, as these may be known from the contemplation of the created world."[4]

The Relationship of the Believer and God

God, as presented in the normative teachings of Islam, is a being or force, and man should obey God's command and laws, worshipping him according to set methods. A prominent Islamicist remarked:

> The Quran demands of the believer, in respect to Allah, reverent fear (taqwā 9:109) and at the same time, piety (birr), the act of which is the same as the act of reverent fear (2:189), gratitude (shukr; in the verbal form: "you may perchance be grateful," as the Book often says, especially in the Medinan period), confidence (tawakkul; frequently in the verbal form: "have confidence in God," e.g., 5:81).[5]

The personal relationship of the believer to Allah is sufficient if the believer submits to these rules. Faith in God (Imān) goes hand in hand with this submission (Islām) for Muslims; Islām and Imān depend on and reinforce each other. What is the relationship of the believer to Allah according to the Quran? Allah is all-powerful and transcendent. He is also immanent. God says of his relationship to man, "We are closer to him than his jugular vein (Quran 50:16)." God sees all man's actions and knows what is in the heart. He cares, since he is pleased or angry with the person's actions. The Muslim relates to God by acknowledging his commands, obeying them, and by calling upon God for help and forgiveness. This relationship takes place both through rituals and through personal petitionary prayer (du'ā). There are also special prayer rituals for seeking God's guidance, help in making decisions, and so on.

Louis Gardet, in his article "Allah," notes that in Islam,

> The forbidding inaccessibility of the divine nature is resolutely maintained; God, omniscient and "near," can only be known by His Word, by the Names, the attributes and acts of His paramount sovereignty, which He Himself reveals. It is indeed in His Sovereignty over every creature that Allah is manifested. The attributes of omniscience and omnipotence relate to God's outward-directed knowledge and power. The declaration of Oneness pertains to the oneness of the divine nature, the godhead as such. God in Himself remains the unexpressed mystery, *ghaib*. [6]

The Islamic Mystics

Within Islam the other main tendencies besides submission and worship which have arisen in terms of personal relationship to God are those common to all humans in relationships to the Divine, the communal and the manipulative. As an example of the former, the mystics strive to experience Allah directly, to "commune" with him. The Sufis, or Islamic mystics, viewed God as beloved, and/or lover, and wanted closeness (*uns*) with him. Their acceptance of this more personal view of God is illustrated in Rumi's (d. 1273) story of Moses and the shepherd. The simple shepherd is overheard by Moses, calling to Allah, offering to cook him dinner, wash his socks, and pick the lice out of his hair. When Moses berates the man for his humanization of the transcendent being, God intervenes and tells Moses that the shepherd's way has profoundly touched him and that he is, even without the proper ritual, among the best of worshippers.

Moses finally says to the shepherd,

> Permission had come (from God).
> Do not seek any rules or method (of worship); say whatever your distressful heart desires.
> Your blasphemy is the true religion and your religion is the light of the spirit: you are saved, and through you a whole world is in salvation.[7]

The Sufi goal is annihilation (fanā) in Allah, which transforms the individual ego to become an instrument of the divine purpose in the world (baqā). Controversial among the Sufis is whether fanā means dissolution of the human ego before the divine, or whether it is absolute union with God, the latter interpretation being condemned by orthodox Islam. A story illustrating the Sufi desire for union with God is told of the Sufi Bayezid Bistami (d. 874). After many years of spiritual austerities and exercises, Bistami was vouchsafed a vision in which he beheld a closed door. A voice, which he knew to be that of the divine, called out from behind the door asking, "Who is there?" "It is I," replied Bistami, but the door remained firmly closed. Bistami returned to his practices until after some time he was again presented with the same vision. This time, however, when the door appeared and the voice asked, "Who is there?" the Sufi replied, "It is Thou." At this the door opened and he was united with the divine presence.

Among the Sufis, monistic and dualistic concepts of the relationship of Allah to his creation are known respectively as *waḥdat al-wujūd* (the unity of existence) and *waḥdat al-shuhūd* (the unity of experience). The former, upheld mainly by followers of Ibn'Arabī, conceived of God as emanating the creation from himself as a self-manifestation. To explain the purpose of creation they cite the Hadith, or saying of the prophet, that Allah said, "I was a hidden treasure and I wanted to be known." Thus, God experiences himself through himself (the world). Despite Ibn'Arabī's note that there is an unbridgeable distinction between the *rabb* (Lord) and the *'abd* (servant), his position tends toward monism. Some contend that Al-Ash'arī's theology in which God recreates the world every instant without any secondary causation inclines toward a monistic theory, and that Ibn'Arabī simply made this more explicit.

On the other hand, according to the Unity of Experience or *waḥdat al-shuhūd,* it is asserted, for example by Shaikh Ahmad Sirhindi, that there is something other than God which exists. Against the background of this "negative" material, we can clearly see God's positive attributes reflected in the world. The goal of humanity, then, should be one of transforming the negative nonbeing, that is, evil, in ourselves. Thus, according to Sirhindi, mysticism involves moral struggle, rather than merely gnostic realization of what we already are.

"Little Tradition," "Folk" Islam

In "little tradition" Islam, the personal aspects of a relationship with God often seem to be manipulative rather than arising from a desire to commune with the divine being. A common manipulative behavior involves making vows or "nadhr." This vowing is a sort of bargain or exchange: "If I get such and such a wish granted or achieve a certain goal, I will fast for several days, give money to the poor," and so on. In addition, petitionary vows are often addressed to saints who function as intermediaries between man and God.

The topic of intercession (*shafā'at*) in Islam has occasioned much discussion. The Quran denies the possibility of one person redeeming another by atoning for his sins. "No laden soul can bear the burden of another" (Quran 17:15). However, intercession is allowed with God's permission, in the sense that someone may pray for God's forgiveness of another. "No intercession avails with Him save for him whom He permits" (34:23). Thus the prophet is believed by many to intercede for Muslims, as are saints, and in Shi'ite Islam, the Imams. Descendents of saints and the prophet are also considered, in popular Islam, to have a certain influence in gaining their ancestors' favor to intercede. The widespread manifestations of the cult of saint worship in Islam are seen as fulfilling a need for a more personal, intimate relationship with a powerful Being. They fill a gap left when Allah's transcendence and the ritualistic and legalistic dimensions of Islam are stressed to the exclusion of a role for personal communication with the supreme being.

Contemporary Presentations of the God-Concept

Neither of these trends (communal or manipulative) is presented as normative in mainstream Islamic theology or education. The contemporary situation in this Islamic milieu defines strictly what should be thought about God and discourages speculation about other aspects of his being. For example, the Egyptian modernist Muhammad Abduh in his *Theology of Unity* writes, "to turn to the transcendent Being, the ever-eternal, is to be aware, not merely of puzzled wonder, but a complete incapacity and otherness." He cites the well-known Hadith, "Ponder the creation of God, but do not think excessively about the Divine Essence, or you will perish."[8]

Muslim education is very detailed in describing what should or should not be thought about Allah. It stresses the signs of God as a source for knowing about Him, as has Islam from its very inception. A recent book titled *Allah,* explains that there are three main signs of God:

1. The creation (its marvelous contents, the way it is precisely ordered).
2. The Quran—as God's revelation.
3. The miracles performed by God's prophets.[9]

Interestingly, the author says that we can know certain attributes of God based on our self knowledge, citing the Hadith, "Whoever knows himself knows his Lord," usually preferred by Sufis. From this comparison, he explains that we may expect God to possess knowledge, will, and power, as do humans; however, these will be at a much higher level.

Disbelief in God, the author notes, is due to ignorance, self-aggrandizement, going astray or plain badness. It should be noted that Islam, which stresses that its tenets are clear, simple, and rational, has always taken the position that faith in God does not involve any mystical sort of leap. In addition to restating Quranic and theological positions on God, recent works such as this often incorporate discussions of scientific concepts, for example the laws of thermodynamics, as proof of the existence of a creator.[10]

The emphasis in Islam on describing in detail what can be said or thought about Allah undoubtedly has a profound influence on the relationship of individuals to their concept of the deity. It helps determine what kind of relationship a person may have and what sort of being one believes he or she is in relationship with. In comparing Islam with other religions, the traditional Islamic concept of God is significant, as is the way this concept is reinforced in the various Islamic countries through education and other means of cultural transmission.

Existing Studies on the God-Concept

Having sketched the above outline of the God-concept in Islam, in the second part of this chapter I would like to offer suggestions regarding the potential significance of research on the God-concept among Muslims for the study of comparative religion and the varieties of religious experience. In the case of the personal religious experience of contemporary Muslims, the basic research is lacking which would allow us to make even preliminary comparisons between Islam and other Abrahamic traditions. A similar lack of data concerning the individual relationship with the personal deity or God/ultimate concept exists in the Eastern religions.[11] The type of information required for such comparisons is by nature qualitative as well as quantitative.

As far as quantitative research is concerned, several studies previously carried out among Christian or Jewish groups provide an initial basis for comparison with Muslims. This work has explored the influence of parental images on the God-concept, thus addressing Freud's hypothesis that God is, to a large extent, a projection of the individual's image of the father.[12] This thesis is reflected in Freud's statement that, "God is in every case modelled after the father, and that our personal relation to God is dependent upon our relation to our physical father, fluctuating and changing with him, and that God at bottom is nothing but an exalted father."[13]

The research carried out in contemporary Western (Christian and Jewish) environments has been limited by methodological shortcomings. Nevertheless, some consistent trends in findings may be noted. There is clearly a similarity in the description of God "images" and parental "images." While some studies indicated a greater similarity between the God-image and the image of the opposite-sex parent or the preferred parent, one study conducted by Vergote et al. found a stronger link with the father image among 180 American students.[14] This study also found that the God-image contained both maternal and paternal elements. Most of these studies tested individuals by means of semantic differential techniques or other methods of evaluating ratings of a set of characteristics.

Studies of a cross-cultural nature were carried out by Spiro and D'Andrade who compared eleven representative primitive societies.[15] "They found strong correlations between parent nurturance and belief in benevolent gods and between parental punitiveness and belief in punitive gods."[16] Again this supports a theory that parental projections play a role in the formation of God-concepts.

Another study by Larsen and Knapp[17] found differences between females and males when rating God as benevolent or punitive.[18] These findings have also been interpreted as supporting the projection hypothesis.

It should be noted that these studies address Freud's theory of religion as it applies to the psychology of religion among contemporary individuals rather than on his hypothesis regarding the origin of monotheistic religion as described in *Moses and Monotheism*.

Research on the God-Concept and the Experience of God/the Ultimate among Muslims

From the above research it is clear that studies among Muslims provide useful data for comparison to results among Christian and Jewish subjects. These results also provide cross-cultural data with which to evaluate the hypothesis that the concept of God is influenced by projections of parental images, whether ideal or as actually experienced by the child. In addition, studies among culturally differing Muslim populations, for example, in an Arab country and in South Asia, provide data for evaluating the interaction of "greater tradition" normative religious factors with cultural and individual variants in forming an image of God/the Ultimate. The work of James L. Peacock is cited in this context. In a study, *Muslim Puritans,* he examined cultural and individual factors shaping a tendency to adopt Islamic fundamentalism in Malaysia and Indonesia. This study used extensive interviewing and questionnaire techniques to elicit data. Peacock's specific concern was not individual religious experience, but rather the interaction of ideology and cultural practices. His work stands as a valuable contribution to an understanding of religious experience among Muslims.

In terms of studying personal religious experience among Muslims, there may arise challenging factors not present in the original God-concept studies among Christians. For example, in terms of a God-image, most Muslims will strongly deny that they have a mental image of God and may feel uncomfortable offering any personal description or feeling not sanctioned by tradition. The author of this chapter prepared an exploratory questionnaire which asked Muslim college students in Jordan to perform a semantic-differential task by rating a set of attributes as applicable to their mother, their father, and to Allah. These were to be ranked on a scale from one to five. Even to suggest such a task for Muslims may be sensitive, particularly in the current atmosphere in the Middle East. Therefore, the questionnaire could not be distributed with institutional approval and some of the respondents, who were approached informally by friends, still found the task uncomfortable or impossible to carry out. Some pointed out that only certain attributes could be used appropriately, others that negative traits such as harshness, anger and so on, were possible for God in regard to nonbelievers (kāfirūn) only. The attributes used in the study were chosen from ones known to be applied to God such as Raḥīm (Merciful), or variant forms of these such as ('Alim) instead of ('Alīm). In future studies it would be advisable to omit items which also function as Divine Names, as in Arabic-speaking Muslim cultures these by definition may not be applied to humans.

Among the thirty respondents, all females between seventeen and thirty years of age, one clear finding was that responses varied for each attribute of the mother and father, indicating strong individual differences in parental images. A problem with the research design was that the "ideal" traits of mother and father should have been generated rather than responses to actual mother and father, or at least both types could have been solicited. Responses concerning God's attributes, however, tended to be all or nothing, with little individual variation. Attributes from among, or similar to, those commonly employed as attributes of God rated the highest level of agreement, a "5" (i.e., this characteristic applies to God *always*). The few which varied, such as "severe" (qāṣin), "rough" (khashin), "content" (qani'), likely did so because they were ambiguous or seemed overly negative if applied non-specifically. An additional aspect of their personal experience of the God-concept which the questionnaire asked of respondents was whether they felt that God was near or far. All respondents indicated that they felt that God was near them, an indication that God's non-personalness does not conflict with his immanence for Muslims. Asked for evidence or examples of this nearness, many individuals cited help from God in situations of difficulty. One person remarked on her awareness of Allah's proximity in times of both happiness and difficulty, again asserting a sense of immanence.

Ana-Maria Rizzuto, in her studies based on clinical interviews in America on psychoanalytic and object relations theories, concludes that a God-representation is formed by all children in the Western world. This representation functions throughout the lifetime of the individual as a "transitional object," which may undergo change corresponding to changes in the person's own self-representation. In the case of the god-representation, "This must be revised to keep pace with change in self-representation, otherwise it becomes asynchronous; either ridiculous or irrelevant for the person or else threatening and dangerous." She notes also that each life offers the opportunity to revise the God represention at critical times, particularly the oedipal stage, puberty, and the last part of adolescence.[19]

Dr. Rizzuto's research indicates an important direction which future studies on representations of God and individuals' relationships to the Ultimate could take. Additional cross-cultural data must be gathered and examined in order to assess the universality of her conclusions and the significance of cultural and individual variation. The importance of other spiritual beings in a person's religious life—such as angels, jinn, and saints as intermediaries—also should be examined.

Some preliminary interviews conducted among Muslim students in Jordan and the United States, suggest that qualitative studies, involving biographical interviews and discussions of religious experience, could provide data relevant to Rizzuto's suggestions regarding God as a "transitional object." These could also explore the wide variations existing among Muslims in their ways of conceptualizing and relating to God.

As an example of such individual variations, one subject, a female student originally from the Middle East, now in the United States, could recall in her childhood and adolescence imagining God as "an older man, about eighty years old, with a kind face, not foolish. He had a beard, moustache and white hair." She would imagine herself talking to him, but could not sense him responding directly. When asked for her impression of God she first cited traditional attributes such as "He is All-knowing, All-powerful, Creator of everything. Everything follows an order which He has set. He is not separate, and is both here and beyond." As a child she admitted to having thought of him as a father who was all-compassionate, all-loving, and responsible for man. She did not believe stories that God would punish humans for sin since "He must have loved us to put us here." This subject volunteered that she may have gotten the idea of God as an old man from American or European programs or books which she saw as a child.

The answers of this person demonstrate the potential interest of interviews with Muslims who are further from traditional sources and practices, both growing up in the West, or coming here for university studies. My limited experience has been that such persons are much more able to evaluate and describe developments regarding their relationship to a God-concept. In order to study how Muslims in traditional societies form and relate to God-concepts throughout the life cycle, and whether personal identity and its flexibility or rigidity can be related to individual God representation, extensive interviews and observation would be required. However, the results would offer valuable insights relevant to the understanding of the effects of social change on identity, as well as for the study of religious experience.

There is also a need to carry out interviews with children in traditional Islamic societies to study how their God concepts change during the maturation process and with their introduction, through education, to normative religious concepts.

In conclusion, I propose that more comparative research be undertaken on the relationship of the individual with the God/Ultimate representation, in non-Western religious traditions and in Islam. Such research will further our understanding of the role of the cultural environment and the normative religious tradition on individual religious experience.

Some of the issues which this research should address are:

1. the influence of actual/ideal mother and father images on the God-concept where God is not theologically attributed a parental role.
2. the effect of religious education on the formation of a God-concept and the individual's relationship with this concept.
3. developmental factors in the formation of a God-concept and the causes of variability in individual relationships with God/the Ultimate over the life cycle in traditional and Western societies.

NOTES

1. Sa'īd Ḥawwā, *Allāh* (Beirut: Dār al-Kutub al-'ilmiyya, 1981), 143.
2. Louis Gardet, "Allāh," *Encyclopedia of Islam* (Leiden: E. J. Brill, 1953), 1:411.
3. From the *Creed of al-Nafasi,* in *A Commentary on the Creed of Islam,* trans. E. E. Elder (New York: Books for Universities Press, 1980), 49. The Shi'a, following Mu'tazilite theology say that Allah's attributes are part of his essence and cannot be ideas or states of being.
4. Muhammad Abduh, *The Theology of Unity,* trans. I Masa'ad and Kenneth Cragg (London: Allen and Unwin, 1966), 55.
5. Louis Gardet, "Allāh," *Encyclopedia of Islam,* 1:409.
6. Ibid.

7. Jelaluddin Rumi, *Mathnavi,* trans. Reynold Alleyne Nicholson (London: Luzac & Co., 1960), 311–14.
8. Muhammad Abduh, 55.
9. Sa'id Ḥawwā, *Allāh,* 14–20.
10. Ibid., 22–28.
11. For a comparative study of Hindu and Christian concepts of mother, father, and God, see *The Parental Figures and the Representation of God,* Antoine Vergote and Alvaro Tamayo (The Hague: Mouton, 1981), 116–25.
12. Benjamin Beit-Hallahmi and Michael Argyle, "God as a Father Projection: The Theory and the Evidence," *British Journal of Medical Psychology* 48 (1975) 71–75.
13. Sigmund Freud, *Totem and Taboo,* standard edition (London: Hogart Press, 1913), 244.
14. Antoine Vergote et al., "Concept of God and Parental Images," *Journal for the Scientific Study of Religion* 8, no. 1 (Spring 1969): 79–87.
15. As cited in Melford Spiro and Roy G. D'Andrade, "A Cross-cultural Study of Some Supernatural Beliefs," *American Anthropologist* 60 (1958).
16. Beit-Hallahmi and Argyle, 73.
17. As cited in P. H. Larsen and L. Knapp, "Six Differences in Symbolic Conceptions of the Diety," *Journal of Projective Techniques,* no. 28 (1964): 303–6.
18. Ibid.
19. Ana-Maria Rizzuto, *Birth of the Living God* (Chicago: University of Chicago Press, 1979), 200.

REFERENCES

Normative Islam

Abduh, Muhammad. *The Theology of Unity,* trans. I. Musa'ad and Kenneth Cragg. London: Allen and Unwin, 1966.

Gardet, Louis. "Allāh," *Encyclopedia of Islam.* Leiden: E. J. Brill, 1953. 1:406–17.

Ḥawwā, Sa'id. *Allāh.* Beirut: Dār al-Kutub Al-'ilmiyya, 1971.

Pickthall, Mohammed Marmaduke. *The Glorious Koran.* New York: New American Library, Mentor Books, 1962.

Qur'ān Karīm. Cairo: Matābi' Al-Ahrām, 1972.

Rahman, Fazlur. *Islam.* Chicago: University of Chicago Press, 1979.

Rahman, Fazlur. *Major Themes of the Qur'an.* Minneapolis: Biblioteca Islamica, 1980.

Smith, Jane I. and Yvonne Y. Haddad. *The Islamic Understanding of Death and Resurrection.* Albany, N. Y.: State University of New York Press, 1981.

Taftazani, A. *Commentary on the Creed of Islam.* New York: Books for Libraries, 1980.

Watt, William Montgomery. *The Formative Period in Islamic Theology.* Edinburgh: Edinburgh University Press, 1973.

Psychology

Beit-Hallahmi, Benjamin and Michael Argyle. "God as the Father Projection: The Theory and the Evidence." *British Journal of Medical Psychology,* 48 (1975): 71–75.

Freud, Sigmund. *New Introductory Lectures on Psycho-Analysis.* New York: W. W. Norton & Co., 1933.

———. *The Future of an Illusion.* London: Hogart Press, 1950.

Guntrip, Henry J. *Schizoid Phenomena, Object Relations, and the Self.* New York: International Universities Press, 1968.

———. "Religion in Relation to Personal Integration." *British Journal of Medical Psychology,* 42 (1969): 323–33.

Rizzuto, Ana-Maria. *The Birth of the Living God.* Chicago: University of Chicago Press, 1979.

Seigman, Aron W. "An Empirical Investigation of the Psychoanalytic Theory of Religious Behavior." *Journal of the Social Scientific Study of Religion,* 1 (1961): 74–78.

Spiro, Melford. "Cross-Cultural Study of Some Supernatural Beliefs." *American Anthropologist,* 60 (1958): 456–66.

Vergote, Antoine, et al. "Concept of God and Parental Images." *Journal for the Scientific Study of Religion* 8, no. 1 (Spring 1969): 79–87.

Winnicott, Donald Woods. *Playing and Reality.* New York: Penguin Books, 1971.

———. "Transitional Objects and Transitional Phenomena." *International Journal of Psychoanalysis* 34 (1953): 2.

Anthropological Perspectives on Islam

Eickelman, Dale. *The Middle East: An Anthropological Approach.* Englewood Cliffs, N. J.: Prentice-Hall, 1981.

Geertz, Clifford. *Islam Observed.* New Haven, Conn.: Yale University Press, 1968.

Peacock, James L. *Muslim Puritans.* Berkeley, Calif.: University of California Press, 1978.

11

Our Experience and Knowledge of God

WILLIAM L. POWER

Among contemporary theologians, perhaps no one has thought or written more about our experience and knowledge of God than John Baillie. Those familiar with his life and work as a theologian know that this one issue was the focus of his interest from the time of his early manhood until his death in 1960. Beginning with his first published article in 1915 and ending with his posthumously published Gifford Lectures of 1961 to 1962, one can follow the trajectory of his reflection on this issue.

As a graduate student in the early sixties, I first became acquainted with Baillie's theology through a reading of his now classic *Our Knowledge of God,* prompted by my own interest in the problems occupying his mind. This initial acquaintance led to further reading and a decision to write a doctoral dissertation on his theology focusing on his understanding of our knowledge of God, the nature of God, and the function of theological language. Although my understanding and assessment of Baillie's theology has changed somewhat over the years, my interest in and appreciation of his theology has remained constant.

I continue to be impressed with Baillie's understanding of revelation and faith. Equally impressive is his unequivocal affirmation of the universal availability of God's saving grace and of genuine faith in non-Christian religions in particular and in human life in general. I am also impressed with his acknowledgment of signs and symbols as decisive factors in the representation of God and in the expression and evocation of faith.[1] I appreciate his Anselmic interpretation of theology as faith seeking understanding, and the irenic and ecumenical spirit in which he constructed his own theology. Last, but by no means least, I appreciate Baillie's positive evaluation of philosophy and logic, and the roles they play in clarifying and critically justifying theological statements.

Time marches on and much ink has been spilled over the problem of religious experience and its epistemological status since 1960, especially in the field of philosophy of religion. We have heard or read that there is no uninterpreted experience, be it sensuous or non-sensuous. We realize there are distinctions among theistic, monistic, and naturalistic types and/or interpretations of religious experience. We know that the object or subject of religious experience is personal or nonpersonal. We also know that saying one has had an experience of God or the Ultimate does not prejudge the case as to whether the experience is veridical or delusory. We have heard that rational justification is appropriate in some types or interpretations of religious experience while it is not in others. We have also heard that the case for religious experience can be strengthened by relating it to other arguments for the reality of God or the Ultimate. It can also be strengthened by relating it to conceptual or linguistic frameworks exhibiting the intelligibility of the notion of religious experience and the notion of God or the Ultimate. In short, we are familiar in one way or the other with Stace, Zaehner, Smart, and others who have entered into the more recent discussion.

Although these recent attempts to understand religious experience are based on sophisticated historical and philosophical analyses, in many ways Baillie's insights are still to be preferred. Baillie was well versed in the history of religions. He had a profound grasp of the history of theology, especially nineteenth-century theology which provided the parameters for early studies on religious experience. On the basis of this historical knowledge, Baillie made some wise and penetrating criticism of the contributions of such early interpreters of religious experience as James, Pratt, and Otto among others.[2] Baillie was also aware of most of the issues cited above. His analysis of them was often clearer and more nuanced in reasoning than that found in more recent literature. Because I find his theology is fundamentally sound, in this chapter I will draw upon his legacy and attempt to carry his program a step further. This involves a presentation of the essential core of his theology in section I and an assessment of his contribution to our understanding of human experience and knowledge of God in section II.

I

According to Baillie, "God is the Omnipresent Other, the Eternal Thou, by whom we are at every moment being addressed."[3] Such an address is God's revelation of himself and his aims to each human being, and is the primary source of our knowledge of God. Indeed, "the only humanity known to us is the humanity which has already, in some degree at least, has been confronted with the reality of God and disturbed by the challenge of his holy presence."[4] The revelation or self-manifestation of God "essentially consists not in the communication of truths about God but in the self-revelation of the divine Personality, the truths about Him being abstracted by ourselves from the concrete reality with which we thus become acquainted, and our knowledge of his existence being given in and with the revelation rather than guessed at in advance of it."[5] Revelation is the mystery of the *parousia* of God. He discloses himself as the supreme spiritual being who is with us and for us in the most intimate of relations. Revelation can be understood only in terms of a relation between two centers of consciousness. In Baillie's words: "Revelation is a category of personal relationship and can therefore have place only within a situation in which God speaks personally to the individual soul."[6]

Revelation should not be understood as an encounter of two separated beings. It is a personal communion of the divine spirit and the human spirit in which the human self *is* only in its relation to the divine subject. "The truth is that there is in man no *nature* apart from *revelation*. Human nature is constituted by the self-disclosure to this poor dust of the Spirit of the Living God."[7] The divine Thou and the human I, though distinct, are not separated. When revelation is constitutive of the existence of every human being, the Thou and I are inseparably bound together. Thus, Baillie denies the I-Thou split.

Baillie also denies that divine mystery is incomprehensible or indescribable. While the mystery of God is inexhaustible, God does disclose his identity, existence, and aims to us, not to mention other creatures. In God's revelation to humankind, there is an implicit informational content about "the nature and mind and purpose of god."[8] Without this element there could be no primary knowledge of faith nor the more reflective knowledge of theology.

If God is present to us and with us in his self-disclosure, and if his revelation is the ultimate necessary condition of our existence as human beings and the primary source of our knowledge of him, then it follows that revelation occurs only in the present. God discloses himself in the *hic et nunc,* and it is only in the here and now that we can *be* with God, *become* acquainted with him, and *actualize* his aims for us. One can remember past revelations of God and having been with God. One can anticipate future revelations of God and being with God again. But only in the present can there be actual communion with God. This, as Baillie notes, is the truth in the traditional doctrine of the *testimonium internum Spiritus Sancti.*[9]

If revelation is the self-manifestation of God to each human being, with God's gift and demand in each here and now, then faith is the proper and primary way of receiving and responding to God. Faith is the actual or possible individual response of each human being to God's address or self-disclosure. According to Baillie, faith is our primary mode of apprehending the divine presence or the cognitive element in our authentic experience of God, upon which the accompanying affective and conative elements are completely dependent. By this interpretation, faith is not mere opinion about God; it is a knowledge of God. It is a knowledge by personal acquaintance, the necessary condition for which is God's self-disclosure making possible and eliciting the response of faith.[10]

Baillie's understanding of faith is continuous with a tradition beginning perhaps in the Biblical Period. It receives its classical expression in Augustine, and is further developed and articulated by such figures as Anselm, Bonaventure, and the early Protestant reformers. It is an understanding of faith prominent in recent Protestant and Catholic theology. In this tradition, saving faith (*fides salvifica*) is primarily trust in and loyalty to God (*pistis, fiducia*). This presupposes an acquaintance with God as he reveals himself (*notitia*), and contains an implicit assent to what is revealed (*assensus*).[11] In a different terminology, faith (*fides directa*) means to believe God (*credere Deo*), to believe that God is as he reveals himself to be (*credere Deum*), and to believe in God (*credere in Deum*). Thus, in the single act of faith there are three distinct but inseparable elements.

It is important to realize that the primary act of faith (*fides directa*) is not an explicit but rather a tacit knowledge of God. Faith is the tacit dimension of our genuine experience of God. In reflecting on faith and its object (*fides reflexa*), the implicit is made explicit by relative degrees of clarity. This is the act of faith seeking understanding, in which an acritical knowledge of God becomes critical knowledge. It is important to recognize that for Baillie *fides directa* is not prerational; it is precritical. Thus, Baillie affirms the rationality of faith at two levels: the level of existential apprehension of God's self-manifestation and address, and the level of faith seeking understanding. There is a rationally justified true belief at the level of acritical faith and a rationally justified true belief at the level of critical theology. Apart from the former, the latter could not exist.

Baillie poses the question of the rationality of faith and answers it in a rather interesting fashion. "If our faith in God's existence does not itself rest on argument," he writes, "then how can the construction of an argument lead, as St. Anselm says it does, to the correct *understanding* of that faith?"[12] Then follows Baillie's answer:

> The only possible answer would be to claim that the argument which was afterwards hit upon was no more than the clear explication of a logical structure which had been already 'implicitly' contained in the mental process by which the faith was originally acquired; and though St. Anselm never explains himself on this point, it would appear that something of the sort was in his mind.[13]

That is, theological argumentation "represents only a more detailed explication of the very process of thought which is implicitly present in faith itself."[14] If I may borrow from C. S. Peirce, there is a *logica utens* at the level of *fides directa* and a *logica docens* at the level of *fides reflexa*. There is the acritical rationality of faith and the critical rationality of theology. There is the "argument" of faith, producing certitude, and the "argumentation" of theology approximating certainty.

Even though Baillie speaks of the certitude of faith, he does not say faith is complete. "The concept of faith always contains both the idea of knowing and not knowing fully."[15] In terms of quantity and quality, one can always know more of God and know him better. Nor is Baillie willing to say that faith is infallible. "Whatever is of divine revelation must be infallible as it issues from God, but we can make no such claim for it . . . as it is received by us."[16] Like all human knowledge, faith is fallible. Moreover, some of the things we claim to know of God, we do not know, and some of the things we claim not to know, we know. The same holds true for theology.

Faith is not a modal necessity of human existence. Thus, not having faith is always a possibility due to our ignorance and irrationality, our willfullness, or our bio-cultural conditioning. That is, by error, intent, or happenstance it is possible not to respond *properly* to God's address or self-manifestation. One may not believe God, implicitly assent to what he has disclosed, or trust in and give one's ultimate loyalty to him. The real option is not the negative response of 'unfaith'—for Baillie a modal impossibility—but the *improper* response of idolatry, where one makes some other object the ultimate focus of one's trust and devotion. By so doing, one's capacities for the certitude of faith and the approximate certainty of theology become so atrophied that for all practical purposes they are lost and God is eclipsed. This is the epistemological status of disbelief.

While God reveals himself directly to every human being with his favor and demand, "it does not follow that He is ever present to us *apart* from all other presences." That is, he "does not present Himself to us except in conjunction with the presence of our fellows and of the corporeal world." Indeed, "no one of the four subjects of our knowledge—ourselves, our fellows, the corporeal world, and God—is ever present to us except in conjunction with all three of the others."[17] Because we use signs and symbols in interpreting our environment, it follows that God probably never discloses himself to us apart from signs and symbols. Furthermore, in any given subject of our knowledge, God is "in, with, and under" that subject as the ultimate source of its existence, order, and value.

These remarks reflect Baillie's holistic and sacramental vision of reality. Its interconnected structure is represented in coherent thought and discourse, and the universe bears witness to God's living presence.[18] However, because of death, chaos, and disvalue in the spatio-temporal order, God's presence in, with, and under all things is not clearly discernable. In short, evils within and evils without dim our vision.

There are, however, specific occasions of discernment which are of signal importance for illuminating the reality of God and his significance for the world on the basis of which human beings understand and direct their lives. Baillie utilizes Karl Mannheim's expression "paradigmatic experience" to refer to these special occasions of insight.[19] While he does not explicitly develop the idea, it is obvious that Baillie considers all human beings to have certain paradigms or exemplars which function to represent reality in its various modalities and mixtures of good and evil, and to shape human life on the basis of that representation. Religions or specific religious perspectives arise from these special moments of discernment. The discernment is perpetuated in various rites, artistic forms, and oral and written linguistic symbols. This semiotic conception of religion is another way of saying that there is no uninterpreted experience. It is the heart of Baillie's interpretation of our experience and knowledge of God as a "mediated immediacy".[20] In theistic religions, signs and symbols function to represent the mystery of God, the final source and end of every existing individual. These signs and symbols express, nurture, and explicate faith as well as hope, love, and joy, also basic human responses elicited by the presence of God.

As a Christian theologian, Baillie was specifically concerned with the Christian paradigm which provides "a *frame of reference* . . . within which the believer acts and thinks and feels, and which gives position and significance to each event and each reality as he encounters it."[21] Earlier Baillie wrote "Christian knowledge of God is not given to any man save in conjunction with the telling of an 'old, old story.'"[22] That story is the church's story of Jesus Christ, which in one rendition, is set within a more comprehensive narrative beginning with the story of creation and ending with the story of new creation. This Christian story or *kerygma* is the primary linguistic means of induction into the Christian community or *koinonia*. In the broadest sense the Christian paradigm or frame of reference is more than story or *kerygma*. Its linguistic repertoire contains many genre—among which are *didache* or teachings—both at the elementary and advanced levels of *gnosis, sophia,* or theology.[23] Like most religions, Christianity has its language of the muse and its language of the theoretician.

Baillie disclaimed the view that there are no genuine experiences of God outside of Christianity. He also disclaimed the view that there are no truths in the stories and theories of other religions or religious perspectives. Given his understanding of mediated immediacy, this is predictable. However, he did claim that God's revelation in Jesus Christ is the most complete revelation given to humankind. This claim can be interpreted in two ways. Either God revealed himself more fully in Jesus Christ than he had ever done before or after, or the story of Jesus Christ, more completely and adequately represents who God is, and who God is for us and who we are and can become by properly receiving and responding to God's self-disclosure than do other stories. One obviously need not choose between the two options, *unless* it is specified that the so-called "content" of the Christian story or what the story witnesses to is no different from that given to each human being through God's revelation at any place and any time. With this specification, the Christian *kerygma* or story allows us to discern *better* what others have discerned quite *well*. Baillie did not indicate which interpretation he preferred. Possibly he accepts the first disjunct, and perhaps the second without my inserted specification.[24]

On either interpretation with or without the specification, an interesting observation can be made. Given the idiosyncratic nature of every individual and the differences between people at different places and times, it would seem that God's particular aims for each person would be different. A real possibility for one person or community of persons might not be a real possibility for another. A real possibility at one place and time might not be a real possibility at another. Revelation contains an invariable element as well as a variable one. The former pertains to God's everlasting identity, character, and existence; the latter pertains to God's particular aims for particular people at particular places and times. Another variable element is introduced if God makes a particular response to these people in their responses to him.

There is another interesting twist to this view of revelation. If a particular person or community of persons discerned God's revelation more completely and adequately than another person or group, it seems plausible that God would want that person or group to share that discernment with others. Hence, there may well be good grounds for some type of missionary imperative, although not necessarily that of Christianity.

Epistemologically, the above account of revelation implies both a metaphysical and an empirical knowledge of God. Thus, some statements about God are necessary or analytic statements, and some statements are contingent or synthetic. Although this may not be compatible with classical theology, it is more in harmony with the comprehensive Christian story and logically more credible.[25]

Let us summarize Baillie's theology of mediated immediacy as it relates to the theme of our experience and knowledge of God. The primary source of our knowledge of God is through the revelation of himself and his aims to humanity. Our primary knowledge of God is the knowledge of faith—each human being's actual or possible response to that revelation. Our faith is always expressed and shaped by certain decisive signs and symbols representing that revelation. Revelation is the ultimate necessary condition for our faith or genuine experience of God. Based on this interpretation, God is conceived as a personal being. Our knowledge of God is a knowledge by acquaintance, and our apprehension of God is conditioned by the inherited signs and symbols of our culture and/or religious tradition. Our knowledge of God is a mediated immediacy.

II

Having presented the heart of Baillie's theology, I will assess his theological point of view, designated by John Macquarrie as "post-liberal."[26] This involves a discussion of the strengths and weaknesses of his point of view and of ways to enhance its overall credibility.

In a well-known article, Paul Tillich attempted to identify the two main approaches to the philosophy of religion in Western culture. One he described as "the ontological approach;" the other he described as "the cosmological approach."[27] The former approach affirms that human beings have direct or firsthand knowledge of God; the latter approach denies this and affirms that our knowledge of God is indirect or "secondhand." Under the cosmological approach are those who ascribe to the cosmological, teleological, and certain ontological arguments as our only foundation for knowledge of God. Adopting the ontological approach are those who appeal to religious experience or mysticism as the only foundation of our knowledge of God. Tillich maintained that altering assumptions created mixed types.

Tillich categorizes Baillie's theology under the ontological type of philosophy of religion.[28] However, Baillie never collapsed the distinction between God and the universe as does Tillich in this article; nor does he accept the Kantian dictum that all existential judgments are synthetic. Furthermore, he does not share Tillich's neo-Platonic proclivities for speaking of the God above the personal God of theism. However, Tillich's article is significant because it poses relatively clearly the issue of the religious adequacy or strength of the ontological approach to our knowledge of God.

The ontological approach attracts those sharing the conviction that God is found in the most fundamental human experiences and in the living faith of simple and sophisticated folk alike. Many claim that all of the world's greatest religions emerge out of this primal understanding or experience of the divine. It is incorrect to claim that the adoption of the ontological approach is due solely to successful modern criticism of traditional arguments for the existence of God, as found in the works of Hume and Kant. Although Baillie is not one of them, there are some philosophers and theologians who argue for the primacy of the ontological approach and still find the arguments for the existence of God sound or quite strong, either in their traditional or revised forms.[29] In these cases, the arguments do not function to shore up a weak faith. Instead they explicate what is given in faith or explain more completely than empirical sciences the common world disclosed through experience. Baillie in some ways views St. Anselm's argument in his *Proslogion* in the former sense, although he says little about the argument's validity and soundness.[30]

Aside from Baillie's rejection of the proofs of God's existence, the major strength of his point of view lies in the fact that he attempted to explicate the most fundamental dimension of human experience and exhibit its rationality. Thus, not only is it rational to have faith, but faith is also rational.

Another strength of Baillie's contribution toward understanding our experience and knowledge of God lies in his recognition that all religions or religious perspectives cannot be categorized as theistic, monistic, or naturalistic. This traditional typology, further developed by Zaehner,[31] is of limited utility. In certain cases its application actually misrepresents or distorts the belief system being investigated. For example, Baillie recognized that Theravada Buddhism and Jainism cannot be so typed nor can other religious options.[32]

While attempting to keep his distinctions clear so as not to distort or misrepresent religions or religious points of view, Baillie knew that all religious notions are not compossible. Given the necessary refinements of terminology, the truth claims of the religions or religious perspectives of the world cannot all be true, although they all may be false. Each religion does make a claim for the adequacy of their stories and theories to represent reality, even if not the exclusive claim that its truths are the only truths. Baillie's own claim for the non-exclusive adequacy of the Christian story and theology to represent the reality of God and his relation to the spatio-temporal order can be understood in this way.

Baillie also correctly saw that there was considerable continuity and overlap within and between cultures. Part of that cultural uniformity consisted in shared criteria allowing us to assess the truth value of the various statements found in different religions or religious perspectives. He was no conceptual solipsist or linguistic relativist. Thus, Baillie could accept religious pluralism, truth in other religions, and human fallibility without falling into what Kai Nielson has called "Wittgensteinian Fideism."[33] This too is a strength of his theology.

Baillie uses the expression "religious experience" to designate one's cognitive, conative, emotional understanding of, and response to the Ultimate Reality. That understanding and response is shaped by the signs and symbols of a particular religion or religious perspective. Baillie's belief could be called a semiotic conception of religion. Baillie was unfamiliar with semiotics as a theory of signs and symbols, and the term 'semiotics' does not appear in his writings. Yet, with his understanding of religious experience as a mediated immediacy, Baillie is in accord with most current inquiry's insistent claim that there is no uninterpreted experience.

Baillie acknowledged that there is an interpretive component in all experience. This component is inseparably related to one's semiotic, linguistic, social, and historical contexts. Whatever is given in experience is always received, understood, described, and interpreted in terms of some conceptual or linguistic framework. In short, our acculturation conditions our consciousness of or acquaintance with reality.

To affirm that the structure of human experience is triadic rather than dyadic does not deny that more is given in experience than we have signs or symbols for. We know more than we are able to express. Our conceptual and linguistic frameworks are constantly altered to accommodate elements for which there are no signs or symbols but of which we are aware. *Mutatis mutandis* the same is true of our knowledge of other human beings, ourselves, and other entities in the universe. Our knowledge of God is always structured by our acculturation. Yet the mystery of God can never be exhausted. We know that it is possible to know more of God than what our signs and symbols allow us to say at any given place and time. Thus, it is wise to recognize that we often do not know something until we have expressed it, and equally so to recognize that we always know more than we can express.

These comments lead to one last note on the strengths of Baillie's theology. Baillie's heralded importance of the tacit dimension of experience, the place of imagination in religion, and the acritical knowledge of faith will be applauded by those who appreciate the post-critical motifs in the philosophies of Wittgenstein and Polanyi. These elements of human experience have often been neglected in the various rationalistic viewpoints of the modern world. Quite early in his career as a theologian, Baillie became aware of the acids of modernity. Such philosophers as Cook Wilson, G. E. Moore, and John MacMurray among others helped shape the post-critical motifs in his own thought. Yet Baillie was wise enough, as some of our contemporaries are not, to admit the need for critical thought as well. This sense of balance between the tacit and explicit in human experience and religion can be found throughout all his writings.

The major weakness of Baillie's theology lies in his confusing, if not confused, assessment of the traditional proofs of God's existence. Granting the primacy of the ontological approach to our knowledge of God, one need not dismiss the traditional proofs too quickly. Apparently, Baillie was willing to do just that. For him, not only the traditional proofs but all proofs cannot withstand criticism. He agrees with those who say that "the invalidity of these proofs has long ago been demonstrated *ad nauseam*," and he accepts the assumption that we cannot "logically proceed from nature to God." In short, he has accepted the criticisms of Hume and Kant.[34] Assuming the criticisms of Hume and Kant are decisive, which I do not, Baillie's complete rejection of all proofs appears inconsistent with his assessment of Anselm and with his understanding of the created order.

Baillie viewed Anselm's argument in the *Proslogion* as an attempt to explicate the tacit knowledge of faith. If such is the case, then it is strange to question the argument's validity or its soundness. Because Baillie does not clearly distingush between validity and soundness, his analysis of Anselm's argument leaves something to be desired. Anselm's argument in the *Proslogion* is a deductive argument. It appears to exhibit the valid argument form of indirect proof or *reductio ad absurdum*. If one accepts Anselm's assumption that the statement "God exists" is not a contingent or synthetic statement, and if one accepts his assumption that the theistic conception or definite description of God is not inconsistent, which Baillie does, there is little reason not to accept the argument as sound and therefore as a critical justification of the statement "God exists." Even if God's revelation is the ultimate source of our knowledge of him and faith is the acritical knowledge of that revelation, that does not change the fact that at the critical level of reflection one still must assess the argument in terms of its validity and soundness. If the argument is valid and sound, then it constitutes a good deductive argument. If Baillie were willing to grant this, then why are the objections of Hume and Kant so decisive?

If the function of Anselm's argument is not to establish faith but to understand more completely what we already tacitly know, there is no reason in principle why the same could not be said of the cosmological arguments of St. Thomas. Surely one of the cardinal doctrines of monotheism is that God is the creator of the universe. It may well be that we have good acritical reasons for believing that this is so. However, if one is to be critical in such matters, then one might attempt to critically justify the belief that God is the creator or the ultimate necessary condition for all spatio-temporal existence, order, and value by means of arguments similar to St. Thomas's *quinque viae*. This is not to assume that such knowledge of God is direct or firsthand any more than it is to assume that St. Thomas allows for a knowledge of God by acquaintance, although Baillie acknowledges that his view of grace implies something of the sort.[35] Rather, it suggests that a complete understanding of the spatio-temporal order may necessitate the existence of one and only one entity who is self-existent, intelligent and good, and who is the ultimate necessary condition for the existence, structure, and goodness of the universe.

Baillie seems to approve of something like this in his discussion of St. Bonaventure. According to Baillie, St. Bonaventure affirms that

> *some* direct knowledge of God is native to every human soul prior to the construction of all arguments to prove His existence. Such arguments, he explains, may indeed be constructed, but they are never the real point of departure. God is indeed knowable to us through the things which He has made (*per creaturas*), but He is still more clearly known to us through His presence (*per praesentiam*) and in Himself (*quantum est de se*).[36]

It is difficult to determine why Baillie did not draw upon St. Bonaventure's insights. In Bonaventure's case we have a good example of one who accepts the primacy of the ontological approach to a knowledge of God without giving up an ancillary use of the cosmological approach. Baillie did not reject philosophical speculation altogether. He acknowledged the important contribution of Greek philosophy in the formulation of Christian dogma. He affirmed that "except in regard to the one great un-Greek insight [that one can know God by faith] I still remain a Christian Platonist."[37] Once again, for Baillie the criticisms of Hume and Kant were decisive for even an ancillary use of the cosmological approach.

I do not believe Hume and Kant's criticisms of the traditional arguments for the existence of God are as strong as many presume. They both beg far too many questions. For example, when Hume and Kant restrict all existential statements to synthetic ones, when

Hume claims that only synthetic statements are about extramental reality, and when Kant denies the possibility of metaphysics, I am not convinced. Granted both men should be placed in their historical context, but to continue to argue for points of view which are both logically and philosophically unwarranted blocks the road to further inquiry. Still, Baillie's position is puzzling at an even more basic level. If Baillie is not in principle opposed to metaphysics or ontology, then how does his "Platonism" square with Hume and Kant's rejection of metaphysics. Much of their critiques of the proofs for the existence of God depend on this fundamental rejection. Unfortunately, Baillie never resolves this apparent conflict. This constitutes a further weakness of his theology.

If Baillie actually believed that the foundations of dogma must be laid in a rational metaphysics or ontology, it would seem that certain Kantian elements of his theology would have to be rejected. Were they rejected, perhaps one could take the next step and bring his Platonism up to date by finding a metaphysical framework which could more adequately clarify and justify his ontological approach. The framework should also clarify and justify the implicit cosmological approach which is suggested in his understanding of God and the sacramental universe. If it is dogma that God creates, orders, and adorns the world such that the heavens declare the glory of God, then is it not possible to interpret the spatio-temporal order in such a way that we might also come to know God indirectly even if not with the intimacy of the knowledge of faith? Is it not possible that the insights of St. Bonaventure are more accurate than those of Baillie and that God discloses himself in the world as well as to the soul—if only we have the eyes to see and the ears to hear?

NOTES

1. In this paper, I will use the term "sign" to designate anything that can stand for some object for an interpreter and the term "symbol" to designate any linguistic sign whether oral or written.

2. John Baillie, *The Interpretation of Religion* (1928; reprint, Nashville, Tenn.: Abingdon, 1956), 214–19, 246–55.

3. John Baillie, *Our Knowledge of God* (London: Oxford University Press, 1939), 221.
4. Ibid., 17.
5. Ibid., 175.
6. John Baillie, *The Idea of Revelation in Recent Thought* (New York: Columbia University Press, 1956), 75.
7. Baillie, *Our Knowledge of God,* 41.
8. Baillie, *Idea of Revelation,* 28.
9. Ibid., 104–8, and *Our Knowledge of God,* 184–85.
10. John Baillie, *The Sense of the Presence of God* (New York: Scribner's, 1962), 60–73.
11. Baillie, *Idea of Revelation,* 100.
12. Baillie, *Our Knowledge of God,* 141.
13. Ibid.
14. Ibid., 142.
15. Baillie, *Sense of Presence,* 5.
16. Ibid., 6.
17. Baillie, *Our Knowledge of God,* 178.
18. Baillie, *Sense of Presence,* 41.
19. Ibid., 75.
20. Baillie, *Our Knowledge of God,* 181.
21. Baillie, *Sense of Presence,* 132.
22. Baillie, *Our Knowledge of God,* 180.
23. John Baillie, "The Given Word: The Message of the Unvarying Gospel," *International Review of Missions* 36 (1947): 452–66. Also, see my article "Story and Theory in Christian Theology," *Encounter* 41, 1 (Summer 1980): 205–18.
24. Baillie, *Sense of Presence,* 189–212. One must, of course, take into account the issue of *many* Christian stories and *many* Christian theologies which seek to interpret these stories. Do any stories have a normative status, and which theologies are more credible?
25. On this issue, see my forthcoming article "The Doctrine of the Trinity and Whitehead's Metaphysics" to be published in *Encounter.*
26. John Macquarrie, *Twentieth-Century Religious Thought* (New York: Harper & Brothers, 1963), 340–41.
27. Paul Tillich, "The Two Types of Philosophy of Religion," *Union Seminary Quarterly Review* no. 4 (May 1946): 3–13.
28. Ibid., 9.
29. For example, one can cite the works of Schubert Ogden and the Recent Gifford Lectures of Frederick Copleston, *Religion and The One* (New York: Crossroad, 1982).
30. Baillie, *Our Knowledge of God,* 134–43.

31. Robert C. Zaehner, *Mysticism: Sacred and Profane* (New York: Oxford University Press, 1961).

32. Baillie, *The Interpretation of Religion,* 386–89.

33. Kai Nielson, "Wittgensteinian Fideism," *Philosophy* 42, no. 161 (July 1967): 191–209. Also, see my article "Analysis and Theology," *Sophia* 17, no. 2 (July 1978): 16–26.

34. Baillie, *Our Knowledge of God,* 118–30.

35. Ibid., 113–14.

36. Ibid., 170–71.

37. John Baillie, "Confessions of a Transplanted Scott," in *Contemporary American Theology,* ed. Vergilius Ferm, 2d ser. (New York: Round Table Press, 1933), 52.

12

God in Gikuyu Religion and in Christianity: What is New?

SAMUEL G. KIBICHO

This chapter examines briefly the initial encounter and interaction of the Christian concept of God and that of the Gikuyu people of Kenya. After giving brief descriptions of the Gikuyu concept of God and the main media of revelation in Gikuyu religion, it is shown that there are important basic similarities between the two conceptions which contributed towards easier acceptance of Christianity by the Agikuyu.[1] Some of the other main factors which attracted the Agikuyu to the new religion are also pointed out, especially the new modern education (symbolized by literacy and seen as part and parcel of Christianity) and the new medicine.

As in some earlier articles by the author,[2] the continuity of the Gikuyu conception of God into and throughout Christianity is stressed. The main focus of the present article, however, is on the question, "What is new in Christianity?" The main new teachings of Christianity, as far as the Agikuyu were concerned, are identified, and the response of the Agikuyu is indicated briefly.

Finally, the author suggests that Christianity needs to focus more than it has done heretofore on some of its radically novel teachings, and on the revolutionary transformation they are meant to have on individuals and on societies. Such teachings include especially the doctrines of Jesus Christ as the incarnate son of God, his church as new people of God for our times, and the role of the church as God's instrument through the risen Christ (or the Holy Spirit), to effect his revolutionary mission of transforming both individuals and societies to conformity with his kingdom of peace with justice, righteousness, and love.

The Agikuyu people form the largest ethnic group of the Kenyan peoples. Today they number over two million. They are part of the Bantu linguistic group, found in East, Central, and Southern Africa.[3] Originally they lived in the central highlands (most still live there) a land interspersed with hills, valleys, and ridges. The land is fertile, with adequate rainfall and an especially pleasant climate due to its high altitude: between 4500 and 8000 feet above sea level. The temperature may go as low as 6°C while the maximum is normally in the twenties.

The Agikuyu were mixed agriculturists—that is, they grew various types of crops and kept livestock—cattle, goats, and sheep. When the British colonialists came, they fell in love with the land and alienated some of it along with other groups' highlands and declared it White Highlands (for whites only). This was a significant causative factor for the troubles and conflicts the Kenyans had with the British, and which ultimately led to the Mau Mau guerrilla war of liberation.

The Gikuyu had a democratic government, run by councils of elders and the age-grade system. One ruling age-set governed for a period of about thirty years, and then transferred leadership to the next age-set in a very solemn religious ceremony called *Itwika.*[4] For neighbors, there were the Meru in the south, the Kamba in the west and the Maasai in the north and east.

As Kenyatta has explained, Gikuyu religion falls into two main divisions.[5] The first focuses on the worship of God, *Ngai;* the second focuses on communion with departed or ancestral spirits. A third, less primary division deals with rites of passage and other related ceremonies. There is also a fourth division—ethical and ceremonial rules and prohibitions.

The Gikuyu Conception of God

Long before the coming of Christianity, the Gikuyu believed in one God. The Gikuyu concept of God was definitely monotheistic. They believed there is only one God, the Creator of the world, of all people and of everything. They did not have creation myths as such. But their legend of origin[6] presupposes creation of the world and of all men. It states that in the very beginning of things, God, Ngai, appeared to Gikuyu, the founder of the nation, and took him up to his presence on the top of Mount Kenya (*Kiri Nyaga,* mountain of brightness, the most sacred shrine of the Gikuyu). From there, God showed him a particular region of the land below, beautiful land with forests, hills, valleys, and ridges, all well watered. God told Gikuyu that this was the land he had allotted to him. God further instructed him to descend to that land and go make his home at a particular spot full of fig trees that he had pointed out to him. Again, he told him that he should always communicate to him his needs, and call on him through prayer and sacrifice, raising his hands towards the holy mountain of mystery.

When Gikuyu came to the spot God pointed out, he found there a beautiful woman. He knew that she had been given to him by God to be his wife. He named her *Mumbi* (molder, creator). Gikuyu and his wife Mumbi had nine daughters, but no son. Gikuyu prayed to Ngai about this problem of having no heir. Ngai instructed him to offer a sacrifice to him under a sacred fig tree, and to offer it as a family. When they came back home from the place of sacrifice they found there nine handsome young men, ready to marry the daughters and also to live with Gikuyu and Mumbi as part of the family. To this day there are nine (plus one) Gikuyu clans,[7] and all are named after the first daughters of Gikuyu and his wife Mumbi. Whether Gikuyu had other wives later the legend does not tell us. Otherwise, polygamy was the usual thing among the Agikuyu for any man who could afford it, that is, before the introduction of Christianity. Even within Christianity some Agikuyu groups resisted strongly the imposition of monogamy by European Missionaries. They argued that besides the fact that there was no such law in the Bible, some of the most important personalities in the Bible were polygamists, including Abraham and Jacob.[8]

As is true of most African peoples, the Gikuyu names of God reveal much about their concept of the nature of God.[9] The main name of God is Ngai. Three other neighboring groups also use the name Ngai for God. These are the Maasai who spell it *En-Kai,* the Meru, and the Akamba. Some earlier writers thought that the Gikuyu borrowed this name from the Maasai. However, it is difficult to determine with certainty who borrowed from whom, since there was much interchange of concepts and practices among neighboring groups.

In its Gikuyu usage, the name Ngai is derived from the stem *gaya,* which means to divide or distribute. The name Ngai therefore means the great or the supreme divider or distributer, signifying the fact that God, as the creator, owner, and ruler of all things is the one who gives and distributes everything to his children everywhere, as he wills. *Mugai* is another name of God derived from the same stem, *gaya,* and having the same meaning as Ngai. However, while a human divider or distributer can be called Mugai, the name Ngai can never be used with reference to humans. The name Mugai, when used with reference to God, has a greater element of intimacy.

Other names include the following: (1) *Mwene-Nyaga,* the owner of brightness or of the sun, and of all great mysteries. These mysteries are symbolically represented by the sun and Mount Kiri-Nyaga (Mt. Kenya), the mountain of mystery and the main holy mountain of the Gikuyu. This mountain was also God's main temporary abode when he came down on his regular inspection tours. (2) *Nyene:* the great owner. A human owner would be described as *mwene.* Nyene, in this case, is the superlative of mwene, and signifies that God is the owner of all things. (3) *Murungu,* the meaning of which is not clear, signifies the attributes of incomparable greatness and power, or omnipotence. This name is one of the oldest Bantu names of God, and is to be found among a number of Bantu groups especially in east and central Africa.[10] (4) *Githuri,* the great elder. This is a rare term, and is used sometimes in addressing God in worship.[11] It has a significant note of intimacy. (5) *Baba,* Father. It is normally used in combination with Ngai: thus, *Ngai-Baba,* Father-God; and even more than Githuri, it has a great sense of intimacy and trust.

From what we have said so far, especially in relation to the Gikuyu legend of origin and their names of God and also from a study of their worship, a number of attributes of God come out clearly. Ngai is regarded and experienced as the supreme being, the creator, the provider and sustainer of the people and of all things, as well as the very foundation of their history and of the family—their most important and sacred institution. He is unique (in a class all by himself), omnipresent, and all-wise.

It is also clear that the Agikuyu thought of God as a personal being. Thus they can talk to him in prayers and he responds and meets their needs. Although transcendent and mysterious, he is also experienced as very close: there is a father-child intimacy and trust which comes out also in worship ceremonies and in the prayers. Examples of some of the prayers include prayers at the important turning points of the life of every individual (birth, second birth, initiation into adulthood, marriage, the various stages of elderhood or womanhood, and death), sacrifice and prayers for rain, prayers in case of epidemics or persistent illness, prayers and sacrifice for the blessing of a new crop before people begin eating it, thanksgiving prayers and ceremonies for harvest.[12] And, of course, there are instantaneous prayers by anyone at any time of need.

Another basic attribute in the Gikuyu experience of God is that he is ethical and benevolent. He and the good ancestral spirits are approached to assist in the people's constant struggle against evil. God is also regarded as the ultimate upholder and sanction of justice, punishing the wicked and rewarding the righteous here in this life. He is all powerful and in absolute control of things, although he does allow both humans and spirits a lot of freedom in running their legitimate affairs. Even in his assistance to people, there is great emphasis on freedom and self-determination. Thus, the Agikuyu believe that God should never be bothered unnecessarily with things one can do for oneself and with the assistance of other humans.[13] Hence the saying: "God helps the person who is helping himself," or "when he is helping himself." Praying and waiting for God to do things for you is ruled out. Prayers for divine assistance and intervention must always be combined with initiative and determination in self-help and self-reliance. Consequently, the main focus of religious beliefs and activities is not seeking God or exhorting people to cultivate their knowledge of and their relationship with him, as we find in Christianity.[14] Rather, the emphasis is on the struggle against all manner of evil threatening the people and the society, and on the enhancement of righteousness, peace with justice, and the general welfare of society.

Media of Revelation for the Agikuyu

If the old people are asked how and why the Agikuyu came to believe in the existence of God, they show great surprise that anyone should ask such a question. God seems axiomatic to them: only a fool would question his existence. If anyone needs to give reasons for his position, it is the atheist or the agnostic (who did not exist among the Agikuyu). Otherwise, to anyone with a sound mind, the very existence of the world with all its mysteries, mountains, sun, moon, and stars, life in man and animals, and things, "wonders and mysteries of God," point to God as creator, sustainer, and the ultimate controller of all things. His creation also shows his incomprehensibility, his mystery. He is the greatest mystery. For this reason the Agikuyu have never had idols, or any kind of representation of God because they say that no one really knows or can imagine God's form or likeness.

The second medium or means of revelation among the Agikuyu, related to the first, is something in human nature. It is reason, but goes even deeper than reason (*meciria*). It is something in the core of man's innermost being, speaking to him intuitively of God as one who ultimately holds his destiny and the destiny of all men and things, and that he is benevolent. This is why the Agikuyu kept their faith in God even in the face of great sufferings and calamities.[15]

The third medium of revelation among the Agikuyu is their tradition with its rituals, ceremonies, and beliefs. Through this tradition and its praxis, their faith is enshrined, preserved and perpetuated. Here the roles of wise elders and uniquely gifted persons are important—especially the roles of the great diviner-doctors, seers, or prophets. A good example of such is prophet *Mugo wa Kibiru* who foretold the coming of the white people and their eventual expulsion from the land.[16] God spoke to such select individuals directly through visions. It was said that sometimes God took them up to his presence. At such times they would disappear mysteriously and then reappear later, to deliver their message. Such messages forewarned people of coming disasters, preparing them to deal with such disasters as colonialism, thus giving them hope and encouragement.

The following prayer is a good illustration of Gikuyu prayers, showing what they thought about God:

> Reverend elder (God) who lives on Kiri-Nyaga. You who make mountains tremble and rivers flood; we offer to you this sacrifice that you may bring us rain. People and children are crying; sheep, goats, and cattle (flocks and herds) are crying. Mwene-Nyaga, we beseech you, with the blood and fat of this lamb which we are going to sacrifice to you. Refined honey and milk we have brought for you. We praise you in the same way as our forefathers (*ndemi na mathathi*) used to praise you under this very same tree, and you heard them and brought them rain. We beseech you to accept this, our sacrifice, and bring us rain of prosperity. (Chorus or response): Peace, we beseech you, Ngai, peace be with us.[17]

Missionary Impression of the Gikuyu Conception of God

After overcoming European prejudices adequately, it did not take missionaries long to appreciate the fact that the Agikuyu had a remarkable monotheism that had remarkable similarities to Jewish monotheism at its best. The following quotation from Father Cagnolo, one of the earliest Consolata missionaries, illustrates this point. He wrote in 1939:

Since our arrival among these people, we found that the Kikuyu believes in a Supreme Being, spiritual, Ruler and Governor of the universe. They believe also in the survival of the soul . . . they distinguish exactly two orders of ultramundane beings: Ngai . . . with singular only—as Supreme Being and source of all things, and the Ngoma or the innumerable spirits of the dead, with no connection with God, but with us.

They do not know the forms and features of the Supreme being, nor did they ever attempt to make material representations of Him . . .

The Supreme Being is believed to be good per se and generally He is not invoked. Only in cases of public calamities, epidemics, droughts . . . is God had recourse to in public prayers and sacrifices . . ."[18]

Cagnolo goes on to state that in cases of calamities and misfortunes, the Agikuyu do not blame God but accept them as God's will. Sometimes they may use God's name in the form of an oath thus: "If I do not say the truth, may God thunderstrike me." Finally, Cagnolo concluded that the new doctrine of Christianity "found a suitable soil for its growth, *monotheism:* therefore the graft took hold and thrived." The above quotation and other attributes mentioned earlier also show clearly that there are basic similarities between the two conceptions: oneness or monotheism, transcendence and immanence, creator, ruler, and governor, benevolence and omnipotence.

What is New in Christianity?

Some of the important aspects of the Christian faith which were new to the Agikuyu are the following:

The first is the idea of the history of salvation through Israel as God's chosen people, culminating in the person and the mission of Jesus as the Christ. This of course raises problems for the Agikuyu as well as other people with their own religious traditions. The main problem arises when this doctrine emphasizes exclusion of these other people, for example, the Agikuyu from the history of salvation. However, this is unwarranted. The emphasis should include the doctrines of the histroy of salvation, of Jesus Christ as the incarnate son of God and of the mission of his church as God's new people in today's world. The conclusion of this chapter will elaborate on these points.

The second and perhaps the basic, most novel aspect is the complex idea of the Trinity. The idea of the complex nature of God's personality and unity was initially present in the Gikuyu thoughts about God. For instance, when it thundered the Agikuyu said that there were two gods disputing whether it should rain or not, the good god saying it should and the bad god saying it should not. As it almost always rained when it thundered, the good god won and was thus more powerful. At other times they would refer to the Maasai god as evil and the Gikuyu god as good. Despite this dualistic reference, the Agikuyu insist that God is one. Thus these mythical dualistic elements could be interpreted as pointing to the complex nature of God's unity and personality. However, the idea of the Trinity and the related notions of the two natures of Jesus (human and divine) were new to the Agikuyu.

A third new aspect is the idea of the church as separate from the state. Related to this is also the idea of a religion as an institution separate from other aspects of life. In fact, the Agikuyu had no term for religion and the missionaries had to borrow the Swahili word *Dini* to translate the English word religion.[19] This does not mean that the Agikuyu had no religion. It means their religion existed as a way of life and was interwoven into every aspect of the fabric of life. It is ironic that one of the problems facing Christianity today, in Africa as elsewhere, is that of Christians divorcing religion from the other spheres of life—economic, political, and social.

A fourth new teaching in the Christian faith for the Agikuyu is the doctrine of eschatology, including the notions of the present world coming to end and the final judgment resulting in the righteous (particularly Christians) going to heaven and the rest going to hell. For the Agikuyu, the destiny of every individual is to become a spirit at death; otherwise the world continues as usual. The living receive their rewards for upright living and punishment for their sins in this present life. Those who were good in this life become good spirits after death. They do not come back to trouble their living relatives, but are sources of help to them. The bad ones, at death continue to be bad as spirits: they are the ones who come back to trouble their living relatives and have to be appeased or dealt with and overcome in other ways.[20]

The fifth new teaching is the idea of a unique, regenerative mystical union of true Christian believers with the risen Christ, with each other (the body of Christ), and with God through Christ, in their life and mission in the world. The sixth is the belief that the risen Christ through the Holy Spirit, commands and enables the mission of propagating this new faith with its transforming power among other people. The final new teaching in this list is the idea of holy book, that is, the Bible, believed to contain the word of God, and the consequent initial linkage of Christianity with literacy and modern education, including modern medicine.

How the Agikuyu Took These New Teachings

As with other Kenyan and East African peoples, Christianity came to Gikuyu country at the same time as colonialism. Among the Agikuyu this was at the turn of the century. The Gikuyu spears, bows and arrows, and swords soon proved to be no match for the gun. The Agikuyu were quickly subdued, colonized, and parts of their best land were taken by force for white settlement. Colonialism and the introduction of money economy, taxation, and the imposition of foreign patterns of government disintegrated the stable traditional community life the Africans previously enjoyed. Within this set up, Christian missionaries, especially those of the Church Missionary Society (CMS), Church of Scotland Mission (CSM), various groups of the Roman Catholic Church, the Gospel Missionary Society (GMS), and the African Inland Mission (AIM), started their work among the Agikuyu.

There was initial resistance to the new faith, especially since these missionaries and their early converts taught against cherished Gikuyu customs and practices. Their dances, their ways of worship, prayers, and ceremonies connected with departed spirits, circumcision of girls (this came a bit later), beer drinking and brewing, polygamy—all were impermissible under the new teaching of Christianity. The older folk particularly opposed this new teaching. Christianity began to make a breakthrough and see some hope of progress only after the impact of colonialism brought the resultant disintegration of traditional society.

Another important related point is that Christianity was introduced as part and parcel of the new knowledge of literacy. At least some (teacher-evangelists-to-be) could read the Bible and possibly were able to teach others. This educational aspect was Christianity's basic attraction, especially among younger men, due to the resulting social benefits: better-paid employment and some prestige. This linkage of Christianity and education (religion-cum-education) were referred to by the Agikuyu as literacy or education (*Githomo*).

The transitive *Guthoma* means "to read" and also, "to become converted to the new religion-cum-education." The sentence "*Ndathii githomo*" means either "I am going to school" or "I am going to Church-service." The younger generation quickly saw education as the key to survival and progress in the new situation of colonialism. Soon there were complaints about the inadequacy and lack of quality in the education the missionaries were doling out to the Africans, particularly in comparison to that given to European and Asian children. Schools, as other things, were segregated along racial lines. One result of this dissatisfaction was the emergence of Gikuyu independent schools and churches especially from 1928 on.[22]

Another factor facilitating Agikuyu acceptance of the new religion-cum-education was that the missionaries preached about the same God (Ngai) whom the Agikuyu had always known and worshipped. Praying and singing to him were not new things to them. This, coupled with some remarkable similarities between some practices and beliefs in the Old Testament and those of the Agikuyu, made the acceptance of this new religion easier than it otherwise might have been. When Gikuyu religion resurfaced tremendously during the Mau Mau guerrilla war of liberation, especially among the Mau Mau freedom fighters, relevant sections of the Old and New Testaments were syncretized with Gikuyu religion.[23]

Still another point aided Agikuyu acceptance of the Christian faith. This is the fact that aspects of Gikuyu religion were demonstrably discredited at some vital points by the new religion and enlightenment. This was particularly so in the area of healing ministry, and some Gikuyu beliefs and prohibitions.[24]

My father was one of those who initially resisted the new religion, especially due to its prohibitions against Gikuyu dances which he cherished. He also held strongly to other Gikuyu beliefs, ceremonies, and prohibitions. Like many others he had great faith in the Gikuyu diviner-doctors (*Ago*). His own mother died during his early childhood, and he was thus brought up by his father's second wife. This stepmother fell ill at the time Christian missionaries and their early converts were proclaiming the new faith and enlightenment, persuading people to abandon their faith in diviner-doctors and accept instead the new teaching and its new medicine. My father, at that time newly married, and his step-brother persisted in their faith in the diviner-doctors, and continued consulting them about their mother's illness. In the process, they also slaughtered a number of sheep and goats as the diviner-doctors directed. The final diviner-doctor they consulted came one day to their mother's home. By this time she was very ill. He performed his divination, and at its conclusion, he told his assistant in a proverbial language which was meant to convey the message to him alone without revealing the truth of the situation to the rest: The assistant should look at the sun and at the diviner-doctor, and be "discerning." He should accordingly wrap the meat of the sheep slaughtered for them, with its skin, and then the two of them should pack up and leave quickly, for "this person is ours with God." This latter statement in Gikuyu, "*Mundi ni witu na Ngai*" is a proverbial way of saying that the patient was beyond the diviner-doctor's power, and had to be left to God's will.

The diviner-doctor and his assistant then left quickly with their meat. Within an hour of their departure, the sick woman died. This experience—with all its agony and expenses in sheep and goats slaughtered as well as in payments to the various diviner-doctors they had consulted—shook my father's faith in diviner-doctors and in related Gikuyu beliefs to the roots. From then on he became a Christian and resumed literacy classes (which he had started earlier as a young man but had later stopped).[25] As the above points show, the new religion-cum-education attracted increasingly more Agikuyu people, especially the younger ones. It seemed to them to be the appropriate religion for these new times, especially in relation to modern education and medicine. It also provided a place where the younger progressive Agikuyu could continue their worship of Ngai in wider inter-ethnic fellowships with other believers in the same one Creator-God as themselves.

As for the new and strange doctrines in this new religion, such as the notions of the Trinity, the son of God, the two natures of Jesus (human and divine), the Agikuyu converts accepted these as part and parcel of the mysteries (or myths) of the new faith. Among the Agikuyu themselves, the idea of converting to another religious system was not new. They had two groups or guilds with different patterns of ceremonies. One was known as the Gikuyu Karinga (or Gikuyu proper) group or guild. The other one was called the Gikuyu-Ukabi or Maasai group or guild. The latter's patterns of rituals and ceremonies were similar to Maasai rituals and ceremonies. One could leave his own group or guild and join the other. To mark and effect such conversion there was a solemn ceremony involving the purification of the convertee from the rituals and ceremonies of his old group, and the incorporation by adoption into the new guild. One had to go through similar ceremonies when one moved his residence and membership from his tribe to another, for example, from Gikuyu to Maasai or Akamba and vice versa. It should be emphasized that in this type of conversion God does not enter the picture, because it does not involve changing one's God. The same God, Ngai, was worshipped in the two Gikuyu ritual guilds as well as among the other tribes they were in contact with. What differed were their patterns and systems of rituals and ceremonies.

In conclusion, it should be stressed that there is a great deal more continuity of the Gikuyu, or African, conception of God (*Ngai*) in and throughout Christianity than many Christians realize.[26] To the Gikuyu converts, the Christian God was the same well-known Ngai worshipped by their forefathers long before the Christianity's advent. God's basic attributes are similar in the two religions.

However, the Christian religion did introduce some radically new teachings. Some of these were pointed out in this chapter. These ideas were accepted without much difficulty by the Gikuyu converts as new teachings of a new religion. They did not involve the introduction of a new God. The thought of a new God is an absurdity among the Gikuyu. For them Ngai is always one: you can never talk of two Ngai's or of a new Ngai. The new religion with its new doctrines and practices, new education, and medicines, were all accepted as blessings of the same Ngai, who is creator, sustainer, and governer of all. Thus, the Gikuyu progressives felt that the new religion provided a better place and means, better suited to these new times, for the worship of the same Ngai whom their forefathers had known and worshipped in somewhat different ways.

Christianity, in its interaction with African religion, should have focused more on teaching its novel aspects, such as Christ as God's incarnate son, the church as Christ's mystical body, Christ's mission through his church of transforming both individuals and societies, and other concepts revolutionary to African religious thinking.

Instead, Christianity became preoccupied with minor religious differences and emphasized the exclusive aspects of salvation and revelation rather than its universal aspects. The universal church of Jesus Christ, transcending as it should all ethnic, national, and class barriers, could fulfill its mission as a regenerative and revolutionary movement. It could bring about not only inner transformation of individual believers, but also revolutionary social change towards more just political, social, and economic structures in our nations and in the world. This is really the focal point and what matters most in all of what is new in Christianity.

NOTES

1. The term "Agikuyu" (sing, *Mugikuyu*) means the *Gikuyu* people. "Kikuyu" is its anglicized form.
2. See especially S. G. Kibicho, "The Kikuyu Conception of God, its Continuity into the Christian Era and the Question it Raises for the Christian Idea of Revelation" (unpublished Ph. D. diss., Vanderbilt University, Nashville, Tenn., 1972). Also, "The Continuity of the African Conception of God into Christianity: A Kikuyu Case-Study," *Christianity in Independent Africa,* ed. E. Fashole-Luke, R. Gray, A. Hastings, and G. Tastie (London: Rex Collings, 1978), 370–88.
3. My first Gikuyu reader, written by a CSM missionary, Arthur Ruffel Barlow, summed up well the European impression of Gikuyu land. It stated: "God has given the Gikuyu good land, which never lacks food or water or forests. It is therefore fitting that the Gikuyu should praise God always, for he has been so generous to them. *Ngai niahete Gikuyu bururi mwega, utagaga irio kana mai kana githaka. Wega no Gikuyu kigocage Ngai hindi ciothe. Ni undi nagitanahira muno.*" The reading primer booklet was popularly called *Gatune* due to its red color. It was quickly out of print and withdrawn from the schools in the early 1940s.
4. For a description of the *Itwika* ceremony, see J. Kenyatta, *Facing Mount Kenya: The Tribal Life of the Gikuyu* (London: Secker and Warburg, 1938, 6th impression, 1974), 187ff.
5. Ibid., 32ff.
6. Ibid., 3ff.
7. The Gikuyu clans are actually ten. But counting of people or of domestic animals was a prohibited thing. The exact number of the clans is therefore never given. Instead, it is stated as "a full nine" (i. e., *kenda muiyuru*). The ten clans go back to the daughters of Gikuyu and Mumbi. They were the mothers of the respective clans. These were: (1) Wangari, (2) Wangeci, (3) Wangui, (4) Nyambura, (5) Wanjeri, (6) Wairimu, (7) Wanjiru, (8) Wanjuku, (9) Wambui, and (10) Wamuyu. See S. K. Gathigira, *Miikarire ya Agikuyu,* (Customs of the Kikuyu) (1934, reprint Nairobi: Equatorial Publishers, 1968), 1–2. Also Kenyatta, 5–6, who gives nine clans.
8. Kenyatta, 271.
9. See Kibichio, "The Kikuyu Conception of God," 58ff. Also, "The Continuity of the African Conception of God," in Fashole-Luke et al. 37ff. The quotations in the subsection are from the latter article. See also L. S. B. Leakey, *The*

Southern Kikuyu Before 1903 (London: Academic Press, 1977), 3: 1075–76. Leakey observes that the name *Baba,* that is, father, was used by the Gikuyu long before the advent of Europeans, and was therefore not a Christian influence as some Europeans including Leakey himself had thought at first.

10. Variations of the spelling of this name include the following: *Murungu,* among the Gikuyu and the Meru of Kenya, and the Sandawe and the Tura of Tanzania; *Mulungu* among the Digo, the Duruma, the Giryama, and the Rabai of Kenya, and among the Bena, the Gogo, the Luguru, and the Sukuma-Nyamwezi of Tanzania, and among the Chewa, the Matengo, and the Yao of Malawi, and among the Yao of Msumbinji; *Mlungu,* among the Bondei of Tanzania, and the Taita of Kenya; *Mlungu,* among the Pokomo of Kenya; *Mungu,* among Sukuma-Nyamwezi of Tanzania, and the Taita of Kenya. For a list of names of God of the various peoples of black Africa, see J. Mbiti, *Concepts of God in Africa* (New York: Preager Publishers, 1970), 327ff. See also, *African Ideas of God: A Symposium,* ed. E. W. Smith, 3d. ed. (London: Edinburgh House Press, 1966), 2–3.
11. See for example, Kenyatta, 246–47.
12. Ibid., 231–68. Also, Kibicho, "The Kikuyu Conception of God," 39–53.
13. See for example, Kenyatta, 234–35, 237.
14. Cf. J. Mbiti, *African Religions and Philosophy* (London: Heinemann, 1969), 98. Also, *Concepts of God in Africa,* 219.
15. See for example, Kibicho, "The Kikuyu Conception of God," 289–301.
16. Ibid., 22–39, 140ff. Also Kenyatta, 41–47.
17. Kenyatta, 247.
18. Quoted in Kibicho, "The Kikuyu Conception of God," 86–87.
19. Cf. Kenyatta, 233.
20. Cf. ibid., 260–63. Also Gathigira, 33–34.
21. See Kibicho, "The Kikuyu Conception of God," 171–77. Also, Roland Oliver, *The Missionary Factor in East Africa* (London: Longmans, 1952), 172, 178, 234.
22. See Kibicho, "The Kikuyu Conception of God," 255–61. Also F. B. Welbourn, *East African Rebels* (New York: The Highway Press, 1958).
23. See Kibicho, "The Kikuyu Conception of God," 289–301. Also Donald L. Barnett and Karari Njama, *Mau Mau from Within: Autobiography and Analysis of Kenya's Peasant Revolt* (New York: Modern Reader Paperbacks, Monthly Review Press, 1968), 104–5, 133, 201, 205, 322–26, 258–61, 367, 446–54, 491.
24. For lists of some of such prohibitions, see for example, Gathigira, 74–76; M. N. Kabetu, *Kirira Kia Ugikuyu* (Customs and traditions of the Kikuyu people) (Nairobi: East African Literature Bureau, 1947, 1966), 105–8. Also, C. W. Hobley, *Bantu Beliefs and Magic* (London: H. F. and G. Witherby, 1922), 103–26, with particular reference to the Kikuyu and Kamba tribes of Kenya Colony together with some reflections on East Africa after the war.
25. This was in the early 1930s.
26. See especially Kibicho, "The Kikuyu Conception of God,"; also "The Continuity of the African Conception of God."

13

The Ultimate: Insight and Reality

EVANGHELOS MOUTSOPOULOS

Definitions

In this chapter I will argue the possibility of an eschatology and archaeology of the ultimate. According to its etymology, the word "ultimate" designates the last conceivable status or degree of presence. It corresponds to the Greek *eschaton* from which the term *eschatology* is derived. It is important to note that these terms are understandable in both a temporal and logical sense. Their meaning is evidently reversible. They may designate not only the last, but also the most remote degree or status of presence. In this respect the *eschaton,* as ultimate, may also be considered as *protarchicon,* that is, as designating the incipient steps of an infinite scale of degrees or statuses. It reflects the fundamental conditions under which (a) what is possible is conceivable and (b) an archaeology of the being is sustainable.[1] In this way, archaeology becomes an eschatology, and vice versa, thus closing a circle which begins with either of these procedures.

Such a reversibility of the ultimate has already been envisaged by Andre Lalande who defines the ultimate as:

> That which one is finally led to in a regressive analysis (and I strongly underline here the word *regressive*—either because it is impossible, though wishable, to proceed further; or more frequently, because one has reached the term beyond which there is nothing more to look after within the order of questions asked. *Ultimate* in this case, is frequently understood as a synonym of *categorical imperative*[2]

It is evident that Lalande reduces the problems which are relative to the ultimate, to these which are relative to the *first,* when he refers to this concept.[3]

In a similar way George E. Moore refers indirectly to the ultimate value, attributing to it the meaning of a fundamental substratum which is *protarchical,* but which consciousness reaches *at* last. In Moore's terms, the ultimate value may be defined as

> the intrinsic value of an entity possessing intrinsic value throughout. For example, a hedonist might say that a pleasant evening at the opera has intrinsic value and yet maintain that only the hedonic tone of the evening has the ultimate value, because it alone has no constituents which fail to have intrinsic value.[4]

Moore's conception of the ultimate concurs with Lalande's in that it recognizes in the ultimate an intrinsic element deprived of all constitutive parts. It is the most basic of all states of being, from which everything is derived. The deliberate avoidance of Neoplatonic views is more than evident here. Both Lalande, through *regressive analysis,* and Moore, through the variance of a manifold superstructure and its underlying elementary simplicity, indicate the ultimate as the final objective (a kind of One) of a mental conversion[5] returning to an objectively real procession.[6] Thus, what, epistemologically speaking, seems to be omega, is in fact alpha.

Likewise, Aristotle conceives of the *prime mover*[7] which, although at motion's origin becomes virtually the last scope of a regressively unfolding chain of causes and effects, towards the motionless cause of any motion, at the level of which, logically and ontologically, it must stop.[8] More than the result of a real procedure, the ultimate is then revealed to be a beginning that only seems to be an end, by virtue of the mental procedure that leads to it. The paradox is only apparent, since the concept involves two distinct levels: one ontological and one epistemological, which complement each other. In the same sense, Paul Tillich understands the ultimate both as an original fact and as a terminal notion.[9]

Plato's conception of the eschatological reality, as depicted in the myth of Er closing the last book of the *Republic,*[10] is the vision of an intermediate status of the evolution of the world, that is, both an end and a beginning. It designates a hidden domain through which all life supposedly passes while waiting for rebirth, under the rule of necessity. Such a mythical vision mingles *telos* and *arche,* without clarifying Plato's concern for the essential cause of the world's existence. The answer of this Platonic enigma is in the *Timaeus,* namely, in the myth dealing with the construction of the world's soul.[11] The transcendent idea of Good is supposed to inspire and to allow, the demiurge to proceed to the cosmic creation. Such a procession is reminiscent of that described by Plotinus. Nevertheless, Plato only implies the real nature of the Good. He conceives it as a kind of alloy, and as a structure;[12] but by no means does he attribute to the Good the character of an ultimate reality. An archaeology of being is envisaged only in Augustine's *Confessions* where, independent of a concern for the essence of the absolute, a quest for existence is clearly suggested.[13] This quest has inspired Christian ontological considerations on this issue.[14] Since the ultimate is considered to be located infinitely far in time, if not beyond time and hence unreachable, one has to define and follow an adequate philosophical method in order to grasp it, surpassing all intermediate terms that separate it from consciousness.

The "Kairic" Method

Such an adequate method must be both *direct* and rational (discursive), due to the nature of the ultimate. This method is practically antinomical. The ultimate is in an unreachable location before time begins. Yet, in order to understand the consciousness must be able to reach the ultimate directly, without intermediate stages.

Two methods are available, in principle, for such an approach. The first method is both an *intuitive* and *mystical* one. From Gregory Palamas to Meister Eckhart, it has been used to assure the ascent of consciousness towards the absolute. No doubt this method originates from the Neoplatonists (and the Gnostics), and goes back to Plato. In the *Symposium,* Plato insists on the importance of ascending dialectics leading from the sensible to the intelligibly beautiful, and hence, to beauty itself.[15] It is obvious that Plato considers this method as presupposing successive stages of approach to Beauty.

Likewise, Plotinus conceives of a similar method of approach to the intelligible world, but denies, at the same time, that there is any possibility of consciousness reaching the highest degree of reality, which is the One.[16] According to Plotinus, the One is beyond rationality, and remains inconceivable. It follows from this that no quality may be attributed to the One. Negative theology derives from such an assertion. Under these conditions, the ultimate may be conceived of, but never thoroughly known. Consciousness may have only an insight, but no real knowledge of it. In the same vein Proclus asserts that, due to the existence of different levels of cognition, knowledge of the One will always be imperfect. Consciousness is impeded from completely reaching the One, due to the interference of the various cognitive functions operating at the inferior levels of the mind.[17] It is only by means of an intermediate factor or symbol that an approximate, though adequate, knowledge of the One becomes possible.

The mystical conception of the problem is that the absolute is not *known,* but *experienced* through the suspension of existence or, at least, when existence is put into brackets. From Schopenhauer[18] to Husserl, this means of suspending existence has been widely commended as the unique means that leads to absolute knowledge without distroying existence. On the other hand, the mystical conception of knowledge of the absolute presupposes the consummation of existence through love. This particular mystical love experience is envisaged by the Arab mystic and philosopher Ahmad Ghazali as leading to an erotic union of existence with the absolute. According to Ghazali, consciousness, like a butterfly, proceeds towards the beloved flame. When it reaches it, it becomes the flame that penetrates it. For one minimal instant, as the butterfly is consumed, it becomes its own lover: it identifies itself with the flame.[19] It is only through such an image that the absolute may be understood. Ghazali himself qualifies this kind of identification as a "mystery";[20] a mystery, however, which obviously does not meet the exigencies of philosophical understanding.

The second method is suggested by Bergson. It is again an *intuitive* method, but *not* a mystical one. Unlike the object of the method of mystics, which is initially located outside consciousness, the object of Bergsonian method is located within the consciousness itself (understood as the consciousness of existence). Bergson rejects the traditional rational method in philosophy, mainly because of its discursive character impeding one from grasping the object of philosophical concern in a direct and immediate way. According to Bergson, reason is able only to surround its object without ever penetrating it. For Bergson, Plato is responsible for having imposed such a method on the whole of philosophical thought, through Aristotle and even through Kant, up to the end of the nineteenth century.[21] Such a method entails the divisibility of the object of any philosophical inquiry.

In order to overcome difficulties in understanding its object, reason resorts to division of particular objects which are basically understandable. However, by proceeding in this way, reason divides a whole into small parts (this aspect of the Platonic method was adopted by Descartes and exposed by him as one of the rules of his own method).[22] Each part may be easily understood, but reason will fail to understand the whole, Bergson insists. Another consequence of the Platonic and Cartesian method is the intrusion of the notion of time into philosophical thought. Time is composed of minimal parts which really do not exist. Time is thus a product of human inventiveness and a mere instrument of measuring, with no corresponding reality.[23] Duration is the only undeniable reality and the very first datum of consciousness.[24] It may not be conceived of, but may be experienced when the consciousness installs itself within its proper duration, in order to grasp reality "from the inside."[25]

The Bergsonian method, in this way, becomes adequate for grasping the reality of duration, but only for this single and specific purpose. By no means is it useful in order to allow the conception of the ultimate, which, by definition, is situated outside consciousness. Furthermore, the Bergsonian method is self-contradictory, since it has recourse to reason after having denied its traditionally accepted epistemological virtues. It is a direct method for grasping the reality of duration, but the intuition it entails is subjective, not objective. Hence, it cannot be applied to the knowledge of the ultimate. The most important contribution of the Bergsonian theory is that time is an imaginary concept which does not correspond to any kind of reality. One has to take advantage of this contribution before looking for a method which is appropriate for both the nature of the ultimate and the possibilities of reason. The "kairic" method meets both of these requirements.

The kairic method is defined as a method of actualization of what is remote. "Kairic" derives from the concept of *kairos* which means in Greek the minimal and optimal moment at which an action gives the best results. The notions of 'not yet' and 'never more' designate the external limits of a zone within which the action in question attains its best validity. Before the kairos and after it, the action fails to fully attain its scope.[26] Besides, the notion of actualization presupposes that of the intentionality of consciousness. This notion is understood not in the Husserlian sense of an opening of consciousness towards its contents nor in the sense of a reference to them, but rather in the Bergsonian sense of intention, of a purpose to be fulfilled, of a particular design of the consciousness to be realized.

The dimensions of time—past, present, future—are thus substituted by the dimensions of the kairos—not yet and never more. Such a substitution and replacement are equivalent to a reduction and restructuring of the notion of time. It leads to the conception of an "intemporality," or rather, of an "atemporality" which has nothing to do with eternity. On the contrary, it liberates consciousness from any kind of obsession due to the notion of temporality. It enables one to proceed to a microanalysis of the atemporal, and to investigate what occurs within a moment which is both infinitesimal and eternal (*aionic*). For this very reason the kairic reduction is favorable, and denotes the transition from the penultimate to the ultimate. The following is one application of this method, meeting the requirements of being both direct and rational, it is suitable for the examination of the two main aspects of the problem of ultimacy: epistemological and the ontological.

The Ultimate as Insight

The kairic reduction allows both (a) a leap of consciousness from the close present to a remote present by removing the latter to the domain of the immediate experience and by excluding any reference to consciousness to the intermediate stages of time, which in a sense it "puts into brackets"; and (b) a direct and immediate intrusion of the remote present into consciousness, which thus experiences it as privileged moment. If by "remote present" one understands the ultimate, it follows that the kairic reduction leads not to the ultimate itself, as an object. It leads to the *experience* of the ultimate, an experience which is equivalent to the identification of the ultimate and of existence itself. Therefore, one may consider such an experience as an insight of the ultimate. Furthermore one may consider the ultimate itself as an insight (rationally and discursively obtained) of what the ultimate is.

An experience of this kind becomes possible due to the two factors, already registered, of the kairic knowledge: first, the intentionality of consciousness, and second, the restructuring of the temporal dimensions, which allows their substitution or replacement by the kairic dimensions.

Intentionality of consciousness, in the kairic sense, has been defined above as opposed to the intentionality according to phenomenological thought. For Husserl, indeed, intentionally designates the ability of consciousness to refer to its own contents. Under such conditions, intentionality is equivalent to receptivity. Its function is in some ways passive, and operates at a static level.[27] The various interpretations of the Husserlian theory insist upon the fact that consciousness tries to *retain* the present which is changed into past, and qualify such a present as a retentional present.[28] It is a past whose former status as present is maintained by consciousness, an actualized past, which exerts an influence upon consciousness. Such an influence is comparable to that of *hysteresis,* that is, of the continuous permanence of past situations, observed in some cases in physics.[29] It is an aftermath of the former experienced present.

Such a model may be reversed in two ways. A first reversion is possible at the level of the opposition between what is leaving the present moment and what is approaching the present moment. By virtue of the kairic categories, one may conceive of a *provisional* (or "previsional") present. This present becomes possible because of the dynamism of consciousness, which advances to meet the approaching moment.[30] Intentionality enables consciousness to conceive of its aim. It also enables the actualization of the scope in question, in which existence, is both approached, and reached. The kairic reduction reshapes the framework of the relation between consciousness and its *object*. The object, when understood as an aim, becomes an *objective*. Thus the ultimate becomes a remote presence whose distance is minimized before being annulled. Consciousness thus installs itself, almost automatically, in a domain that temporally does not exist any more, but that is "kairically" confirmed. What is beyond experience is now experienced in a definite and actual way through existence.

A second reversion of the same Husserlian model is also possible, but at a quite different level. This is, at the level of opposition between the present that becomes past, and the remote past, unexperienced as yet by the consciousness, which seeks to meet it by actualizing it. In the first case, consciousness "sticks" to the past ex-present; in the second case, that of the reversed model, that is that of the kairic model, consciousness jumps into a present ex-past. The whole attitude of consciousness thus changes completely, as well as its possibilities for grasping what seemed to be unknowable before. It experiences what is far beyond experience, residing in an area of reality normally unreachable by any rational method of approach other than the kairic one. The kairic method allows the insertion of consciousness into an area which is otherwise "forbidden". In epistemological terms, what is definitely beyond any conception becomes accessible to reason without any need for consciousness to use a mystical means of approach. The direct character of such an approach is thus easily combined with its rational character.

Both reversions of the Husserlian model are not mere alterations of it. They are deep and radical restructurings of the "temporal" reference of consciousness to its object. Each of these reversions applies to a vision of the ultimate, whether it is considered a pretemporal beginning or as the conclusion of an ascension (or accomplishment) towards the end of some epistemological concern. Be it a beginning or an end, the ultimate is revealed as the *object of an insight* and as an *insight* as well. The kairic reduction entails the use of brackets not in a phenomenological sense, namely as a means of suspension of a phenomenal reality, but in the sense of rejection and exclusion of time as an invention of the mind. The kairic reduction leads the intentionality of consciousness, which is, the intentionality of existence, to assure an actual experience of what seemed to be beyond being.

The Ultimate as Reality

The epistemological approach to the problem of the ultimate illustrates that its ontological approach must analyze the fundamental paradox of viewing the ultimate from a temporal viewpoint. In the logical sequence of thoughts, the ultimate is placed *after* whatever precedes it, since it is reached by means of logical ascension from effects to causes, up to the first and original cause, also the last and final cause. The ultimate is located *beyond* any area in the chain of causes and effects. It is an extratemporal reality.[31]

Suppose that the senses of causes and effects, besides being a sequence and a scale of logical references, are also a succession of data envisaged within the framework of time. Take into consideration that time itself is an invention of consciousness which may be superated by means of the kairic method. It then becomes clear that the whole series of causes and effects, considered from a logical and from a temporal aspect, is merely parenthetical within reality. The existence of such a parenthesis entails that temporality itself including human presence and hence historicity, may also be viewed parenthetically within reality in its utmost essence.

Such an essence is veiled by the parenthesis in question. It appears, then, that reality as we perceive it is only a substratum into which temporality and history are inserted. Reality's existence is unaffected by this insertion. The kairic argument supports such a conclusion.

The ultimate is the pertinent and permanent reality that constantly remains. The insertion of the parenthetical temporal and historical "reality" conceals only a part of the ultimate. Before and after it are two other parts of the ultimate which are not concealed at all. Ontologically speaking, the ultimate is an infrastructure. As an infrastructure, it presents all the characters of every other ontological structure.[32] The ultimate can be understood as located both *before* and *after* temporality and history. One can also conceive of the "before" as "joining," in the "after," and vice versa. It is a process of identification, like an intangible "geometrical" point which is the *arche* and the *telos* of a circumference. Such an image is itself an ingenious, invention.

The points lying ultimately "before" and ultimately "after" temporality and historicity are not the results of identification. On the contrary, they are identical points of the same permanent reality. It is only illusory that they are separated and distinguished from each other by virtue of temporality and history. In fact, they are the only parts of reality that are not concealed by temporality and history. They are not identical with each other, except in that they are both constitutive parts of the continuity of reality itself. Temporality can be described as a means by which consciousness is able to locate human presence in relation to reality, and to interpret the meaning of this presence, and the meaning reality has for it as well.

Along the same lines, it becomes clear that the ultimate reality is found neither only *before* temporality nor *after* it, but *under* it as well. Ultimate reality permeates temporality. Only its two extremes remain outside temporality, absolutely open to insight on behalf of consciousness. The relation of human presence, and hence of human consciousness and understanding, to the ultimate reality comes about only by human presence emerging from the reality in question, an emergence that does not affect this reality at all. Temporality is only a means of interpretating historicity. In turn, historicity is the outcome of the process through which consciousness becomes aware of the reality of existence.

This explanation allows one to evaluate the preceding views as the outcome of an attempt to overcome difficulties resulting from constant opposition between exclusively realistic and exclusively idealistic considerations of the problem. There is no doubt possible about the reality of either the ultimate or of existence itself. What makes it possible to establish a relationship between these two realities is to understand consciousness as an emanation of existence, through which existence attributes meaning to the ultimate reality and, hence, to its own reality.

Historicity is the expression of the reality of conscious existence. Historicity conceals the ultimate reality only because it emphasizes the significance of the reality of existence. Historicity itself is the axiological aspect of the reality of existence. What conceals the ultimate reality is temporality through which historicity becomes conceivable. The kairic reduction enables consciousness to surpass the temporal framework of its own continuity. Thus consciousness can infiltrate the continuity of the ultimate reality by going beyond time to the ultimate's extreme ties—the beginning and end of time. These extremities are not separate from the whole, except through the invented category of temporality. Thus, the kairic reduction is the means by which consciousness comprehends the relation of the reality of existence to the ultimate reality, and through which the meaning of the ultimate reality itself is revealed to existence.

By destroying the temporal superstructure, and by restructuring the image of reality within consciousness, the kairic reduction provides a framework for conceiving and evaluating the ultimate reality, previously an impossible task. Considered through time, that is through a divisible means, the ultimate appeared to have limits, or at least, to begin beyond its own limits: a limit *before* and a limit *after* actuality. By being actualized, thanks to the kairic reduction, the ultimate reveals itself as an unlimited actuality.

Under such conditions, the adequate conception of the epistemological problem of the ultimate allows the revelation of a completely unsuspected visage of the reality of the ultimate. From now on, one has the right to speak not of an *archaeology* or even (in case of inversion of the data) of an *eschatology* (with the traditional meaning of this term) of being, but of a reality that underlies and supports being throughout its presence. There is no *arche* or *telos* of reality (since *arche* and *telos* are only fictitious terms according to which reality is temporalized), according to which existence is ontologically evaluated. By invalidating the temporal conception of the ultimate, I in no way intend to attribute any eternal character to it. My personal viewpoint consists of an attempt to atemporalize the ultimate, leaving the way free to my kind of interpretation of it, without exclusion of any eventual significance of its reality.

From such a perspective, it is impossible to exclude the right of consciousness to proceed to an evaluation of the ultimate as a reality by reference to which it seeks to establish the legitimacy of existence. In this respect, the field of investigation remains completely open. It is the responsibility of philosophical thought to opt for further theistic or atheistic solutions of the problem. What I have tried to do is to define the epistemological and ontological framework within which such solutions should be sought. I have defined the methodological prerequisites of an investigation on the nature and meaning of the ultimate not as a remote reality, but as a pertinent and essential one that invisibly dominates the reality of existence.

Axiological Considerations

As has already been stressed,[33] the ultimate is an essential substratum of the reality of the framework within which the human consciousness operates. As such, it constitutes an infrastructure of existence. It is also the point of reference for consciousness dealing with its own experiences of existence itself. Be it subjective, objective or a combination thereof,[34] any axiology must take into consideration the fact that values are interrelated with their respective conceptual, or even experienced, conscious image. Independently of its ontological status, the ultimate is epistemologically and axiologically the foundation upon which existence bases its own desire of *more-being,* through the fruition of its intimate impulses when these are reflected upon objective realities.[35]

The intentionality of consciousness is an intentionality of existence. It is necessarily orientated towards such objective realities, although these seem to be orientated towards consciousness itself.[36] This dialectic scheme of relations between the intimate reality and the phenomenal motion of values finds its application at the level of reference of consciousness to the ultimate. The axiological foundation of the ultimate has been considered by G. E. Moore[37] as what exists beyond the intrinsic value of what is experienced, but irradiates the dominant tone of the value in question.

It is important to stress that, understood from this viewpoint, the ultimate is eventually beyond the range of consciousness, but not beyond the range of existence. It constantly sustains it and allows it to confirm itself. As a substratum of existence, it manifestly differs from it. Nevertheless, it surrounds it and extends it. The ultimate may be compared, even by means of an epistemological inversion, to the *Umgreifendes* of existence, according to K. Jaspers.[38] Axiologically speaking, the ultimate forms not only the term of reference, but also a field of interest and of attraction. It is the terminal "point" of the process of existence seeking a value strong enough to justify its intimate impetus towards more—being. Such an impetus has nothing to do with Schopenhauer's idea of "blind will," which is intimately related to the concept of life.[39] It is itself reflected in the idea of intensification of existence through the enrichment of consciousness with a constantly growing deal of intimate experiences. The ultimate, thus, becomes, for existence, through reflection, the foundation of value of existing.

It has been sufficiently shown that the ultimate is neither a beginning nor an end. In spite of any kind of appearance, it remains a constant substructure of existence. An insight of this status of the ultimate may be acquired by consciousness through a methodical kairic reduction which eliminates the temporal exigence. The ultimate, then, is confirmed as an atemporal framework as well as an axiological foundation of existence. Theistic or atheistic interpretations of its ontological status, with reference to existence, are equally susceptible to offering an explanation of it and an explanation of existence as well. The ultimate reality remains a term of reference, altogether epistemological, ontological, and axiological, which sustains the reality of existence, and remains the real, though unseizable foundation of every reality.

NOTES

1. Cf. Evanghelos Moutsopoulos, "Une archéologis chrétienne de l'être est-elle possible?," *Diotima* 8 (1980): 184–86.
2. Cf. André Lalande, *Vocabulaire technique et critique de la philosophie,* trans. Evanghelos Moutsopoulos, 7th ed. (Paris: Presses Universitaires de France, 1956), 1158 a–b.
3. Cf. Ibid.
4. Cited by Charles A. Baylis, in Dagobert D. Runes et al., *Dictionary of Philosophy* (Totowa, N.J.: Littlefield, 1960, 1976), 331a; Cf. George E. Moore, *Principia Ethica* (New York: Cambridge University Press, 1903, 1953); George E. Moore, *Philosophical Studies* (London: Kegan Paul, 1922, new ed. New York: Humanities Press, 1952); Cf. Paul Arthur Schilpp, ed., *The Library of Living Philosophers,* vol. 4: *The Philosophy of G. E. Moore* (Evanston, Ill.: Northwestern University Press, 1942); Cf. Charles William Mooris, *Six Theories of Mind,* 3: "Mind as Intentional Act" (Chicago: Chicago University Press, 1932).
5. Cf. John M. Rist, *Plotinus: The Road to Reality* (Cambridge: Cambridge University Press, 1967), 37ff.; Thomas Whittaker, *The Neo-Platonists: A Study*

in the History of Hellenism, 4th ed., after the 1928 Cambridge ed. (Hildesheim: G. Olms, 1961), 29ff.

6. Cf. Jean Trouillard, *La procession plotinienne* (Paris: Presses Universitaires de France, 1955); Evanghelos Moutsopoulos, *Le Problème de l'imaginaire chez Plotin,* publication of the Societé Hellénique des Etudes Philosophiques, série "Recherches," no. 4 (Athens: Grigoris, 1980), 41.
7. Cf. Aristotle *Metaphysics* Λ 7, 1072b, 10–11.
8. Cf. ibid. Λ 3, 1070a 2–4: "anankē stēnai."
9. Cf. Paul Tillich, *The Systemaic Theology,* 5th ed. (Chicago: University of Chicago Press, 1951, 1956), 1:110f; "Revelation as revelation of the mystery which is our ultimate concern, is invariably revelation for someone in a concrete situation of concern."
10. Cf. Plato *Republic* 10: 613e–21b.
11. Cf. Plato *Timaeus* 28aff.
12. Cf. ibid.
13. Cf. Augustine *Confessions* 11: 13, 15ff., ed. W. Watts II (London: Harvard University Press, 1961), 225.
14. Cf. Moutsopoulos, "Une archéologie chrétienne," 184–86.
15. Cf. Plato *Symposium* 209e–211c.
16. Cf. *Enneads* 5:6, 3, 3: "prōton . . . to hen."
17. Cf. Evanghelos Moutsopoulos, *Les structures de l'imaginaire dans la philosophie de Proclus* (Paris: Les Belles Lettres, 1984), pt. 1, chap. 5.
18. Cf. Evanghelos Moutsopoulos, *Dialectics of Will as a Foundation of Aesthetics in Schopenhauer's System* (Athens: Vayonakis, 1958), 53ff.
19. Cf. Ahmad Ghazali, *Sawânih al-'oshâg* (*Intuitions of the faithful of love*) ed. Helmut Ritter, chap. 39; Cf. Henri Corbin, *Histoire de la philosophie islamique* (Paris: Gallimard, 1964), 1:281; Cf. Evanghelos Moutosopoulos, *Phenomenology of Values* (Athens: University Press, 1981), 50–53; Evanghelos Moutsopoulos, "Eros et Thanatos," *Meletē Thanatou* (Athens: Plethon, 1977), 174–91.
20. Cf. Ghazali, *Sawânih al-'oshâg.*
21. Cf. Evanghelos Moutsopoulos, *La critique du platonisme chez Bergson,* publication of the Société Hellénique des Etudes Philosophiques, série "Recherches," no. 3 (Athens: Grigoris, 1980), 40ff.
22. Cf. René Descartes, *Regulae ad directionem ingenii,* Regula 5, 379, ed. Adam and Tannery, ". . . Atque hanc exacte servabimus, si propositiones involutas et obscuras ad simpliciores gradatim reducamus et deinde ex omnium simplicissimarum intuitu ad aliarum omnium cognitionem per eusdem gradus ascendere tentemus"; cf. *Discours de la méthode,* 2ème règle. Cf. Jules Simon, *Oeuvres de Descartes* (Paris, 1892), 11: "Le second, de diviser chacune des difficultés que j'examinerais en autant de parcelles qu'il se pourrait et qu'il serait requis pour les mieux résoudre."
23. Cf. Moutsopoulos, *La critique du platonisme,* 48ff.

24. Henri Bergson, "Essai sur les données immediates de la conscience" (1889), *Oeuvres,* Edition du centenaire (Paris: Presses Universitaires de France, 1959), 68–74.

25. Ibid.

26. Cf. Evanghelos Moutsopoulos, "Maturation et corruption. Quelques réflexions sur la notion de 'kairos'," *Revue des Travaux de l'Académie des Sciences Morales et Politiques, et Comptes Rendus de ses Séances* 131 (1978): 1–20; Moutsopoulos, "Sur les dimensions 'kairiques' de la structure de l'être," *Hommage â Francois Meyer* (Aix-en-Provence: Publications de l'Université de Provence, 1983), 121–33.

27. Evanghelos Moutsopoulos, "Temporal and 'kairic' Categories," *Scientific Annuary,* Faculty of Philosophy, University of Athens (1962): 412–36.

28. Moutsopoulos, "Irréversibilité du présent chez Husserl?," *Diotima* 11 (1983): 193–94.

29. Cf. J. H.-Y. Tai, *Pulsed Sine Wave Hysteresis Loops* (Washington, D.C.: Catholic University of America Press, 1957).

30. Moutsopoulos, "Irréversibilité."

31. Cf. Moutsopoulos, "Prospective et historicité de la présence divine," *Il senso della filosofia cristiana oggi, Atti del XXXII Convegno del Centro di Studi Filosofici,* Gallarate, 1977, (Brescia: Morcelliana, 1978), 103–4.

32. Cf. Moutsopoulos, "Sur les dimensions 'kairiques' de la structure."

33. Cf. ibid.

34. Cf. Moutsopoulos, *Phenomenology of Values,* 27–44; Moutsopoulos, "Fondement ontologique et fondement existentiel des valeurs," *Diotima* 11 (1983): 149–52.

35. Cf. Evanghelos Moutsopoulos, *Pleasures: A Phenomenological Inquiry in Some Privileged States of Consciousness* (Athens: Grigoris, 1975), 74ff.

36. Moutsopoulos, *Phenomenology of Values,* 53–54.

37. Cf. Moore, *Principio Ethico* and *Philosophical Studies;* Schilpp, and Morris.

38. Gerhard Knauss, *Gegenstand und Umgreifendes* (Basel: Verlag f. Recht, 1954).

39. Cf. Moutsopoulos, *Dialectics of Will,* 54–55.

Part Three
PHENOMENOLOGICAL TECHNIQUES

14

Ineffability and Religious Experience

DAVID E. COOPER

"Experience" is a vague and ambiguous term. It hovers between a subjective and an objective connotation. "Experiencing hostility" may refer either to the subject's hostile feelings or to his sensing the hostility exuded by another. Typically we expect a description of an experience to look in both directions. A traveler recounting his experiences will tell of what he encountered, but also of his reactions and feelings towards this. A good travel book is neither a geographical treatise nor an exercise in pure introspection. This applies to religious experience as well. To count as such an experience it must, it seems, be an experience of objects of a certain kind—a God, a spirit, hell, or whatever. If it is to be more than an account of a mere thought, a description of it will tell of how the experience was for the subject, of his feelings, his sense of awe, and so on. The description of a religious experience must, apparently, have its objective and subjective dimensions.

From ancient prophets, through St. Bonaventura, to a modern philosopher of religion like John Hick, it is religious experience that provides the strongest ground for religious belief. For the person who experiences God, writes Hick, a proof of divine existence would be as sensible as a proof of his wife's existence would be for the husband.[1] And for those who do not enjoy such an experience, the accounts of those who have can inspire greater conviction than the arguments of natural theology. Assessment of such accounts is, therefore, of primary importance; it is upon it that a person's conviction may turn.

I want to focus upon one element in that assessment: the seeming lack, in those accounts, of enlightening descriptions of the objects of the experiences. We might call this "the ineffability problem." Descriptions of putative religious experiences are frequently rich in detail on the subjective side, vividly communicating the flavor of the subject's emotions and reactions, and in a way that contrasts with the meager depiction of what the experiences are *of*. Sometimes this is merely alluded to as a *voice* or *light*. It was scarcely unreasonable for Moses' followers to be initially unimpresssed by their leader's claim to have encountered a God who would volunteer no more information than "I am who I am." In Zen, this apparent indescribability of the object of experience is turned into a virtue and a studied refusal even to embark on such description. "What is the Way?" asks Joshu of Nansen. "Do not seek it, study it, or *name* it," comes the reply. Another Master, asked the same question, proceeds to describe the local scenery.[2]

This inability to describe the objects of experience is due not to a contingent deficiency in vocabulary or in observational acumen, but to the nature of what is allegedly experienced. "The idea of the Creator," said Saadya, "must of necessity be subtler than the subtlest, more recondite than the most recondite, and more abstract than the most abstract."[3] Today the situation is more complicated. Elements that might, in an earlier time, have been construed as belonging to the object itself are now ascribed to the subject's imagination. Time was when a vision of hell could be thought of as a genuine encounter with the place, but the contemporary view is the one expressed by Thomas Mann: "The secret delight and security of Hell [is] that it is not to be informed on, that it is protected from speech, that it just is. . . ."[4] Thus, the terms used to describe it, like "soundless" or "hopeless" are only poor, weak symbols, which are revealing of the subject's state of mind and not of hell itself.

How serious is the problem of ineffability, this "protection from speech," for the possibility of religious belief? If a traveler signally fails to describe the lands he purports to have visited, we shall suspect that he has not left the confines of The Travelers' Club. Is a similar suspicion warranted, even required, in the case of alleged religious experiences? At least three maneuvers can be used to ward off this suspicion. Each takes the form of an analogy with some familiar and undisturbing kind of ineffability—undisturbing in the sense that ineffability of these kinds does not prompt doubts about the existence of what cannot be described.

We are all familiar with occasional, strange bodily sensations and experiences that we can't put into words, and for which we can do little more than provide coordinates—"It's the feeling you have in . . . , when you. . . ." It is hard to see, however, what bearing this experience has on our problem of ineffability. The question our problem poses is not whether certain experiences occur, but whether they are of the objects they purport to be. In the case of weird bodily sensations—despite the grammatically transitive nature of expressions like "experiencing something strange"—no distinction is made between the subject's experiencing and the object experienced. There is nothing in such experiences whose ineffability is analogous to the objects of religious experience.

A second maneuver would appeal, by way of analogy, to what philosophers call 'simple qualities', such as colors. Precisely because they are simple, it is unclear what can be said about them, *qua* items of experience, other than that they are the colors they are—red, or whatever. Nobody thinks that this inability to say more threatens the reality of colors. Colors are genuine objects of experience, distinguishable from the subject's experience of them. In this respect, the analogy with them sounds more promising than the one with ineffable bodily sensations. Some theologians, notably Aquinas, have ascribed part of the difficulty of describing God to his absolute simplicity. "Substantive terms," according to Aquinas, can only be applied to God "defectively," since they denote complex entities. It is equally defective, unfortunately, to apply 'formal' terms, like adjectives, since these do not signify subsistence. God, being a simple substance, escapes description by both complex and non-substantive terms—yet these are the only ones we have.[5] Thus the analogy with simple qualities is unhelpful. The sense in which they are ineffable is a very special one with little bearing on our problem of ineffability. Clearly we can say a great deal more about experiencing a color beyond simply giving its name. We can say how it contrasts with other colors in the visual field, how it shimmers, and how it seems to alter as we move position. A sensitive appreciator of painting can spend pages on a colored patch that you or I would leave at calling a bit of yellow. Colors are only ineffable in that there are no words in terms of which their names may be defined or analyzed. There are no criteria for something's being red: it just is. Now it may be, as Aquinas was perhaps suggesting, that God is ineffable in this sense; but this does nothing to explain why descriptions of God as an object of experience are so thin. If it did, we should expect the ineffability (unanalyzability) of colors to entail the ineffability (indescribability) of experiences of them. But with colors ineffability in one sense does not entail, explain, or excuse ineffability in another. Someone pursuing Aquinas's point might complain that the analogy should be with simple substances, not simple qualities. The trouble is that the simple substances favored by some philosophers—Leibniz's monads, for instance—are themselves too obscure to serve as unproblematical examples of the ineffable.

A third maneuver and analogy is possible. The description "ineffable" is most frequently applied to commonly experienced nouns such as "charm" and "grace." Expressions like "ineffable charm" verge on the idiomatic and clichéd. A quality like charm differs from one like color in at least two relevant respects. First, the quality cannot be abstracted from other qualities, in the way that color can be abstracted from shape, texture, and the like. Charm is something we experience *through* the way a person smiles, talks, gestures, or laughs, and not in logical abstraction from these. Second, it is not a simple quality, and so not ineffable in the same sense as colors. Dictionaries can do something by way of analyzing "charm" in a way they cannot with "red." For both these reasons, charm is the more inviting analogue for the ineffable objects of religious experience. In the more pantheistic traditions, what is experienced is not described as some discrete, isolable phenomenon, but more as a quality with which familiar objects are imbued. An analogy between exuding charm and exuding the holy offers initial promise.

The next step is to discover what makes charm ineffable, so hard to put into words. The answer must refer to the *subtlety* of charm. One does not speak of ineffable boorishness or jollity. These qualities are displayed in striking ways that scarcely fail to register. However, charm may be characterized by such elusive qualities as the gentle play at the corners of the mouth, the hardly perceptible raise of the eyebrows, or the fine modulations of voice. The composite result of charm is hard to describe. Certainly the signs of charm are sufficiently subtle for different observers to disagree what the signs really are. What is charming to one person might be signs of oiliness to another. At this, the analogy with objects of religious experience seems to totter, for encounters with the holy are often portrayed as vivid, explosive, and unmistakable. The explanation of ineffability could not, therefore, be the same as in the case of charm. If the analogy holds at all, it could do so only for those quiet experiences of a nature imbued with the holy that Wordsworth and other pantheists have tried to capture.

We have failed to defuse the problems of ineffability by comparing the objects of religious experience to some perfectly familiar and untroubling instances of ineffability. In these familiar cases, either there are no genuine objects of experience at all, or the sense in which there is ineffability is a special and irrelevant one, or the explanation of ineffability does not transfer to the religious case. Suspicion about the credentials of alleged religious experiences remains in order, even mandatory.

The word "suspicion" seems too mild. There are many who would want to turn the screw tighter, arguing that the ineffability of an object is a conclusive reason for denying that the object is genuine. In his poem "Das Wort," Stefan George finds that what he cannot express trickles out of his grasp, and concludes: "*So lernt ich traurig den verzicht: / Kein ding sei wo das wort gebricht.*"[6] (Sadly I learned this renunciation: / no thing exists where the word is missing). Hans-Georg Gadamer more prosaically affirms "We can express everything in words"; thus what we cannot express is not there to express.[7] The point could be put in the form of a paradox of ineffability, of which there are both slick and serious versions. The slick version of the paradox runs: no sentence of the form "X is ineffable" can be true, since if it were we would be saying something about X, thereby contradicting what the sentence asserts. This version could be dissolved by heeding the distinction between levels of language, between talking about things and talking about talk. The serious version could be put as follows: in order to state significantly that X is ineffable, we must be able to identify X as a possible object. This requires us to have beliefs about X that serve to distinguish it from other possible objects. However beliefs can only be identified if they are expressible in language. I shall not adumbrate the arguments in favor of the final step in this version, but some of them are persuasive.[8] It is clear that if the arguments are well taken, then ineffability must be severely limited. We must be able to say enough about X for us to significantly assert that other things cannot be said about it. The familiar cases of ineffability glanced at above are constrained in this way. For example, we were able to say enough about uncanny bodily sensations, by giving coordinates for them, to significantly deny that further elaboration of *them* was possible.

"But what is the relevance of all this?" someone might ask. Let us grant that if God were totally ineffable, we could not say anything about him, including even this. Let us grant that a totally ineffable God is an absurdity. What we are assuming to be ineffable is not God himself, but the nature of experiences of him. Clearly, there is much we can say about him. He is one, perfect, omniscient, and so on. This is enough to support the claim that it is experiential encounters with him, and not something else, which are ineffable. It is because he is the kind of being described that experiences of him cannot be put into words. He is, to recall Saadya's words, "more abstract than the most abstract." The mathematician Ramajan claimed to enjoy personal relations with numbers. That he was unable to say much about these does not show that numbers are ineffable; only that they are not describable by an *experiential* vocabulary.

The reply is that we can say enough about God as object of reason to identify him, and so lend credence to the idea that it is *he* who is encountered in ineffable experiences. The God of natural theology is introduced to lend significance to God-as-revealed. The trouble with the reply is its overconfidence in the effability of the God of natural theology. The terms describing God fall, arguably, into two categories: terms like "One" or "Absolute," which belong at the same obscure level, and terms which are irredeemably analogical or figurative. The former are obviously unhelpful, while the latter constitute a serious problem. Aquinas, Kant, and others, argued persuasively that if God is to be conceptualized at all, then he must be describable in words that are analogical or symbolic extensions of their uses in connection with familiar objects and persons. "All our knowledge of God is merely symbolical," writes Kant. To treat the symbols literally is to lapse into anthropomorphism, while to eschew their use altogether is to lapse into a "deism, by which nothing at all is cognized."[9] What neither Kant nor Aquinas convince us of, however, is that the idea of a being who can *only* be described analogically, figuratively, or symbolically is a viable concept. We need a straight description of something before we can identify it as that which can be analogically or figuratively depicted. In Aquinas's example, foods are called healthy by analogy with the healthy bodies they nurture; in Kant's example, political states are described symbolically in organic or mechanistic terms. But foods and states, of course, are things that can be given straight descriptions independent of these extended predications. Not so with God, according to these writers.

Faced by the problem of the apparent ineffability of God of natural theology, of his apparently irreducible, analogical nature, a not uncommon response has been to turn back to the God as encountered in experiences. If we can directly experience God, then the fact (if it is one) that reason can capture him only figuratively is not devastating. However, given the assumptions of our earlier discussion, this response gets us nowhere. The problem assumed earlier was precisely the ineffability of God as object of experience. The idea, a short while ago, was to blunt the edge of this problem by appeal to the God of natural theology, a being about whom we could say enough to explain his experiential ineffability. Clearly that idea falls apart once we concede that sense can be made of this being only via experiences of him. The circle would be complete: we can allow an ineffable God of experience only if we can identify an effable God of reason, but we can do the latter only if we can first make sense of, and therefore communicate, the former.

Let us rehearse the position reached. We began by echoing disappointment at the meager descriptions typically given of the alleged objects of religious experiences in accounts of these. Unsuccessful attempts were made to ward off suspicion about these objects, and to explain or excuse the meagerness by assimilating the problem to familiar and untroubling cases of ineffability. Disappointment and suspicion then modulated into a challenge to the very intelligibility of ineffable objects of experience. The attempt to ward off that challenge by appeal to the God of reason could not work if he too is ineffable. We do no more than pirouette if his ineffable nature is in turn explained by reference to God-as-experienced, since the latter's ineffability and obscurity was the original problem.

What, then, becomes of religious experiences, or rather accounts of them, as a ground for religious belief? It certainly remains open to debate that such experiences are remarkable and not accountable for in natural terms, and thus must be explained by reference to an extraordinary being, a God or some other non-natural entity. But whatever the (obviously questionable) merits of such an argument, it is no longer the traditional argument from experience. It makes of God an *inferred* entity, a *deus ex machina* invoked to explain the extraordinary or highly improbable. The argument belongs in the same bag as the arguments for miracles, the origin of the universe, the improbable existence of pattern and order in the world, and so on. Religious experience becomes one more of those phenomena which, like the genius of Shakespeare according to some, require a non-natural agency by way of explanation. Earlier we saw how the traditional argument from experience contrasted with those that treat God as an inferred entity. God was compared to the wife whose existence need not be inferred, since she is directly encountered. It is true that for someone who has not had a religious experience, conviction can only be obtained on the basis of an inference from the reports of others. But traditionally, all that is deemed necessary for that inference is faith in the authenticity of those who profess to have had religious experiences. This is not an inference of God as the best possible explanation of something uncanny. Likewise we normally assume that a man has a wife because he appears honest in talking about her, not because her existence would be a plausible explanation of his words.

The following section will challenge the previous approach to the problem of ineffability and the critique which stemmed from it. It should prove much more interesting than the above attempt to salvage something after the critique of ineffable experience. So far I have sympathetically presented that critique; now I turn to sympathetically elucidating, without assessing, a method of challenging it. This method derives from remarks of Wittgenstein on ineffability.

Unlike members of the Vienna Circle, we now know from notes written at the time, that a main purpose—though hardly an explicit theme—of the *Tractatus Logico-Philosophicus* was to *preserve* the domain of the ineffable. It served to demonstrate the limits of thought and language, not with the aim of dismissing what falls outside them, but of protecting this domain against improper incursions of talk and metaphysical speculation. One should be silent about, but not dismissive of, that whereof one cannot speak. For what cannot be spoken may yet be *shown*. Wittgenstein's most helpful comments on this obscure notion of showing come not in the *Tractatus,* nor in his lectures on religion, but in his remarks on art, especially poetry. In a letter to a friend, he writes: "The poem by Uhland is really magnificent. And this is how it is: if only you do not try to utter what is unutterable then *nothing* gets lost. But the unutterable will be—unutterably—*contained* in what has been uttered."[10] Elsewhere he writes that the attempt to *state* the sense or impression conveyed by a poem or piece of music is not so much fruitless as positively pernicious. Such an attempt implies, absurdly, that the sense is detachable from the work itself—in which case why not just have the sense and forget the work? Two works having the same sense should be interchangeable, like identical tins on a supermarket shelf.

How then does one convey the sense or impression of a poem? He writes:

You may read a stanza. . . . I get the definite impression that "None of [you] has got hold of it." Suppose then I read it out to you and say

"Look, this is how it ought to be." Then four of you read this stanza . . . in such a way that I say: "Each one is exactly certain of himself". . . . I might say in this case that you four have got hold of it. I would have conveyed something to you. I would perfectly correctly say, that I have exactly conveyed to you the exact experience I had.[11]

A couple of pages earlier, he wrote that reading out a poem in a certain way, playing certain bars in a certain manner is equivalent to *describing* what the words or notes convey. He thinks that the familiar viewpoint that aesthetic impressions are indescribable is due to a narrow notion of description modeled on the paradigm of stating a content. Such a description is appropriate in the language-game of science, but not art. In the latter case, the relevant notion is more akin to the sense in which a geometry teacher describes a circle on the blackboard—letting the circle show itself. (Wittgenstein, here, is criticizing his earlier stance; for the model of indescribability in the *Tractatus* was indeed that of unstatability.)

An art-work may show itself yet not be stated; it is ineffable only if we are fixated upon a one-sided model of description. What bearing do these preceding thoughts have upon the problem of the ineffability of religious experience? They have at least three bearings. They suggest, first, that the reason people *fail* to rise to the challenge of describing the objects of these experiences is that the challenge is illicit. The failure is analogous to that of the person who cannot state the sense or impression conveyed in a poem or piece of music. However, in the aesthetic experience, the person may show his impression through the way he reads or plays. Thus someone "describing" a religious experience may do the same, by not talking about the objects experienced, but by the way he speaks his lines, and tells his story.

The second point suggested by our artistic analogy is that we may have been looking in the wrong place for the most authentic descriptions of religious experience. If Wittgenstein is right, the place to find the sense of a poem or piece of music is in the work itself, or a performance of it—not in some piece of literary or musical criticism in which an author tries to state that sense. Similarly, reports of visions and the like, with their attempts to state the objects encountered, may not be the best place to look for descriptions of religious experience. Where else, then? Perhaps in the narratives told in the Bible and in other books of peoples living lives of simplicity and hardship, experiencing a sense of divine presence and protection. Perhaps we can find descriptions of religious experience in works of art, and not necessarily ones of a self-consciously religious nature. In all great art, says Heidegger, the Gods are "let be." More people have been brought to a sense of the holy through listening to Bach, reading Wordsworth, or even looking at Van Gogh, than by accounts of visions, road to Damascus conversions, or apparitions.

The final bearing is that the very distinction between subjective and objective dimensions of religious experience, with which I began, may have been badly drawn. The distinction was supposed to be one between two kinds of statements figuring in reports of religious experience: one kind describing the subject's feelings and reactions towards the experience, the other describing the object experienced. Wittgenstein's remarks on aesthetics allow for some distinction between subjective and objective. We might, for example, distinguish features of a performance which display personal or idiosyncratic responses to the music from those which seem to capture the very sense of the music itself. Such a distinction is not between kinds of statements made. In Wittgenstein's terms, the performer will be "describing" the sense of the work in the way he plays it—by letting it show through, not by saying anything about it. Similarly the objective dimension to religious experience should be sought, not in statements expressly designed to talk about the alleged objects of the experience, but in the way that a whole performance—the telling of a story, the composition of a mass, the reading of a prayer—lets a sharable sense of the holy show through. If this is so, then we were rash at the beginning to bemoan the meagerness of the objective descriptions of religious experiences. It is like complaining that a musical performance has not conveyed the sense of the piece because it was not punctuated with statements about that sense. This sheds new light on the Zen Masters' "studied refusal" to talk about the objects of religious experience, and to talk instead about mountains and lakes, or not to talk at all, but rake their gardens. Perhaps this was no refusal at all, but merely the refusal to describe in a particular and inappropriate way. Perhaps it is in the descriptions of mountains in Haiku verse, or in the careful raking of the stones of a monastery garden, that we should look for demonstration of the holy.

NOTES

1. John Hick, *Philosophy of Religion* (Englewood Cliffs, N. J.: Prentice-Hall, 1963), 61.
2. *Zen Buddhism* (White Plains, N. Y.: Peter Pauper Press, 1959), 13, 38.
3. Saadya Gaon, *The Book of Beliefs and Opinions* (New Haven, Conn.: Yale University Press, 1948).
4. Thomas Mann, *Doctor Faustus* (London: Penguin, 1971), 238.
5. Thomas Aquinas, *Selected Writings* (London: Everyman, 1964) 144f.
6. Stefan George, "Das Wort," from the collection, *Das Neue Reich,* vol. 9 (Düsseldorf: Gesantausgabe, 1964).
7. Hans-Georg Gadamer, *Truth and Method* (London: Sheed and Ward, 1981), 493.
8. See, for example, the papers, "Mind and Verbal Dispositions" by W. V. Quine and "Thought and Talk" by Donald Davidson, in *Mind and Language,* ed. Samuel Guttenplan (Oxford: Oxford University Press, 1975).
9. Immanuel Kant, *Critique of Judgement,* trans. J. H. Bernard (New York: Hafner, 1966), 198.
10. Quoted in W. W. Bartley III, *Wittgenstein* (London: Quartet Books, 1977), 51.
11. Ludwig Wittgenstein, *Wittgenstein: Lectures and Conversations on Aesthetics, Psychology, and Religious Belief,* ed. Cyril Barrett (Berkeley, Calif.: University of California Press, 1967), 40.

15

Appearance and Disappearance of God: Some Phenomenological Remarks

WILLIAM EARLE

The spiritual masters of the world have almost universally confessed to a distressing experience: while God is the alpha and omega of creation and in himself eternally actual, nevertheless he is not always—and in cases only very rarely—present to them. Therefore the presence of the very core of their spiritual life is intermittent. The vision fades, prayer goes flat, the symbols lose their symbolic sense, the world sinks into mere empirical fact. Words which before had an evocative power now retain only their literal and questionable sense. The spirit experiences an acedia or dark night, and is left with despondency, self-loathing, and an essential worthlessness. For the religious, it is despair; for the metaphysical philosopher, it is a fall into the meaninglessness and absurdity of thought. There remain pastimes, of course, for the religious, preaching and the doing of good works; for the philosopher, argumentation, study, and book reviews. But these occupations must lose their savor if their epicenter has vanished from the spirit.

Before we can discuss the disappearance of God, a word is in order about his appearance, for what can disappear which has never appeared? The Greeks said, he who sees God must die. It is said that he who has no sense of God has never been spiritually alive. The question remains then of *appearance.* The appropriate procedure for investigating modes of appearance will be called phenomenology. For our present question, our concern is not whether God exists or not, but solely the way in which God appears and has any *meaning* whatsoever, whether his being is affirmed or denied.

Whether God has ever appeared to man is a matter of belief and faith. But there is obviously a prior question: what are the *modes* of appearance, and what is the essential nature of that which *can* appear in any particular mode? This chapter is written from a philosophical or phenomenological viewpoint. From that angle this discussion will proceed. Consequently, when men "see" or "experience" God only when the sun shines, the flowers bloom, or their fellow citizens are just and righteous, the sense of God manifested under those conditions, is correlatively conceived as a benevolence in nature. Such a God appears when things go well and suffers an eclipse when the clouds cover the sun, the grain withers, or their fellow citizens become cruel and murderous. Prayer is understood as a petition to a pantocreator to alter the course of nature or history by a divine intervention. To the philosophic mind there is absolutely no difference in principle between such activities and rain dances of the Hopi, rain prayers of Iowa farmers, prayers for the health of loved ones, and Presidential prayer breakfasts for the release of hostages, re-election, or balancing the budget. They are the crudest form of superstition. The God of the superstitious mind is to the philosophical mind sheer blasphemy. The fact that superstition has always occurred and no doubt always will occur is hardly an argument in its favor. The God of no philosopher works in any such way and would not be worthy of worship if he did. The appearance of God in any such mode is easily followed by his disappearance when things change in the course of the world, as change they must. However, neither the appearance nor disappearance of such a God could be anything but a summary judgment of happiness and unhappiness on earth. To dismiss such modes of appearance and disappearance is not an indifference to God, least of all an indifference to sunshine, health, and justice. It only clarifies what is pertinent to any conceivable philosophical question. Even for a dry philosophy, prayer still serves a single and essential function, to wit, to alter our own hearts by urging them to alter or purify themselves by what Spinoza calls the "intellectual love of God." The philosophers' God then has the phenomenological sense of *moving* us by being loved, and appears to that mode of consciousness. He does not move the world by rolling back the seasons, abolishing illness, or vengefully chastising those who either hate or ignore him. Their hate or ignorance *is* their punishment, and it is essentially and necessarily involved in their turn of mind. In a word, they are *punished* by what they have lost, the divine origin and goal of what exists, and what might be. The God of the philosopher, then, neither appears nor disappears in this manner. An additional correlate is that if many philosophers are either atheists or total indifferentists, the sober truth is that the God they deny is most probably deniable, and the God to which they are indifferent would indeed be a frivolity. They are clear and right. The remaining question is whether absurd or trivial conceptions of God come close to any serious metaphysical question, or more precisely whether it isn't our own triviality of mind which has so evacuated the question of sense.

The symbol or metaphor is another appearance or mode in which men become aware of God. Some believe it to be what men are ultimately condemned to. If the direct experience of God as good luck in history is somewhat ludicrous, perhaps a deeper sense of God can be touched through the metaphor, a form of utterance which is addressed to what we shall crudely call the imagination. There would be little point in a catalog of the metaphors for God. As everyone knows, the symbols range from light, to storms, sacred trees, sacred ponds and mountains, favored animals, crosses, stars, and holy men, some of whom are not regarded as symbols of anything but rather the very incarnation and presence of God. The mode of appearance in these cases is either to a transcending imagination, or to what is sometimes called the "eyes of faith." Karl Jaspers calls this particular access to what is transcendental "reading the writing of ciphers."

If we call the symbolic appearance of God an appearance to the imagination, it must be obvious that the imagination so invoked has very little to do with Hume's definition of it—a faculty of forming images which themselves are either decayed sense-impressions or compositions of them. Instead perhaps Schelling should be our guide, one of the very few philosophers who declared that not reason but imagination was the spiritual organ of philosophy. Such a faculty could hardly be an ability to form before the mind images or compositions of images of what had been, or in principle, could be seen. Thus how can imagination be conceived such that it is adequate to such an infinite task?

In the first place, whatever is present to the mind through symbols must be read *through* the visible body of the symbol itself. This is true even of reading print, which obviously is not staring at black marks nor running one's eyes along a horizontal string of marks in order to evoke what Marshall McLuhan used to call "linear thought" (which isn't thought at all but merely a species of sensation). What is seen must be read or interpreted as meaning what is not seen. The reading of symbols as symbols makes available to the mind that which is not seen directly. It goes beyond the merely visible to what has its own sense beyond the physical senses. It offers to the imagination or interpretative consciousness an occasion to make present to itself that which would otherwise be absent. It offers an occasion to the freedom of spirit without compelling it. The invitation may be accepted or rejected, in which latter case, the symbol collapses from being a symbol to being only its own miserable, experienceable body. The cross to the Christian becomes nothing but a geometrical diagram he has seen once too often, and the Bo Tree to the Buddhist is nothing but an old relic of vegetation. The appearance of the divine has vanished, and nothing remains but flat fact. So it is with the language of faith; the miracles of Christ were miracles only to the eyes of faith; when that faith dried up, nothing remained but most dubitable magic tricks or collective hallucinations.

Finally, there is a long tradition in world philosophy of something like a direct assault on divinity: mystic experience. Through it God is encountered not as happiness in the world, nor through symbols of no matter how ancient a lineage. The direct vision of God himself promised death to the Greeks. Doubtless this intuitive and unmediated vision was also accompanied by symbols, images, and sentiments. But our present question concerns that part distinguishable from such psychological or historical accidents.

This aspect of experience is usually consigned to mystics of a specifically religious stamp. However, I would like to point out that the intuition of God—not by way of sense experience, symbols, or as the conclusion of a tortuous argument—also happens to be the very essence of philosophers ranging from Plato, Aristotle, Plotinus, throughout the middle ages and through the rationalists of the seventeenth century up through Hegel and a certain number of philosophic contemporaries. The terms "mystical," "intuitive," and "vision" may be rejected, but the essence of the idea is there. It is essential to their metaphysics which must be defended and developed by argument, but which do not rest upon it. Not everything can be proven. Obviously if one demands a proof for everything including the premises of proof, nothing whatsoever can be proven at all. The proof regresses ad infinitum, and therefore the whole is left hanging in the air, an empty exercise in what Hegel calls the "bad infinity" or the indefinite.

For our present purposes, let us look at some varieties of metaphysics in the seventeenth century. Our question concerns the relations between the subjective idea, and the object of that idea. For both Descartes and Spinoza, any mind of the human order already had in it the idea of God. For Descartes, it was an innate idea, that is, was neither acquired from experience, nor constructed by either the rational or imaginative faculties. It was constitutive of the very essence of rational mind. For Spinoza also the idea was innate, and proper philosophical method consisted only in recovering this idea by a reflexive examination of the various kinds of ideas found there in order to discern this primordially *adequate* idea. For both, in spite of differences of vocabulary and the usages to which their philosophies were put, the idea of God or Substance or *Natura naturans,* was clear, distinct, and adequate. For Spinoza an *adequate* idea was an idea adequate to its object, the *ideatum.* For Descartes, such an idea was clear, that is, the object of the idea showed what it was to reason, and was distinct from any other object with which it might be confused. Such ideas could not be false to their object, since they immediately apprehended that object. The further claim that the object of such an idea, God in our present case, existed not merely as the object of an idea, but also independently of the mind, was of course the burden of the ontological argument. It is basically a *via negativa.* To deny the real being of the object of the idea of God is to fall into instant absurdity. The ontological argument did not intend to generate the idea, which would be impossible in principle, but to defend its truth against attacks. The defense was, to put it into a nutshell, that those who denied the truth of the argument simply did not know what either the idea or its object were.

The direct conceptualization of God, without the intermediary of either happy experiences in the world or imaginative symbols, but only the bare and simple apprehension of God as an object of the idea is called *intuition.* The great metaphysical constructions of the seventeenth-century rationalists rest upon the absolutely simple and absolutely true rational apprehension of a most distinctive object, 'absolute being'. An infinity of consequences follow from this apprehension, as the systems themselves bear witness to. What does not immediately follow from such apprehension but which requires experience, hypotheses, and indeed a certain amount of guesswork, is sharply distinguished from the fundamental idea and all given their proper places, no matter what we think of such explanations today.

Consequently, rationalism in its proudest and most self-assured form hinges upon the immediate access of the mind or reason to God. This God *is,* is *necessarily* in his own being and is *eternally actual.* Indeed, for Spinoza, our mind's thinking God is one and the same as God thinking himself. There are not two distinct acts, one conducted by ourselves and another by God or Substance, which happen to resemble one another. There is only one, God's, which in this unique case is present also in our own minds.

We can hardly review the enormous mystical literature in which similar views are repeated, namely, that the innermost self of the mystic's soul is in identity with God himself, and knows itself to be so.[1]

If these philosophical considerations seem arid, perhaps the subject can be warmed by considering what is commonly called the *heart,* the faculty of loving, hating, and remaining indifferent. It also hopes, despairs, can be filled with self-loathing or self-affirmation. We had best let the poets speak of the variety of its modes of life. But the matter is not wholly forgotten by philosophers, and so it is not wholly irrelevant to say a few things about this more *human* side of philosophy, hoping philosophy will not dehumanize it, too. Our question now is: Can God appear to the heart as an object of love or adoration?

At the onset, we must understand that these varieties of the human spirit, named "faculties," are not independent of one another, although distinguishable from one another in their own functions. In a word, the cognitive faculties of perception, imagination, and reason do not operate on their own steam. They are directed in their activity by the heart, or the desiderative faculty, which in turn is activated by what the cognitive faculties present to it. Nevertheless, operating in mutual cooperation when successful, they may be distinguished for our own artificial purposes. Hence the question is, what does the heart desire? Or, if not what does it desire as an empirical question, what may or ought it desire? If the proper object of the cognitive powers is the truth of being, ultimately God, what is the proper object of the heart if not the good or the holy or sacred? God, as the name of the holy or sacred, appears then in a new mode, not as an object of dispute over his existence, but as that which may be loved or adored. Whether that which is eternal and infinite, considered as absolute being, is also that which may be ultimately loved, is a separate question to which we shall return. The heart will thus be considered as another mode of the appearance as well as disappearance of God.

The heart, or Eros as Plato calls it in the *Symposium,* is the child of poverty and plenty. It is a longing for what it once had in some form, but in this life does not have (it could hardly long for what it never knew). If it longs for the identity with God, or in Plato, the good, it must now have an intimation or vague recollection of what it once had, living now in the aftermath of its previous glory but with hope for a reunion. Our own old, human hearts long for many things, just as our cognitive faculties try to perceive, know or guess about many things. Our present question touches not the longings of the heart for the love of human beings, but the heart's longing for God, or for us to be seen in a divine light. Here we are concerned with the presence of God himself to the heart, or the thinking and loving heart, which Spinoza summed up in a remarkable phrase, "the intellectual love of God." Whatever it signifies, it is clear what it does *not* signify: anything remotely approaching an appetite or lust for God, or the use of God for any purpose whatsoever. Nevertheless, this appearance of God to the human heart, not as cognitive object or mere being, but as the correlate of love of a distinctive order, must be considered. It is perhaps most frequently the God appearing in this mode which disappears most easily.

Kant, who regarded the ontological argument as a "miserable tautology" giving no genuine knowledge of anything but the meaning of our own idea, nevertheless reintroduces God in his second critique as a postulate of the moral will. In short, the most appropriate locus for the discussion of the subject was not in the domain of knowledge, but the domain of what we, but not Kant, are calling the heart. Even then, for Kant, God is not an appearance or phenomenon, but a postulate, a hope. Later in the third critique, God again has a distinctive role. It is "as if" the world were created by an infinite and holy spirit not absolutely unlike the best in our own inwardness, gathered together under the idea of teleology.

What we are calling the heart then has God as its essential correlate, showing a bit of his face under the rubric good, holy, and sacred, categories which do not fit into any objective or scientific schema. We are then touching upon what is often called the *living* God, who moves us by being loved. Such is his *appearance* to the heart, even though appearance now has undergone a severe shift of meaning from anything that might be called experiential, phenomenal in the narrow sense, or an *object of any sort*. He now is likely to be called a "person," or, with Hegel, "absolute spirit." The encounter of our own persons with God defined as a person or as absolute spirit can take as many forms as the history of philosophy discloses: hate, indifference, adoration, worship, fear and trembling, or shuddering. Each of these responses of the heart correlatively defines its subject, God, and obviously God turns as many faces to us as there are different modes of ourselves. Each discloses something, or in an extended sense of the term, is an *appearance* of God, which defines equally well a certain mode of *disappearance*.

God then disappears in as many ways as he appears, and the explanations of his disappearance are as various as the modes of appearance, and the sense of God which consequently appears. Kierkegaard, from his diaries, wanted nothing so much as to sit on a cloud and sing hallelujah all day long, but what of the night? Spinoza desired nothing so much as to comprehend all things *sub specie aeternitatis*. To live in the light of eternity is then the inherent desire of both the heart which wishes union with God, and the intellect which wants to see and see as God sees. But then, once seen, the vision as immediate intuition passes, and we are left with a recollection, an infinite nostalgia, a horror of metaphysical or moral vacuum. Jesus on the cross asks, "My God why hast Thou forsaken me?" And so we now turn our attention to the disappearance of God and some purported explanations of this most common and human of disasters. The God we are considering is eternally actual in himself. He is not and cannot be a flickering, intermittent being who dies and is reborn like the phoenix, nor anyone with a changeable will, subject to flattery or wheedling, who chooses to reward the just and punish with wrath those who either despise him or ignore him. The book of Job should dispel any such idea. In short, God is eternal and we, while we can indeed encounter both intellectually and in the heart such an eternal being, nevertheless are not ourselves in our totality eternal. Indeed, we could hardly live at all unless we paid proper attention to the perceptible things of the world and the transient objects of our desires. In a word, we are caught between two domains of being, the finite and the infinite, being an extraordinary synthesis of the two, as hateful as this must seem to a purely formal logic. And so the answer to the disappearance of God seems easy at the start; God does not disappear in himself but we divert our attention and minds from him. The accounts therefore of the turning away from God by his devotees, individually or communally, have been various.

Disappearance to the Transcendental Intellect

Intuitive reason or the transcendental intellect finds the idea of God inherently in it as constitutive of reason itself, innate. It is that idea which comes and goes; who indeed can pretend to live in the constant presence of the God of the philosophers? The intellect in which this idea is found is transcendental to existence itself, not generated or determined by anything whatsoever in natural existence. Intellect is, of course, an act of transcendental ego. Its transcendence of natural existence in time and space is another way of expressing the absolute freedom of the transcendental ego. The ego and its proper and authentic acts are free from the influence of anything whatsoever in the world of nature. It determines itself, or is *causa sui* as Spinoza puts it. Therefore when the idea of God disappears from its intellect, the cause cannot be sought in any psychological, physiological, or existent influences. Hence to say that we lose the living rational presence of God because of fatigue, boredom, brain damage, distraction, or because of anything external to the transcendental ego itself is pure error. We cease to animate this unique thought because we choose to do so, and that is almost the end of the matter. It is not the intuitive reason which chooses anything. The pure light of reason cannot choose anything to consider this or that, or to bring anything into explicit consciousness. It is indeed pure light. Descartes calls it the "light of nature," *lumen naturale*, but it is not natural at all, nor a product of any conceivable motion or commotion of natural existence. The light of nature must be understood as an essential and eternal conjunction of a particular idea and its object, it is the idea of God which, as Spinoza said, is God's idea of himself. Such an idea is inherently an eternal actuality, even though within ourselves it comes and goes at our pleasure.

If thinking of God inherently tends to objectify him, and if God is the absolute spirit, that is, an absolute subjectivity, the very act of forming an objective idea of the absolute spirit transforms its object, an absolute subject, into an absolute object. This is exactly the mode of thought in which subjectivity disappears. The same is true of ourselves: forming an objective idea of another abolishes the free subjectivity of that other for that experience. One's awareness of this failure rests upon another mode of thought altogether: our reflexive participative consciousness. Empathy for ourselves, thinking God for ourselves are a reflexive recovery of transcendental self-awareness, not phenomenological "intentionality."

Since nothing makes sense when abstracted from its immanent and absolute cause, why does the transcendental ego choose to blind itself and fall into absurdity and confusion? In a myth Plato suggests this is due to birth into becoming, or natural existence, crossing the river Lethe (forgetfulness). This birth and crossing throw eternal clarity into confusion. Doubtless this is true. But from time to time we recollect what once we saw, and this is the purpose of the Platonic dialectic. It is a remedy against the illness of existence, an existence which Socrates neither shunned nor pursued. So far, we have sought to pinpoint why the intellectual soul seeks to blind itself, though not permanently, and is free to do so. We shall trace this a bit further below.

The Transcendental Heart

Mutatis mutandis, the heart has its own freedom. Heart is defined as the act of the transcendental ego by which it wills, chooses, or loves. If it is transcendental, it is the love of God, the absolute spirit, or the omega of all spiritual striving. But who could possibly boast that he loved none but God? Were it that simple, why a *commandment* to do so? Yet equivalently, who could *justify* anything else? The naturalist answers, "I was overcome by desire, by egotism, by rage, by the wish for fame, by the glitter of the goods of the world." Each time, we find ourselves asserting that the heart of the transcendental ego is overcome by something external to itself, like some sort of bacterial infection; it couldn't help itself. In short, while it remains free to love whatever it wants to love, nevertheless it is overcome by what is not itself, and succumbs to what is less than good. In fact, it falls victim to what it perceives perfectly well as the worse. But being overcome and succumbing must be false solutions to the problem. It is impossible for the transcendental ego to be overcome by anything other than its own choosing. Freud's principle of Eros and Thanatos, traced to supposedly physiological sources, is merely a recent attempt to relieve the *transcendental ego* of its own freedom and responsibility.

Our problem then is not so much the love of the good but the hatred of the good, that is, vice. To solve this problem, Plato offers unsurpassable but enigmatic solutions. "Vice is ignorance," he repeats, for who indeed could apprehend the good itself and not desire union with it? Would it not be, he suggests, as absurd as a healthy man desiring to be sick and decrepit? Aristotle claims the ethics or philosophy of the good would help man achieve it, providing him with a target *happiness,* which otherwise he would hit only by chance. Such confidence in the power of rational education or philosophical ethics provides the justification for our courses in and books on ethics, rights, and happiness, down to the present day. Why engage in such activity if it were vacuous or positively evil by way of distracting one from concern with what was genuinely good? Needless to say, both Plato and Aristotle perceived the limitations of their confidence, and neither could very well be called optimistic. Plato asks almost in spite of himself, "If virtue is knowledge and knowledge teachable, why so often have the most righteous of men the most worthless of sons?" For Aristotle, ethics and politics were not in themselves fit subjects for young men; more suitable for them was precept and example, and good habits fostered by a good society which honors them.

If Plato put his finger on the justification of philosophy, namely, that it could lead to the intuition of the good at midnight among friends, a good from which everything proceeded, another tradition puts its finger on the other side of the coin. That side will now preoccupy us. In the Judeo-Christian religions, the evil man is not he who is ignorant of the just and good, but precisely the opposite. He has seen it in full. His enjoyment of evil consists of his hatred of good. Socrates in his apologia remarks that if he has taught evil doctrines, he should be instructed rather than killed. The Judeo-Christian tradition does not find evil in ignorance or some defect of reason, no matter how generously extended in meaning. The Judeo-Christian tradition finds evil in a turn of the faith, will, or what we are calling the heart. An evil man is not in need of instruction so much as punishment or repudiation, or best, forgiveness. What must be altered, rebuked, or forgiven is not his intellect but his heart. Our great moral and political conflicts are not conflicts of reason to be resolved by better reason, but oppositions of the heart or will.

Then how can what is intrinsically good be hated? We must first remember that the good turns its face only toward what loves it; it is ultimately the phenomenological correlate of love. Love loves what it perceives as the loveable, and the perceived loveable is the perceived good. Love's aim is to unite itself with its object so that they become one. Similarly, hate hates the hateable, and desires its abolition. In religious language, transcendental love loves God and all his works; transcendental hate hates God and all his works, including itself. In the story of Lucifer we have an infinitely profound myth of an angel, a spirit whose characterizing essence was lucidity. Lucifer, the bringer of light, was once "closest" to God. Being closest and being composed of pure light, he was the first to turn directly away from his own creator, by no predestination or compulsion, but of his own free will, exercising pride. Now if Lucifer, the brightest of the angelic beings, could not perceive the transcendental goodness and beauty of God, he was simply blinded, his syllogisms bent out of shape, and what he needed was instruction. But that is precisely what he did not need, nor could it have availed. He had most clearly of all others seen the Godhead and revolted from it. That eternal instant redefined him as Satan, and his dwelling was transformed from heaven to hell, where his particular palace was pandemonium. All of this must have been foreseen by the most lucid of angels. And could it have been prevented by further dialectical refutations from the equally divine Socrates?

To turn away from the holy itself or the good itself and will the contrary implies a double layer in hate. It must first see what is good, i. e., love it, in order to then reject it. It is like nonbeing, unthinkable unless there is a being of which it is not. This does not refute hate of a transcendental or even finite order, but only situates it metaphysically. We must take for granted that such a transcendental hate, as well as a transcendental love, exists in us. This is hardly a huge assumption given the literature on the subject. The literature includes the book of Job. Descending rapidly down to modern times, it includes writers such as Shakespeare, Milton, Dostoyevsky, Melville, Conrad, and lastly Baudelaire, whose *Flowers of Evil* tempt as much as repel.

Baudelaire knew perfectly well what he was talking about. It was certainly not that good might by chance, or even by poetry, burst forth from evil, much as the lotus with its roots in mud rises to display a flower to the sun and us. Evil was itself a flower.

Some Concluding Reflections

Is it possible for the transcendental intellect and the transcendental heart (the former reflecting God as being, the latter, God as the good or holy) to negate their essential activities, namely, knowing and loving, and activate the opposite, a transcendental nescience and hatred? If so, these two acts are acts of another aspect of ourselves, the transcendental ego in its *absolute* freedom. The freedom of the ego is to know or not know, love or hate, and with that freedom it is entirely responsible for the appearance and disappearance of God. If one looks for *causes* of these radical choices, there are none; the very idea of causing freedom negates the freedom itself. What is free is a cause of itself. Descartes said our freedom of the will was *infinitely* free to will what it willed. In this infinite freedom it was the same as God's freedom. This freedom within the transcendental ego, in its identity with God's freedom, is another way in which God appears to us. The absolute freedom of God and our own absolute freedom are strictly correlated. In fact they are one and the same taking two different paths.

This leads to a remarkable if not heretical conclusion: God in his absolute freedom is also free to turn away from any given face or attribute of his, and be, *for himself,* the opposite. The mystics are well aware of this paradox—if paradox it is. If God is light to us, and therefore light to himself, he is also darkness to himself, a "cloud" or "abyss" as mystics call it. Thus, the idea which God forms of himself is a true idea of himself. Yet that which is illuminated still is not illuminated. Indeed, how can absolute freedom be illuminated?

The same paradox applies to his goodness or holiness. If God moves or creates the world by being loved, he also works by being hated. The source of any transcendental hatred must be one aspect of God's freedom, a self-hatred. This is mythically preserved in the eternal being of Satan, once God's favorite, sustained eternally by God and whom God still permits to go about on earth tempting Job and the rest of us. Men are not exactly unacquainted with the terror and wrath of God. The fact that these faces of God are not punishment for our sins is clear enough from the book of Job. The emergence of this antithetical character in the godhead would hardly have surprised Hegel or some of the less sentimental mystics.

The antithesis has been sketched out; still reason looks for the final synthesis to preserve the absolute unity of God who lives eternally in absolute freedom. But the absolute spirit or God is eternally *actual* or alive. For Hegel, actuality and life are themselves illustrations of becoming, the synthesis of being and nonbeing. The "synthesis" is *eternally in act,* and not a final resting term. Similarly, for Spinoza, God (or substance or nature) is *Natura naturans,* the eternal act. Freedom, another name for the transcendental being of God, can be just as easily said to be known as not known, or to be good as well as evil, "beyond good and evil." In short, the disappearance of God to either intellect or heart is not *altogether* a fact of our own finitude, instability, vice, or failures in the work of mind. They reflect very well final aspects of absolute spirit. These final aspects, if they cannot be precisely known or loved, can at least be intuitively touched upon by a sufficiently transcendental heart and intellect.

NOTES

1. For further discussion of these ideas, see William Earle, *Mystical Reason* (Lake Bluff, Ill.: Regnery-Gateway, 1980).

16

Commemoration in the Eucharist

EDWARD S. CASEY

Even the merest acquaintance with eucharistic practice and theory reveals it to be considerably complex with regard to commemoration. The following is an essay to bring out its leading components.

I

"Do this in remembrance of me." This is the recurring theme of the Eucharist. It is important to examine it closely for a moment before proceeding. Let us begin by guarding against three possible misinterpretations: (1) bring back to mind certain definite recollections of scenes (the Last Supper, the Crucifixion, etc.); (2) use this formula as a *reminder* of Christ; (3) regard this formula as itself liturgically efficacious.

In reply to these possible readings the following needs to be said: First, having specific secondary memories is neither a necessary nor a sufficient condition of following the formula in a liturgically adequate way. It is not to be expressly discouraged, and it may even aid certain worshippers as part of their *private* ritual by initiating a conducive state of mind. By the same token, it can be obstructive of the ritual process because of its focus on the inward landscape of recollection. As we may observe in other kinds of commemoration, evoking a stock of secondary memories is at best a contingent concomitant of the appropriate practice.

Second, is the eucharistic rubric (as we shall call the above formula) a reminder then? This is more tempting to believe, especially if "reminder" is taken in a sufficiently broad fashion, for example, as an admonition to keep in mind. But at the core of reminding there is always a mnemonic function. This presently existent object is to be taken as a sign of another presumptively existent object. Christ is not just presumptively existent in the minds of believers but actually existent—overwhelmingly so—and thus no mere reminder would be adequate as signifying such existence.[1]

Third, the rubric is not intended to be memorially efficacious. It is memorial in status, since it repeats Christ's own words as reported by Paul and Luke, but its referent is to the partaking of the bread and drinking of the wine which precede its utterance (twice repeated in Paul's version). It is tempting to regard the rubric as performative in status and so in the same class as "I thee wed" and "I promise you." Yet the demonstrative "this"—and the injunction "*Do* this"—render it less than fully peformative by giving the entire expression a referent which is an activity apart from the uttering of the sentence itself. It says in effect: *if* you do this (take the bread and wine in the liturgically correct way), *then* you will have remembered me. It is to be classed as a hypothetical injunction whose consequent is an act of remembering. (Would not commemoration in this case consist in the whole complex of rubric uttered *plus* enjoined action executed? If so, we are again shown how much more diffuse commemoration can be in comparison with discrete acts of remembrance.)

Having made these exclusions, we must begin to discover what, in a more positive way, constitutes the memorial and memorializing character of the rubric—and through it of the eucharistic practice as a whole.

Let us first focus on the word *anamnesis* in the rubric: *"toûto poiête eìs tèn èmèn ànámnensin."* Aside from its usage in 1 Corinthians 11:24, 25 and Luke 22:19, it appears in the New Testament only in the Epistle to the Hebrews 10:3. It, along with *mnemosunon* (from which it is not distinguished in English renderings), translates the two Hebrew terms *azkarah* and *zikkaron,* both of which mean "memorial." The root of these latter is the verb *zakar,* which has a cluster of senses related to remembering.

> Its different meanings may be summarized thus: to think of something known and past, a material something, a sin or the blessings of God; to recall a duty: in reference to God, to recall man's sin, the covenant, love, and fidelity; in reference to man, to recall God or to invoke Him; to recall something in favour of someone or against him; to recall something to someone (e.g., the needs of the people to God); utter a name (that of God); and finally, to recall before or remind God by means of a sacrifice and especially the memorial of incense.[2]

Thus the word *anamnesis,* stemming from *zakar,* recalls all of these meanings. It is commemorative by virtue of its own etymological polysemy. This does not even touch upon any Platonic echoes in *anamnesis,* which would be difficult to exclude entirely from a word as philosophically loaded as this.[3] It must be stressed, that the word "remembrance" in the rubric serves as a point of reference for memorial rituals relevant to religious practices of many kinds (and not just the Eucharist). Remembrance remembers more than its own name; it brings with it a host and history of rememberings.

Just as the single word *anamnesis* takes us back ineluctably to Old Testament origins, the rubric in which it is embedded does so as well. The expression "Do this in remembrance of me" was part of Jewish liturgy long before Jesus appropriated it for his purposes. It was in particular part of the paschal meal at Passover. Thus in Exodus 12:14 we read: "This day shall be unto you as a remembrance (*le-zikkaron*), and ye shall keep it a feast to the Lord." The ingestion of food and drink conceived as sacraments was a memorial of deliverance and exodus from Egypt, commemorated by ritualistic word and action.

Note what is happening here: the New Testament use of the rubric commemorates its use at Passover, which in turn commemorates the events of deliverance and exodus. This concatenation of commemorations is something we sometimes also encounter in works of art (e.g., Caruso-Toscanini-Verdi). It illustrates one of the ways in which commemoration is more diffuse than ordinary remembering. It has an expansiveness evident in the example now at hand.

This expansiveness is not limited to the repetition of the ritualistic rubric. The bread and wine of the Eucharist carry forward the same sacraments as paschal—with modifications which we shall explore—while the same elements in the paschal meal itself refer us to still more ancient origins: The bread "is the manna of Exodus 16, the drink is the water from the rock of Exodus 17:1-7 and Numbers 20:1-13 and 21:16-18."[4] The sacraments are as much commemorative as the words by which they are consecrated and put to use. Thus we observe how a given commemoration can itself commemorate another commemoration.

We must ask a very basic question: why is a *meal* the commemorative event in both the Passover and the Eucharist? Can this be a chance setting? Clearly it is not. Rather than providing only one scene of action among other possible scenes, the communal meal creates a sacred space or more exactly a *liminal region*[5] in which sacred and profane meet and merge. Eating is an activity in which merging occurs in a very palpable way: ingestion is assimilation of; digestion is suffusion by and with, the food and drink taken in. Thus in eating we *partake* and the activity is an embodiment of that more general action which Levy-Bruhl calls participation.[6] The purpose of participation is to achieve mystical unity with a totem or god. In the case of the Eucharist or paschal meal this mystical participation is at once symbolized and enacted in the partaking of bread and wine. The partaking, though physiologically actual, is at the same time symbolic since the bread and wine have become sacraments, that is, consecrated in such a way as to be suitable *commemorabilia* of a sacred figure or action.

Contrast this situation with a recent circumstance; I was working late at Sterling Library, and stopped at Naple's Pizza (formerly George & Harry's) for supper. The specialty of the evening was listed as "Corn Beef and Cabbage—$3.95." A rush of recognition came over me. This is precisely what I had often ordered at the same restaurant on the same evening of the week (for I had formerly worked late on Thursdays as a regular habit) and even at the same price after an interval of five years! I had no choice but to order the corned beef and enjoyed the meal immensely, even consuming it at a table which I had often used. Was this a commemorative meal? In some respects it *felt* commemorative. It led me to think warmly about other such evenings at the same restaurant—evenings of happy productivity in my work. It seemed to honor these former occasions. Paying tribute is an important part of any memorialization. A serious reflection on the past is also an important memorial attribute. I reflected, not without considerable nostalgia, on the earlier times when life was less distended and distracted. There was even the material factor of memorialization: namely, the meal itself. Present also were elements of the four preliminary conditions of commemoration: time for reflection, allusion to a pre-existent actuality, bodily action, and communal ambiance (this last in the form of the other customers, who seemed timelessly the same). Notably lacking, however, was the factor of solemnification. On the one hand, there was no social sanctioning of the event of my having dinner at this restaurant. However meaningful it was to me personally, it was in the end a contingent occurrence of my own choosing and delectation. On the other hand, there was no sanctifying of the meal or the space in which it took place. For both of these latter reasons, my present activity at Naples Pizza cannot be considered ritualistic in any strict sense of ritual. (It is a repetition of an activity which previously was ritualistic in a purely secular and private sense; but just this sense means that such an activity is less than fully commemorative.)

II

Let us return to the question of the origin of the Eucharist in older traditions, above all that of the Passover. It can hardly be denied that "at its origin, Christianity was a Jewish religion . . . in their practice, Jesus and his first followers conformed to a large extent to Jewish customs."[7] Much effort was expended in recent decades in establishing the sources of the Eucharist in the Passover meal.[8] But the question of the Eucharist's origin is more than a matter of tracing historical roots. It is a question of indicating how one institutionalized form of commemoration sprang from another commemorative action.[9] It was a commemorative not only of deliverance and exodus, which were its explicit *commemoranda*. It was also commemorative of other ceremonial meals. The Eucharist borrows from a set of customs common to many such meals, especially that of the Sabbath, when grace was pronounced at several points during the meal. *Berakah* is the term for this prayerful blessing, and the following pattern was traditional:

1. First cup of wine accompanied by *berakah:* this seems to be the origin of Luke 22:17 ("And he received a cup, and when he had given thanks, he said, 'Take this, and divide it among yourselves'");
2. Breaking of bread along with another *berakah;*
3. A last cup of wine, mixed with water, followed by a more elaborate blessing consisting of three *berakoth:*
   1st *berakah:* blessing for nourishment; for creation of life.
   2nd *berakah:* thanksgiving for having been given the promised land; for redemption.
   3rd *berakah:* supplication for the coming of the Messiah and the establishing of the kingdom of God.

It is evident that this last *berakah* is the source of the institution narrative's stress on the coming of the kingdom of God in and through Christ's second coming (Matt. 26:29; Mark 14:25; Luke 22:16, 18; 1 Cor. 11:26). It is also the point at which commemoration includes a possible future. An important variation on the same *berakah* was often substituted on high holy days:

Our God, and the God of our fathers, may the remembrance (*zikkaron*) of ourselves and of our fathers and the remembrance of Jerusalem, thy city, and the remembrance of the Messiah, the son of David, thy servant, and the remembrance of thy people, the whole house of Israel, arise and come, come to pass, be seen and accepted and heard, be remembered and be mentioned before thee for deliverance, for good, for grace, for lovingkindness and for mercy on this such and such a day. Remember us, JHWH, our God . . . [10]

The prominent use of *zikkaron* throughout this prayer leads to another aspect of commemoration at work in the Eucharist and its origins. This is called *objective commemoration,* contrasting with the merely subjective commemoration effected by the human commemorators. In objective commemoration, *God* is urged to commemorate in this plea: to remember us by honoring his pledges to his people. The remembrance or memorial (*zikkaron*) is possessed by him, not by his worshippers. They are only bringing it to his attention. (In this regard they *are* reminding him of his commitments.) Thus Bouyer writes:

It is in this sense that the "memory" of the divine actions which the people have kept faithfully can urge Adonai to "remember" his people. For our subjective commemoration is merely the reflection of an objective commemoration, established by God, which first of all bears witness to himself of his own fidelity. Hence this prayer formula, which is so characteristic and which was to pass over from the Synagogue into the Church: "Remember us, O Lord."[11]

Two comments are in order. First, the eucharistic extension of objective commemoration takes the form of making Christ's sacrifice into a memorial placed before God, in addition to the already existing memorial of his other redemptive actions. Thus, the Eucharist is "not just a liturgical action that makes the Lord present, it is a liturgical action that recalls as a memorial before the Father the unique sacrifice of the Son, and this makes him present in his memorial, in the presentation of his sacrifice before the Father and in his intercession as heavenly High Priest."[12] God's objective commemoration is thus doubly determined in the offering of the Eucharist, implored twice over. Second, and of more consequence for the understanding of commemoration in general, both in the Jewish and New Testament cases we witness an instance of *reciprocal commemoration.* The subjective commemoration of those participating in the Christian or Jewish ritual calls for the objective commemoration on God's part to honor his promises to the participants. Just as the high holy days commemorate the *mirabilia Dei* of creation and redemption, so the Eucharist commemorates Christ's sacrifice and its power to remit sins. As we commemorate God—mediated in Christianity's case through Christ as himself an objective memorial—so he commemorates us. One form of commemoration, human and finite, is complemented by another, deific and infinite.

Why then a meal as the occasion of such mutual commemorating? Could not such reciprocity be carried out in the mind alone—aided perhaps by a few prayerful words? We are confronted, however, by the requirement for a concrete, and explicitly material, *commemorabilium.* The grounds for this requirement are twofold. First, only a material object, such as a loaf of bread or cup of wine, is capable of being efficacious in the daily lives of worshippers. Its concreteness ensures its potential efficacy. Thus the Passover meal can be considered "the efficacious sign of the perpetual activity within itself of the *mirabilia Dei.*"[13] The Eucharist follows suit in being a forceful sign *in concreto* of Christ's redemptive power. Second, as the material objects are forms of food and drink, their incorporation during the meal further signifies the reciprocal commemoration at work throughout. Thus we read in *The Book of Common Prayer:* "Grant us therefore, Gracious Lord, so to eat the flesh of they dear Son Jesus Christ, and to drink his blood, that we may evermore dwell in him, and he in us."[14] Just as Christ is present in the consecrated bread and wine, so the communicants in consuming these sacraments become "members incorporated in the mystical body of Thy son."[15] As the commemoration is two-way, so is the incorporation, which can thus be said to be its corporeal analogue.

At this point, the deep parallelism between the Passover (and other holy meals) and the Eucharist begins to lose its strictness. The transubstantiation of the sacraments gives them an additional meaning in the Christian service. When Jesus said, "Take, this is my flesh . . . this is my blood, of the covenent, shed for you,"[16] he was identifying himself with his very *commemorabilia.* These latter are the vehicles of objective commemoration.

"Do this as my memorial," the concluding rubric to the words just cited,

> in no way means a subjective, human psychological act of returning to the past, but an objective reality destined to make some thing or some one perpetually present before God and for God himself . . . It is an institution, we may say, established by God, given to his people and imposed on them by him, in order to perpetuate forever his salvific interventions. Not only will the memorial assure the faithful subjectively of its permanent effectiveness, but above all it will assure this very effectiveness through a pledge which they can and must represent to him, a pledge of his own fidelity.[17]

Thus the eucharistic practice, though complicating matters by complicating the matter consecrated in the service itself, is in the end continuous with its Jewish heritage, and commemorates it even as it changes it. This supports Bouyer's view that the "words of Christ which were to give rise to the Christian Eucharist arise from a whole structure underlying the Gospels, [namely,] the Jewish liturgy in which they were inserted."[18] It is a commemoration in words, in actions, and above all, in its incorporative activity. The incorporation, however, is not of the sacraments alone. It is of the tradition out of which the Eucharist arose and from which it borrowed its main movements.

III

As fully ritualized commemoration, the Eucharist manifests that temporal structure designated as *"perdurance"* (a form of temporal continuity located between eternity and finite human temporality). Perdurance is operative in Christ's concluding words at Corinthians 11:26, "For as often as ye eat this bread, and drink the cup, ye proclaim the Lord's death till he come." It is also at work in the idea of perpetual memory as found in *The Book of Common Prayer:* Christ "did institute, and in his Holy Gospel command us to continue, a perpetual memory of that his precious death and sacrifice, until his coming again."[19] But we must consider more closely the exact temporal structure that subtends the Eucharist and gives to it its own peculiar form of perdurance. This form is one that contains two pasts, a present, and a continually projected future. Set forth schematically:

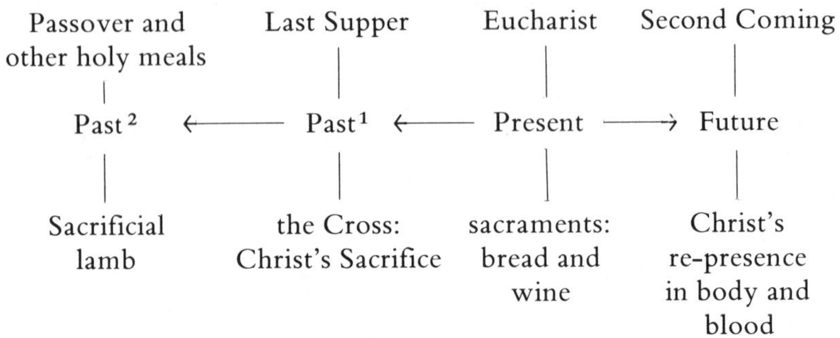

A few words of explanation are in order. The Last Supper, whether or not it was a Passover feast,[20] commemorates Passover and other holy feasts in the manner described in sections I and II above. In this way what is itself past (Past^1) in relation to the event of the Eucharist refers us to a still more ancient past (Past^2). The comparatively definite datability of the former—only the exact night of the week is in serious dispute—contrasts with the indefinite origin of the later, whose institution stems from time immemorial. The Eucharist always takes place in a moving and repeated ceremonial present, an eternal now. The role of such a present is analogous to that of the bread and wine and of the altar. The sacraments concretize the vehicles of commemoration. The altar establishes a sacred space for their consecration and consumption. The ceremonial present opens up a moment in time (a genuine *Augenblick,* a moment of truth or vision) wherein the commemoration can be consummated, the ritual realized. Such a present is neither definite nor indefinite in historical terms; it is simply *open* to continual re-enactment. This latter opens onto a future of coming re-enactments—as well as signifying the second advent of Christ. Such an advent is different from the pasts and present just delineated. Its status is that of an *eschaton* bringing an end to time as we know it, thus ending the temporal divisions on which my analysis relies. It will also be quite commemorative in character. For the Second Coming is equivalent to the definitive building of Jerusalem as projected in the Old Testament. In this way, the end point brings us back to the beginning point, to Past^2. Between the two stand the Last Supper and the Eucharist itself—as if to mediate between two unimaginable extremities, one radically indefinite and the other all too definitive.

Another viewpoint emphasizes the Janusian character of the

Eucharist. On the one hand, it looks ahead to redemption and resurrection: "Will not this fulfillment [i.e., in the Second Coming] be not only promised but also prefigured in the eucharistic celebration in which we become the 'body' of Christ by being nourished with his 'flesh' and his 'blood', believing in his resurrection?"[21] On the other hand, it looks back—first to Christ's sacrifice on the cross, following the Last Supper, then on back to the sacrificial lamb of Jewish holy meals: "He handed himself over to [the cross] at the Last Supper as an immolated oblation, like that of the Passover lamb."[22] This bidirectionality is made possible by the sacraments, the bread and wine whose very corporeality is at once a re-embodiment of Christ's presence and a pre-embodiment of his Second Coming.

The perdurance in all this consists in the constant concatenation of the factors distinguished in the above diagram, in their mutual interplay and continual support of one another in temporal terms. In a more particular sense the per-during *qua* lasting-through is effected mainly by the sacraments as the mediating elements par excellence. It is *through* the sacraments that both pasts and the future become active visions. They are memorials of such visions, their efficacious *anamnesis*. They are the primary *commemorabilia,* the effective bearers of the continual remembrance, the accomplishment of all significant commemoration. Only through such items, concretely situated in a sacred space and continually enacted in a ceremonial present, can the ritual of the Eucharist become a genuinely commemorative event.

IV

The Eucharist is paradigmatic for a study of commemoration due to its collective and its communitarian character. It is a ritual carried out in common and shared by all who participate. From the very beginning of its practice, it was considered a "plenary session [which could] not begin until all are assembled."[23] It both presupposes and creates a community of worshippers. Worshippers convene at a particular time and place, and once gathered together, a deeper bonding comes about. How does such bonding arise in and by the service of the Eucharist itself?

It arises in two essential steps. First of all, a "vertical community" is established between Christ and his worshippers: "The Eucharist establishes a fellowship (*koinonia*) between Christ and the Christians."[24] How is this done? Once more through the sacraments, but now with a special emphasis: "The cup of the blessing [over] which we bless [God], surely it is a common sharing in the blood of Christ? The bread which we break, surely it is a common sharing in the body of Christ?" (1 Cor. 10:16). The emphasis is on the way in which partaking of the sacraments is partaking in the parts of Christ's body. The physical community of the sacraments—their actual proximity in the eucharistic ceremony and their complementarity to each other, that is, *qua* material: as liquid and solid—at once signifies and realizes a community with Christ's body as material, as having its own density (flesh) and liquidity (blood). Whether we adhere to a doctrine of transubstantiation, consubstantiation, or symbolization,[25] the sense of an abiding vertical community is powerfully present. By ingesting the bread and wine, the individual believer realizes a dyadic union with Christ's body. The remembering-through effected in such commemoration is accomplished in and through this ritual participation in which Christ's body is re-membered by rejoining of bread and wine with one's own body. Note how the sacraments are thoroughly mediatory. Infused with Christ's body, they are conveyed to the participant's soma, where their internal, physiological comingling re-enacts the external-historical compresence of body and blood in the actual Jesus. Thus we get the following schema of community^1:

Christ's physical being: body and blood	⟵	sacraments: bread and wine as bearers of community^1	⟶	participant's body: re-gathering of 'body' and 'blood'

What I have just called "vertical community" or "community^1" is by no means the whole story. It omits a specifically horizontal "community^2" of worshippers in their compresence to one another. Only this latter is a genuine *communitas* in a strict sense. Only within the actual contemporaneity of believers co-participating in the Eucharist is the contemporaneity with Christ adumbrated in community^1 fully realized. As Jones says: "The common sharing of the particles of the one, broken, loaf symbolizes and effects the union of the participants not only with Christ but *also with one another. The eucharistic body creates the ecclesial body.*"[26]

This ecclesial body constitutes (in Sartre's term) a "we-self", as is underscored in the frequency with which the "we" and the "us" appear in the eucharistic liturgy contained in *The Book of Common Prayer:*

And we must humbly beseech thee, O merciful Father, to hear us . . . that we, receiving [the sacraments] according to thy Son our Savior Jesus Christ's holy institution, in remembrance of his death and passion, may be partakers of his most blessed Body and Blood . . . And here we offer and present unto thee, O Lord, our selves, our soul and bodies, to be a reasonable, holy, and living sacrifice unto thee; humbly beseeching thee that we, and all others who shall be partakers of this Holy Communion, may worthily receive the most precious Body and Blood of thy Son . . . and made one body with him, that he may dwell in us, and we in him.[27]

From such passages, it is evident that the vertical community realized with Christ (being "made one body with him") is accomplished only by the communal activity of all of the assembled worshippers. Such activity is commemorative in character, as is clear from another passage from the same liturgy: "[Christ] did institute, and in his holy Gospel command *us to continue,* a perpetual memory of that his precious death and sacrifice, until his coming again."[28] We communicants are in a position—are properly empowered—to commemorate Christ's death and sacrifice. By means of such communal remembering-through Christ is kept in mind not only as a past presence but as a presence to come: "His coming again" will be a coming to such a community of believers. As we have just seen in section III, commemoration draws in the future as well as the past; but it can do so only in its specifically collective character. In what, then, does this consist?

A closer analysis of the eucharistic ritual itself is in order. The celebration is collective on *both* sides of the altar. Not only are the communicants gathered together in their readiness to receive the sacraments, but the celebrants are plural as well:

At all celebrations of the Liturgy, it is fitting that the principal celebrant, whether bishop or priest, be assisted by other priests, and by deacons and lay persons . . . It is appropriate that the other priests present stand with the celebrant at the Altar, and join in the consecration of the gifts, in breaking the Bread and distributing Communion.[29]

The interaction of these celebrants proposes to the congregation an important model for their own interaction. From the onset, the emphasis is on bodily action closely coordinated in the company of others; it is a matter of "inter-involvement" in Merleau-Ponty's word.

Added to this are moments when the two collective entities—

celebrants and communicants—interrelate and form a single more encompassing community:

1. "The Peace" (all stand and the antiphony follows): "The peace of the Lord be always with you" (celebrant) "And with thy spirit" (people)—after which there is the instruction: "Then the Ministers and People may greet one another in the name of the Lord."[30]
2. "The Offertory": which follows just after "The Peace"; the offering of the people are taken over by the celebrants and placed on the altar to be blessed: a literal 'inter-change'; "representatives of the congregation bring the people's offerings of bread and wine, and money or other gifts, to the deacon or celebrant. The people stand while the offerings are presented and placed on the Altar."[31]
3. "Holy Communion" wherein the interaction becomes still more intense and significant; the worshippers come forward to the edge of the altar and are given the sacraments there by the officiants, who *hand over* the bread and wine to the awaiting communicants: at this moment, the bodies themselves of the two collectivities come into contact with each other (or more exactly, into contact *through* the sacraments, which are touched by both parties in the ceremony).

Citing these modes of aggregation does not imply that the eucharistic community is restricted to those literally present. The role of "intercession"—i.e., prayers for those who are unable to attend but who are in some specific need—indicates that the scope of the community is very large. It also indicates that the active commemoration is not confined to Christ alone. The ceremony and its commemoration implicate the entire worshipping community, whether or not every member is literally present. It even includes those who are not yet members but who shall become so: "we, *and all others who shall be* partakers of this Holy Communion . . . [32] This act not only ensures perdurance and gives increased scope, but it enforces the *unity* embedded in the word "community." In doing this, the Eucharist rejoins many other rituals as well. As Cassirer remarks, "the true accent of the sacral act is on performance by the community *as a whole*."[33]

In the Eucharist, wholeness or unity is underscored by the oneness of bread and wine. Paul is explicit about this: "the fact that there is only one loaf means that, though there are many of us, we form a single body because we all have a share in this one loaf" (1 Cor. 10:17). The actual breaking of the bread reinforces its unitary nature, since in this way the *one* becomes two or many. Similarly, one cup passed among communicants underscores the unity of those who drink from it: "*this cup* is the new covenant in my blood" (1 Cor. 11:25; my italics). It is precisely at this point that the Christian ritual appears to have departed from its Jewish origins: "the single, common cup, so essential to the symbolism, may not have been contemporary custom, but Jesus' own idea."[34]

The issue of oneness affects both community[1], and community[2]. On the one hand, the literal unity of each sacrament signifies unification of the communicant with the one body of Christ. Again Paul is eloquent on this point: "just as each of our bodies has several parts and each part has a separate function, so all of us, in union with Christ, form one body" (Rom. 12:4:5). On the other hand, Paul adds immediately in the same passage: "and as parts of it [i.e., the one body we form with Christ] *we belong to each other*" (Rom. 12:5; my emphasis). This "belonging to each other" forms a body of believers which is, at the maximum, the entire Church. *This* body, indefinitely numerous in principle, remains one corporate body nonetheless by virtue of the incorporation of Christ's body in actual and potential communicants (and of their corporeality in Christ's). The "new covenant," is at once between Christ and the people *and* among the people themselves—each precisely because of the other. The covenant commemorated in communion through the sacraments is at once vertical and horizontal; so is the sense of community thereby realized. In this way the two modes of community draw together and become inseparable. As Barbara de Concini writes:

> As anamnesis, the Eucharist becomes the distinguishing and constitutive action of the believing community. . . .To "do my anamnesis" ranges, we can now see, beyond the story of Christ's death and resurrection to the whole Christ, the community of believers already redeemed by that saving action. Their story is taken up into and manifested in his. The community both becomes and discovers who it is by remembering liturgically who he is. They become members of his body by re-membering themselves, i.e., re-constituting themselves, putting themselves together in him.[35]

V

Such is the structure of the Eucharist as a commemorative ritual. I have not pretended to fathom the complexity of this structure. My intention has been limited to stressing those features that bear, directly or indirectly, on the way it effects commemorating by its activity of remembering-through the sacraments of bread and wine. These latter, properly consecrated and integrated into the total ceremony (including both bodily actions and words), are the true *commemorabilia* of the occasion and are densely overdetermined in this role. Above all, they keep their communicants mindful of Christ's sacrifice and his continuing presence. In this regard they are genuine memorializations from. (Memor means 'mindful'.) They are also solemnifications wherein their very materiality aids in the process. The result of all this concerted activity is commemoration in one of its richest ritualistic expressions.

As a ritual, the Eucharist draws our attention ineluctably to the collective character of commemorating—especially as it relates to the issue of "liminality." This last term, coined aptly by the anthropologist Victor Turner, refers to the threshold state which is undergone in any significant *rite de passage* (e.g., birth, puberty, marriage, and death). Its most remarkable link is with what Turner has called *communitas,* the Latin expression for what has been discussed in section IV as horizontal community, or community². It turns out that one has a profound affinity for the other; and we will be able to see this within eucharistic ritual itself.

Van Gennep's classical formulation in *Rites of Passage* posits three phases in every rite of transition: separation, margin, and aggregation.[36] Separation often involves purification, strikingly reminiscent of the placement of the "Confession of Sin" *before* communion in the eucharistic service. The worshipper needs to be properly penitent before receiving the sacraments. From the separation implied by such penitence, one can move to a marginal state—a state of readiness for communion expressed concretely by the communicants' movement together to the edge or threshold of the altar, where one spatial margin (that of the domain of the celebrants) becomes contiguous with another (that of the communicants themselves). Temporal margins also touch at this point in the phenomenon of perdurance: past with present, present with future, and past-*cum*-present with future. After the reception of the sacraments, aggregation is realized in the twofold manner examined in the preceding section.

Looking at the eucharistic ceremony in this three-stage way has the effect of keeping the period of marginality apart from community—as if the latter were to be achieved only after the attainment of the former. In fact, there is reason to believe that the two are much more closely conjoined than this peremptory application of Van Gennep's phase analysis suggests. If we consider more closely the deep features of the liminal period as this occurs in rituals of many kinds, we begin to suspect that, far from being pre-communitarian, it possesses its own form of community. This latter is precisely *not* the unified community discussed so far but a loosely knit *communitas* in which unity per se is not the overriding theme.

Victor Turner developed the relationship between the marginal phase (or liminality) and *communitas* quite extensively. Let us focus on his account of liminality first of all. As something "essentially unstructured (which is at once destructured and prestructured),"[37] liminality resists facile unifications by virtue of its paradoxical combinations of the 'no longer' and the 'not yet', the living and the dead. People who are in liminal phases, for instance, initiates and neophytes:

> are at once no longer classified and not yet classified. In so far as they are no longer classified, the symbols that represent them are, in many societies, drawn from the biology of death, decomposition, catabolism . . . The other aspect, that they are not yet classified, is often expressed in symbols modeled on processes of gestation and parturition. . . . The essential feature of these symbolizations is that the neophytes are neither living nor dead from one aspect, and both living and dead from another. Their condition is one of ambiguity and paradox, a confusion of all the customary categories.[38]

Further contributing to the ambiguity and paradox is a characteristic role reversal demonstrated in the following example. The chieftain-to-be in the Ndembu tribe is reviled and humiliated during the liminal period before he assumes office: "Be silent! You are a mean and selfish fool, one who is bad-tempered! You do not love your fellows, you are only angry with them! Meanness and theft are all you have!"[39] This harangue is spoken by Kafwana, a traditionally passive and weak figure. In this particular ceremony the chief-elect wears only a worn-out waist cloth and must sit with one of his wives in a posture of shame and servility throughout the ceremony. He is enjoined to be continent during the period of his installation, and is called by a name common to many people. He is expected to be submissive and silent. Generalizing from this circumstance, which has so many similarities with the state of penitence in the Eucharist, we can say that liminal persons "have no status, property, insignia, secular clothing indicating rank or role, position in a kinship system."[40] They are in a limbo of nonbeing and nondistinction; they are dispossessed and disoriented. There is a suspension of "all attributes that distinguish categories and groups in the structured social order."[41]

What makes any such liminal experience sustainable and even invaluable are two closely related functions which it serves: commemoration and the creation of *communitas*. First, the commemoration is effected via the tradition prescribing the forms of liminality. The submissiveness exacted is final submissiveness to this tradition conceived as a "total community."[42] In following its injunction, one is in effect commemorating all those who, anonymous as they may be, have been responsible for giving these injunctions their particular shape and sequence. The purified state of the neophyte—analogous to the confessed mind of the communicant—is maximally receptive of tradition and thus ready to commemorate it: "the neophyte in liminality must be a *tabula rasa,* a blank slate, on which is inscribed the knowledge and wisdom of the group, in those respects that pertain to the new status."[43] Sometimes the commemoration is explicit—as occurs in the Ndembu ceremony cited above. When the chastened chief-to-be emerges from his confined state, a subchief offers the following prayer:

> Listen, all you people. Kanongesha [the new chieftain] has come to be born into the chieftainship today. This white clay [mpemba], with which the chief, the ancestral shrines, and the officiants will be anointed, is for you, all the Kanongesha of old gathered together here. [Here the ancient chiefs are mentioned by name.] And, therefore, all you who have died, look upon your friend who has succeeded [to the chiefly stool], that he may be strong. He must continue to pray well to you. . . . The chieftainship has appeared.[44]

Here the theme of rebirth from the commemorated person(s) is stated as expressly as in the Eucharist, wherein the communicants are spiritually reborn through their incorporation into Christ. Both ceremonies illustrate the principle that *commemoration, in honoring the past, revivifies the present,* giving it a new birth—whether of a political or a spiritual nature.

Second, such renascence of the individual participant in commemorative rituals occurs only in the presence of others who, with the participant, form a special community. One of the primary meanings of the Ndembu liminal ceremony of enforced abstemiousness is the setting aside of "private and privative wishes"[45] to facilitate joining together with other members of the community—other co-commemorators. This is an emerging into genuine *communitas.* In the case of the Ndembu ceremony, it is implicit in words spoken by Kafwana to the expectant chieftain:

"We have granted you chieftainship. You must eat with your fellow men, you must live well with them. . . . Do not be selfish, do not keep the chieftainship to yourself: You must laugh with the people . . . You must not be ungenerous to people!"[46]

It is striking that the most concrete activity recommended is to "eat with your fellow men"—paralleling the sharing in the eucharistic meal. In such an activity, the injunction to "live well with [others]" is most readily realized. Why is this? In brief, because in eating together, the common partaking of food and drink suspends rigid distinctions of rank and status that prevail in society at large. In a *communitas,* where unity is less important than fellowship, all who come are welcome. This is the situation in the eucharistic ceremony, in which all are welcome whatever differences of class or education exist otherwise. As much as the Ndembu ceremony described by Turner, the rite of the Eucharist offers a blend of "lowliness and sacredness, of homogeneity and comradeship."[47]

The liminality of both ceremonies fosters such *communitas.* In a threshold state, which suspends the constraints and differentiations separating people in civil society (where ordering and unification are central concerns), comingling occurs. Here people laugh with others, sharing food with them, welcoming them, overcoming separation without organizing into aggregations. Earlier we have seen how rituals are enacted in sacred spaces and effect perduring times. With the notion of liminality, we can understand how rituals in their intermediary being—the "liminal period," says Turner, is "betwixt and between"[48]—make possible such confluences of sacred and profane, and of past, present, and future. In so doing, they favor, and often realize, the commemoration which is also composed of such confluences as these.

This remembering-through, the core action of all commemorating, finds its most fortuitous occasions in ritualistic enactments containing a marked liminal phase. In that phase, the various *commemorabilia*—whether sacraments as in the Eucharist, or words as in Ndembu chieftain initiation ceremony—are best able to conjoin the disparate spatial and temporal factors which compose commemorating. By the same token, the liminality of these occasions creates the kind of community essential to the collective character of commemorating. The *communitas* therein realized is remarkably free from those established social and political distinctions that prevent commemorating from being an activity in which all who wish to honor a given past person or event can freely participate. These distinctions are held in abeyance when we commemorate together on public holidays. They are at least muted at other commemorative moments, especially in rituals of the kind which have been analyzed in the pages above. The liminality of these rituals—expressed in manifold ways—encourages the *communitas* which is the most propitious setting for commemoration in its collective dimension.

NOTES

1. "Jesus could not have intended to say simply: 'Do the Eucharist in order to be reminded of me'. This interpretation of the text is excluded by all leading exegetes": Max Thurian, *The Eucharistic Memorial* (London: Lutterworth, 1961), 1:16. Excerpt by R. T. Beckwith: "Commemoration (or reminding) is the sense of Christ's word *anamnesis,* the reminder being primarily directed towards men," *The Study of Liturgy cit. infra,* 49.
2. Thurian, 25.
3. Thurian prefers to translate *anamnesis* and *mnemosunon* as "memorial." Cf. Thurian, 20–21.
4. C. P. M. Jones, "The New Testament," in *The Study of Liturgy,* ed. C. Jones, G. Wainwright, and E. Yarnold (Oxford: Oxford University Press, 1978), 151.
5. I use the term "liminal" in Victor Turner's sense: see his *The Ritual Process* (Chicago: Aldine, 1969), chap. 3: "Liminality and Communitas." We shall return to liminality in section V.
6. See L. Levy-Bruhl, *The Notebooks on Primitive Mentality,* trans. P. Rivere (New York: Harper, 1978), passim.
7. Beckwith, 39.
8. In addition to Thurian's book, there is J. Jeremias, *The Eucharistic Words of Jesus* (London: Dent, 1966); and L. Bouyer, *Eucharist,* trans. C. U. Quinn (Notre Dame, Ind.: University of Notre Dame Press, 1968).
9. Beckwith, 49: "The Passover was essentially commorative."
10. Cited by Bouyer, 84.
11. Ibid., 85.

12. Thurian, 2:35–36.

13. Bouyer, 85.

14. *The Book of Common Prayer,* 337.

15. Ibid., 339.

16. Matt. 26:26–27, with slight modifications.

17. Bouyer, 103–4.

18. Ibid., 106.

19. *The Book of Common Prayer,* 234.

20. For an excellent summary of this debate, by no means yet resolved, see Bouyer, 99ff.

21. Bouyer, 105.

22. Ibid.

23. Jones, 154.

24. Ibid.

25. I take "symbolization" to mean any signifying relation in which the symbol and what is symbolized possess some minimal *analogical* relationship with one another. (*Caveat:* "analogical" does not require resemblance as such.)

26. Jones, 153. (my italics).

27. *The Book of Common Prayer,* 335–36.

28. Ibid., 334 (my italics).

29. Ibid., 332, "Concerning the Celebration."

30. Ibid., 332.

31. Ibid., 333.

32. Ibid., 336 (my italics).

33. E. Cassirer, *Philosophy of Symbolic Forms* (New Haven, Conn.: Yale University Press, 1965), 2:227 (my italics).

34. Jones, 157.

35. Barbara de Concini, *Remembering: A Hermeneutic of Narrative Time* (Ph.D. diss., Emory University, 1980), 132–33.

36. See Arnold van Gennep, *The Rites of Passage,* trans. M. B. Vizedom and G. L. Caffee (Chicago: University of Chicago Press, 1975), passim.

37. Victor Turner, *The Forest of Symbols* (Ithaca, N.Y.: Cornell University Press, 1967), 98.

38. Ibid., 96–97.

39. Victor Turner, *The Ritual Process* (Chicago: Aldine, 1969), 101.

40. Ibid., 95.

41. Ibid., 103.

42. "This community is the repository of the whole gamut of the culture's values, norms, attitudes, sentiments, and relationships. Its representatives in the spe-

cific rites—and these may vary from ritual to ritual—represent the generic authority of tradition," ibid., 103.

43. Ibid.

44. Turner, *The Ritual Process,* 105.

45. Ibid., 104.

46. Ibid., 101. Turner comments: "Even when a man has become a chief, he must still be a member of the whole community of persons (*antu*), and show this by 'laughing with them,' 'respecting their rights,' 'welcoming everyone,' and 'sharing food with them,'" ibid., 104–105.

47. *The Ritual Process,* 96.

48. "Betwixt and Between: The Liminal Period in Rites de Passage" is the title of the essay from which Turner's developed reflections in *The Ritual Process* take their origin. Cf. *The Forest of Symbols,* 93–111.

17

Mystic Experience and the Technologies of Transformation

ANTONIO T. DE NICOLÁS

The present chapter is an attempt to clarify mystical experience. In this context, mystical experience refers particularly to an experience which comes to us historically through such early Christians as John of the Cross, Ignatius de Loyola, Teresa de Avila, and others. It does not refer to contemporary "oceanic" experiences not yet historical or verifiable. What is true of Christianity in our interest applies equally to Hinduism and Buddhism, which claim as their origin an experience which is strictly beyond time.

The strategy followed in this clarification focuses primarily on images, languages, and the technologies by which ordinary experience is transformed into mystical experience. I will concentrate on Christianity and use as a reference point the model of "creation out of nothing" to clarify the role of creativity and experience. I will also distinguish the different uses of imagination in this tradition in relation both to mystical experience and to the "imago Dei" which humankind resembled before the fall. Finally, I will also analyze the particular epistemologies and their technologies of the two means by which we seek knowledge: the imaginative and the technologies proper to it and the cognitive and the technologies proper to it.[1]

As a reference point I will summarize the argument of this chapter in what I consider the epigram of Christianity: John of the Cross.

John of the Cross

John of the Cross appears to have come to this world to offer in his own life and body the epigram of Christianity. Though he wrote theology for the inquisition of his time, he disclaimed any direct connection between the theology he wrote and his experience, stating at the beginning of his writings that he would be most willing to write something else if the Inquisition so desired or ordered him. Experience was his pursuit—the kind of experience that originated Christianity, the experience of the will of God creating a new world or transforming a world already created. For this purpose John of the Cross rejected all cognitive skills, all sensuous imaginings, all tangible apprehension, and chose to walk "in the dark." He rejected understanding, memory, and will in the manner of their *cognitive* operation and proclaimed his method as the method that makes experience empty of all these skills. But this experience must be understood as a total bodily experience, not just an intellectual intuition. John pursued and prayed that his senses be empty of all normal and ordinary sensing and sensitization. He literally turned his method into desensitizing his own body from the habits of ordinary sensation and opened it to new habits through new technologies. His superiors and the world around collaborated, for he was not persecuted by the world or Islam but suffered abuse and imprisonment at the hands of the priests of his own order and fathers of the church. His body suffered the effects of corruption; it became full of abscesses and sores, it stunk, and it was full of pus. Yet at the moment of his death, this same body underwent a transformation; it became clear, clean, and let out a sweet smell that would communicate to those that touched him as if they "had been handling flowers." John's experience of union did not only involve technologies and habits of the transformation of experience from ordinary to mystic. It also involved transformation of the flesh and the world.[2]

The domain of this experience cannot be found in his prose writings in which he disclaims this transformation. These prose writings are the public domain of the theology of the times, of cognitive skills, and of repetitions of a theoretical world his experience denied. The domain of his writings originated by his mystical experience are found in his poetry and above all, in his own technologies, his path, that when repeated, transformed his ordinary life into that of an epigram of Christianity.

Let us examine another story, this time not of an individual but of a group in pursuit of the same transformation: the early Christians.

The Early Christians

History is the best therapy for pessimism. What is wrong is usually our own choosing and is also what we decide to forget. In this case the forgetfulness lies in the fact that experience and the public domain are originally autonomous; they are opposed to each other.

When the first disciples of Christ decided to write the Gospels and put down their *experience* of Jesus, they could do no better than reduce this experience to the linguistic habits of the Jewish audience. Mark relived the experience of Jesus in his ministries as a verification of the Jewish scriptures, of all that had been prophesied about Jesus the Messiah. Matthew and Luke stretched this narration to cover the childhood of Jesus, making this childhood coincide with the Old Testament stories and expectations. When John, or his community, wrote the fourth Gospel, the audience and the linguistic habits were different and so was the Gospel: a gospel that begins before time in the experience of the Trinity itself. The physical reality of Jesus disappears and the language of his image (and technology) appears. Through this mediation, the experience reaches beyond the physical Jesus, beyond the patriarchs to the Trinity, the second Person, Christ, who was from the beginning the origin of an experience that has already happened.[3] Paul, who never saw Jesus, proclaims his own vision of Jesus on a par with that of the Apostles who knew Christ. Neither Paul's experience, nor that of the Apostles originated on external physical perceptions or images abstracted from those perceptions. Theirs was an inner revelation, a transformation from the inside out and not vice versa. This transformation affected not only the public domain but transformed the flesh and the world: "It is not I that lives any longer, but Christ lives in me," *Vivo autem, iam not ego, sed Christus vivit in me,* in the words of St. Paul. A Christianity without this experience would have been unimaginable to the early Christians. But an experience unable to transcend and transform the public domain would have made Christianity impossible.

Creation and Transformation

The will of God and its epistemology separated Christianity from the many mystery religions, moral reformers, freelance worshippers, and groups that followed specific rites.[4]

This epistemology implied that the world *was,* and therefore *could be,* created out of nothing. It conversely implied that the act of creation, human or divine, required as a first step the cancellation of the existing world, that of God or that of wo/man. This will of God had so limited itself in the act of creation that it gave free will to the humans it created. While the original state of the created wo/man was God's image and was seen by God to be good, the subsequent choice of knowing differently by wo/man introduced in the world a rift and division in the act of knowing itself: it introduced the fall. This was a different and lower form of knowledge dependent on human criteria for rational principles and cultural usages, dependent on separation from God. While the knowledge of the original image is unitary, the knowledge of the fall is diverse and multiple and stands on human abstractions, not God's will, as its ground. Historically, both grounds of knowing are in opposition; their first historical reconciliation is the death of Christ on the cross. The second historical reconciliation is the way of the mystics and the technologies they devised for the passage from human consciousness to God consciousness. Mystics went beyond knowledge of human cognitive skills and ideologies, to knowledge identical with or close to the original image of God's creation and the technologies derived from the model of the original act of creation.

The history of Christianity is a mixed account of public failures and individual or community success in bringing about the redemption of wo/men. The individual successes are the mystic experiences, while the public failures are the lack of a public Christian domain, philosophy, and culture. Nothing resembling these has ever arisen.

The public domain has always been a philosophy from below, a means of knowing through principles of logic, belief, opinion, and ideology where the will of God is absent, forgotten, or even antagonistic. Christians, even the Fathers of the church, are guilty of propagating this domain. Augustine, more Greek in inner technological skills than Christian, was the first to introduce ideology in the will of God by equating the Trinity to the normal faculties of cognition inherited from Greek epistemology.[5] Greece shaped the Western public domain even more than Judaism, as much for Christians as for communists. The history of the public domain consists of the technologies used to vindicate and glorify the state, the father, morality according to rational order, obedience, the law, the book, time, strife, and the masculine perspective so familiar to us.[6] The mystics, on the other hand, offer faith as the most exact and immediate way of knowing the texts, the mother, origins, feelings, sacrifice, continuity, creation, and the feminine. Our future and salvation lie in the reconciliation of these two perspectives.

The Technologies of Transformation

Human experience divides into the experience of 'I' and 'not-I'. The experience of I involves a subject as the beginning, middle, and end of such experience. The technologies that reinforce and habitualize this I experience are those of cognitive skills, fantasy, and sensuous imagining. The different epistemologies of the history of philosophy are designed primarily to reinforce these technologies. Since the time of Plato and Aristotle, these technologies are so termed because their repetition not only creates habits in humans but eventually reduces human capacity to these technologies. It operates on the assumption that by repetitive ingestion of these technologies it is guaranteed identity, permanence, and continuity, till crisis, death, or corruption overcome it.[7]

Fantasy and its technologies are linked to the sense-of-I in that it starts, moves, and ends always in a subject. It lives and dies within the story of that subject.

Imagining, practiced for the sake of a subject, is pure fantasy.[8] Because it originated as an abstraction from the senses, imagining, as Kant already stated, is a sensuous synthesis that makes judgments of fact and their repetition possible.

Creative imagining and the technologies accompanying it are of a different kind. These technologies are a revolution against nothing. These creative technologies first cancel the technologies of the sense-of-I in order to lead to the experience of the not-I or, in our case, of the will of God.[9]

Why have these technologies not been part of Western history of philosophy, or for that matter of theology? The public domain has been in the hands of the technologies and epistemologies of *nature*. Since Plato and Aristotle, through Kant and Husserl, *nature* was the foundation of public discourse and inquiry. It controlled the public domain since the language of *nature* was the only language available for translation of any and all kinds of experiences and findings. This language grounded private as well as public inquiry from theology to astro travel, from the organism to personal life. The inquisition of the sixteenth century, as well as all other inquisitions, relied on this epistemology to proclaim truths of logic to which all experience had to conform, at least in speech.[10]

The veil of the epistemology of *nature* over the epistemology of the *will of God* has been so complete that individuals find it almost impossible to talk of anything that is not natural. Conversely, what is not natural is either heretical or private, or irrational and better left unsaid.

On the other hand, imagining, as the origin, is an experience of the world, the not-I. Its origin, middle and end, its unity is always the world—an immediate, witnessed, exciting, consuming, total world. This experience can be interpreted by focusing on the technologies that make it possible. The Zen master Yasutani Roshi, instructing his disciples, identified the threshold of these transformation technologies. He said: "Your enemy is your discursive thought which leads you to differentiate yourself on one side of an imaginary line from what is not you on the other side of this non-existing line." Thus, the first exercises or technologies are directed toward the cancellation of discursive thought and the worlds and sensations carried with it. The reason for this strategy is simple. The early Christians and the sixteenth century mystics would only accept a world originating and resting in the will of God, not in the human will and intelligence. They transformed the ordinary world, making it a myriad of memory-points of the will, presence, and God's original act of creation. This transformation from an epistemology of nature to that of the will of God is not a conceptual transformation. On the contrary, it is a complete transformation of the world. The experience of that world is transformed into the living presence of the image made flesh. In other words, it is not sufficient to cognize the world. The human experiencer must undergo a whole resensitization process. The exercises and technologies for that human transformation, brought to us by the epistemology of the will of God and its mystical legacy, enhance the possibility of human experience.

Classical physics, taken as our example of the philosophy of nature, initiated our mammoth external technological progress, but at the expense of a dramatic reduction in human capacities. By means of classical physics, sophisticated technologies were developed to verify its existence in the world. However, those same technologies atrophied inner human capacities and dimensions. Through external technology, classical physics established its dominion in our world. However, this same technology debilitated the inner human activities, which became totally dependent on the externality of technologically achieved facts. In time, the only sources of knowledge for the wo/men of that world were external facts and their data (empiricism), while education (positivism) became the gathering of these facts in memory or the ordering of them in imagination. In summary, cognitive skills were at the top of the hierarchical ladder where memory and imagination were placed below and subservient to these skills. Human capacity was thus rendered (officially) impotent to create. It was reduced to an inner technology dependent on the external sensations of an already established world. This technologically defined world hid its fixity by rapidly churning out facts, without altering the world's dependence on this technology.

How can we cancel (or momentarily suspend) these technologies by which and through which we are normally sensitized, and develop the original technologies of the image, the will of God, the original creation?

Give me your will, and I will give you as many ideologies as you need to justify such an irrational gift.

We must return to the will. This return is not theoretical; it involves exercises and technologies autonomous and independent from those of cognition. Eastern traditions, in particular those of Hinduism and Buddhism, may serve as a guide. Sāṃkhya philosophy and yoga, for example, on which Hinduism is grounded and Buddhism derives in its earlier stages, do not possess a cognitive faculty as we understand cognition. Cognition for these traditions is one more sense (*manas*), which with the other five collaborate to make up the experience of the sense-of-I. Hinduism and Buddhism accept the imagination/will (*buddhi*) as the only faculty for human development or freedom. This imagination is not dependent on external objects for its exercise. Inner space (*antahkarana*) activates this memory and imagination in the way Plato used recollection,[11] and in the way mystics used the mysteries of Christianity. The mystics also used the life of Christ to regather the frames of the past in order to build the original image-experience from which the whole culture originated. Every philosophy becomes eventually incarnated through the technologies of interiorization, linguistic behavior, and systematic use of the faculties. Every technology creates habits in us that cannot be displaced except through the use of different technologies that instill new habits. This provides a certain mobility within technologies. It has an effect of a certain detachment from the fruits of action. This correction of physical stillness, this preparation for inner and outer mobility, this plurality of body habits on stale body habits, and the ensuing mobility of such exercises are all legacies of inner technologies of transformation left to us by Eastern cultures and Christian mysticism.[12] These exercises and their repetition—hence the power of their habit formation—are a deliberate effort to open the inner resources and spaces of the imagination by learning how to frame its possibilities on the memory-points of the past. The past is simply the residue of the habits and traces left in our sensations by theories that lived and died through earlier human bodies (the *karma* of history). Culminating the exercises of the imagination, every living point of the world becomes our experience, a living memory of the original image, a unity of experience where body, image, and world share the same boundaries and demarcations. In this experience there is no room for identities or perspectives. It may be called the experience of not-I; some have called it God, others the experience of no-thing. In most cases this experience serves as the model for immortality here and now. It is an experience that lasts beyond and without the assistance of personal identity, though, it is felt as more real than any other kind of experience: I may witness that which has no sense whatsoever of 'mine' or 'I'.

The Text of Meditation

In the following detailed analysis of technologies used in meditation, our first move is to link the image to language. The originating image and those that mediate in meditation, be they mandalas or mysteries, are languages in the sense that they can be articulated, are intentional, and carry meaning—that is, have organizing value for experience. The fact that they appear only as large images is as inconsequential as the fact that ordinary semiotics makes of every object an abstract sign. Both kinds of languages function with different criteria and by different technologies. Furthermore, the language of images, or images as language, point to a human space that is originally an image of the creator, be it God, culture, or simply the origin of human experiencing.[13] This is the true inner space that may be revealed, opened, touched, and uncovered by the unique, original act of creation and by no other creature or object or sensation. The mystic's task in meditation is a movement through memory-points to steal the imagination's horizon, to become that experience that is the origin of human experiencing.[14] The text of meditation as language has its own signs (feelings) original to the image or the background. Their decoding needs as much accuracy and dedication as any signs in any semiotic text. However, in this case, lives are at stake, not only theories or logical truths. The text of meditation, contrary to cognition, is better understood if focused entirely on the transformation in the human body and its sensory appetites. The human body of the meditator comes to the meditation in an apparent false unity of sensation and habits of sensation. These texts, when performed as meditation, as exercises, and not merely read, are a systematic dismemberment of this original false unity of the meditator until his will and body coincide with the larger will and body of the original image, the creative horizon: the Trinity, in the case of Christian mystics; Krishna, the original sacrifice, in the case of Hinduism; the experience of no-thing, Nirvāna, in the case of the Buddhists.

To proceed with some semblance of unity I will generalize these technologies following the sixteenth century mystics, John of the Cross and Ignatius de Loyola.

Dismemberment, Mediation, Death, Transformation

We will bypass the preparatory techniques of meditation, such as location, body positions, and concentration, and focus primarily on the activities or exercises proper that turn meditation into transforming technologies. For clarity's sake, this discussion is divided into four kinds of exercises corresponding with the four weeks of the *Spiritual Exercises* of Ignatius de Loyola.[15] Following the discussion is a summary of the four stages through which ordinary experience is transformed into mystical, common to practitioners of the East and Christian West.

The first state is that of dismemberment.[16] Ignatius places two frames facing each other at the beginning of the first week of the *Exercises*. On the one hand, is the body of the meditator, coming to the meditation in a false unity and identity, with a bundle of sensory habits directed almost exclusively to the satisfaction and unity of the meditator's own will. On the other hand is the Trinity, the creator and his will. The whole course of the exercises is to make both wills coincide as the will of the Trinity, the creator. Since will, emotion, and experience go hand in hand, the coincidence or approximation of both wills results in an experience which is out of the ordinary. It carries in this journey of approximation or coincidence, a body and a different sensitization each time it experiences the point where body/experience/will form a unity.

This journey of coincidence or approximation is not done without a continuous violence in the form of nonphysical dismemberment.

The exercises of the first week set in motion the pattern of the exercises that follow. The meditator's body and senses are systematically dismembered in order to be sensitized to new kinds of sensations. The new sensations are images proposed to the meditator that mediate between his starting self and that larger frame of the Trinity. These images mediate between the two original frames by developing in the body/image of the meditator sensations, emotions, and feelings appropriate to the objects they present, like shame, sorrow, guilt, gratitude, and love. These images of mediation are those of creation, the fall of the angels, of sin, hell, humankind and redemption.[17] What separates the technologies of meditation from those of fantasy or cognition is that in these meditations, the meditator is not a unity present in any one of those images. He is a dismembered sensorium that lends sight, smell, sound, touch, and movement to the frame of the images and the contents of the frame. The meditator lends his senses to the frames, not his unified self. Two types of emotions develop: on the one hand, the meditator is sensitized to these images; on the other, he is slowly becoming desensitized to the original sensations with which he entered the exercises. Will exercises, like examination of conscience and discernment of the movements of the will, are also introduced at this early stage.

Mediation and the Images of the Life of Christ

The same technologies apply to the second week. The only difference is that at this stage the images are imaginings from the life of Christ. In the mystic's intention, Jesus' life is the mediation to the Trinity. Through all the exercises, the Trinity remains a constant frame as the absolute background. The meditation on the mysteries follows the same exercises of dismemberment by lending sight, sound, smell, taste, touch, and movement to the images of meditation. The results are similar to the first week. There is a stronger sensitization to the frames and contents of these images. There is more distance from the objects and images to which the meditator was habitually sensitized when he entered the exercises. The inner signs of the will require a more technical reading as the depth of experience deepens and broadens. Ignatius de Loyola used these inner signs in the meditator at this early stage to make decisions by learning how to use them. Others, like Teresa de Avila, would follow those signs without any hesitation, while John of the Cross would strive not to heed them and continue meditating. From a theological point of view, it is interesting how these mystics center Christianity on the Trinity and the experience of the Trinity, and not on Christ. Christ on earth is the mediator to Christ the second Person of the Trinity: the experience that has already happened.

Death

There is a moment, as the exercises of the third week indicate, where all the striving in meditation ends in the death of all the past habits of sensing, before the birth of the new sensitizations of the exercises. This is the most demanding and violent act of the whole power of these technologies and where most people stop short. It is a complete death to the original unity, to any unity. A new life begins, sensitized from within, rather than from without as it was at the exercises' beginning. This is the passage through the dark night, the bereavement of the past habits and securities. In the dawn of a new life, we are uncertain if it will continue to rise and if it will reappear outside of these exercises, or even in the next sensation. The soul's flight between the old way and the new way is a continuous fight between two loves that at last have recognized their common origin. While the meditator has been busy building frames and mediations for new sensitization, what starts as imagining very soon turns into experience, and signs that lead to new experiences. The background becomes alive and imagination stops where new life begins. This power of transformation is the power of imagining as the mystics from East and West practiced and willed it to us.

Transformation

The fourth week of the exercises of Loyola is the confirmation of this whole transformation. He calls it "Meditations to Gain Love." This is the stage John of the Cross immortalized with his poems "The Spiritual Canticle" and "Love's Living Flame." He immortalized the third week with his poem of the "Dark Night" and the first week with his poem on "Creation."

The mobility of the imagination is faster and more powerful than any mobility induced by ideology. Ideology travels by abstraction, but the imagination travels by embodiment. The passage of the imagination is an eternal and living fabric in our lives. The imagination moves with images, and the images are of the same fabric as the imagination. The ability to discover those primal images is a guarantee that we are not dying of strangulation as victims of only one ideological image.

The passage from image to image, or object to object, or sense to sense, within the frame of one image, is filled with signs and experiences. Ignatius de Loyola could not perceive one without the other, if his *Spiritual Diary* is any guide. There, he lists these signs. He kept this remarkable diary for a year using these signs as a guide to make an important decision for the society he was founding. These signs include tears. In the first forty days of the diary, Ignatius wept over one hundred twenty-five times, an average of four times a day, twenty-six times with intense sobbing. He spoke of joy and spiritual rest; intense consolation; rising of the mind; divine impressions and illuminations; intensification of faith, hope, and charity; spiritual flavor and relish; sightings and spiritual visitations; loved surrender; spiritual dialogue; voices and sounds from the inside; touchings; memories and memory transformation; understanding and clarity without previous cause; increased love; joy for the things of the spirit; peace and rest of the soul in the creator; knowledge and divine inspiration.

Perhaps it is John of the Cross who best and most memorably summarized the whole transformation in his poem "Love's Living Flame" (my own translation):

Love's Living Flame

Songs that the soul sings in the intimate union with God, her beloved bridegroom.

1. O Love's living flame,
tenderly you wound
my soul's deepest center!
Since you no longer evade me
will you please at last conclude:
rend the veil of this sweet encounter!
2. Oh cautery so tender!
Oh pampered wound!
Oh soft hand! Oh touch so delicately strange
tasting of eternal life
and cancelling all debts!
Killing, death into life you change!
3. Oh lamps of fiery lure

in whose shining transparency
the deep cavern of the senses,
that was blind and obscure,
warmth and light, with strange flarés
gives next to the lover's caresses!
4. How tame and loving
your memory rises in my breast,
where secretly only you live
and in your fragrant breathing,
full of goodness and grace,
how delicately in love you make me feel!

Conclusion

These concluding remarks do not mark an end but a beginning. They are offered as an encouragement to every individual to use the way of the mystics as an accessible way in the marking of our own lives. Living is for everyone. Other people's lives are not ours to make. Our own life needs the originality that each of us alone can give it to be ours. To be originals, our lives need to coincide with the original images that originally sensitized them. We cannot borrow those images from the public domain. The public domain is the domain of the fall, ideologies, theories, distances from living, and living by inertia. It is the multiplicity of worlds that need the corrective of the original images for creation to continue. Nor can we borrow our images from the epistemologies of human nature. The rhetoric covers the fact that human nature is only a theory for the control of living, not any nature we originally carry within us. The decisions of history about nature itself are sufficient proof of our lack of any nature. Living begins as an image of a creator, and this is the radical decision that Western history has obscured. The corrective of this oversight, of this impasse, the corrective of everything that we feel is wrong with our lives, is only one memory-point away in the history of our own background.

As a model, the image of the origin—be it named creator or not—has always remained hidden. Yet it has been creating *originally* and continuously. The reason is simple—the image of the act of creation and the human species are an original and potential unity linked to each other from the birth of the species. The manifestations of this image appear *collectively* in the different primordial, *paradigmatic* images that gave birth to different cultures. These cultural paradigms have acted *distributively* on each life to the degree that they appear, individually, as the embodiment of a cultural primordial image. The manifestation of these paradigmatic images, culturally and distributively, makes possible the kind of public articulation we are here involved in. It also explains the unity of the first acts of wo/man—Adam and Eve—etc., as involving not only themselves but the whole of the species. This image of the primordial act of creation has acted subconsciously in every act of human creation. These primordial images are encoded in our brain and tissues in such a manner that conscious and guided imagining involves a transformation of holographic or "holomoving" intensity. These primordial images not only sensitize us to their information, but our lives—worlds—are as large as the total holomovement. The complete sensation of the total image is contained not only in each of its parts, but each of the parts of the imagining living body is also sensitized to the total image. What the original image contains in potentiality, each individual may attain distributively through the use and application of the technologies described above. Conversely, the distributive form in which the image appears in the mystics through history gives a more accurate picture of the encompassing power of the images of origin and the technologies of transformation. Ultimately this is the original image: a generative power of an experience beyond time. The experience becomes time in the imagination, and transforms time by infiltrating the secondary images of wo/man's fall, through technologies that transform worlds and body-sensations into a continuation of the original act of creation. The mystic experience, and the technologies used to reach it, is a model of human creating whose time has come. Human history, as a model of human possibilities, may yet succeed where the computer and the rat have failed as universal models of the same possibilities. But these technologies depend on the decision of individuals for their use; they—we—hold in our power the ultimate modulation. It is up to each individual to decide. Hopefully, he/she will find a community to share the darkness and joy of the journey.

NOTES

1. The philosophical lineage of this article falls in line with contemporary interests in phenomenology and hermeneutics or interpretation of cultural activities. From Husserl I am interested in his claim that reality may be bracketed, Edmund Husserl, *Idea* (London: Allen and Unwin, 1931), 110; *Logical Investigation* (London: Routledge and Kegan Paul, 1970). I am forced to go beyond the fixity of his *eidos* or essences with authors of this tradition like Heidegger and more closely José Ortega y Gasset. These two take the interpretation of texts as the radical activity and context of human decision making. Ortega, furthermore, establishes the text as the primary unit of instrumental interpretation—embodiment—of theories and cultures. He further implies that a text once interpreted may open up a systematic domain of concepts and values necessary in the interpretation of culture and in the establishing of a native background before objects appear as objects for us. I will clarify, as we go along, the different ways the word text is used in the paper. See also: Edmund Husserl, *The Crisis of European Sciences and Transcendental Philosophy* (Evanston, Ill.: Northwestern University Press, 1970); Martin Heidegger, *Being and Time* (New York: Harper & Row, 1962); José Ortega y Gasset, *Obras Completas* (Madrid: Revista de Occidente, 1946).

2. San Juan de la Cruz, *Vida y Obras de San Juan de la Cruz* (Madrid: Biblioteca de Autores Cristianos, 1960); Gerald Brenan, *St. John of the Cross* (Cambridge: Cambridge University Press, 1973), 82–83.

3. See in this respect the work of Raymond E. Brown in particular, *The Birth of the Messiah* (New York: Image Books, Doubleday, 1977).

4. See in this respect the works of Charles Williams, *Witchcraft* (London: Faber and Faber, 1941); *Descent of the Dove* (Grand Rapids, Mich.: William B. Eerdmans, 1939).

5. Augustine in his work *De Trinitate,* book 14, introduces chapter 4 with the following thesis: "The Image of God is to be sought in the immortality of the rational soul. How a Trinity is demonstrated in the mind." This is the thesis we oppose here.

6. From the beginnings of Western philosophy with Plato and Aristotle, later with Augustine, Aquinas, Galileo, Spinoza, and in our time, Einstein, there had been the belief that nature is a book written from the start in its complete final form, and that science, be that the science of theology or natural science, is the actual form of that reading. But with the fixity of nature other values were also fixed and held supreme—the state, the father, the rational order, morality, the law, the book, time, in a word the masculine way of knowing. But nature is not a book written in final form, it is rather a text generated to respond to a human form of enquiry linked more closely to cultural interests than natural ones. The so-called natural interests depend more on the time and place and cultural interest of the scientific group than on the natural interests of the same group. In fact, in view of the history of natural science, there are no natural interests per se, but only cultural ones. See in this respect the work

of Patrick A. Heelan, *Space-perception and the Philosophy of Science* (Berkeley: University of California Press, 1982); "Natural Science as a Hermeneutic of Instrumention," *Philosophy of Science* 50 (1983): 181–204.

7. For discussions of *techne* one needs only read Plato's *Gorgias* and Aristotle's *Rhetoric* and *Poetics*. See in this respect the summary work of: Jacqueline de Romilly, *Magic and Rhetoric in the Ancient Greece* (Cambridge: Harvard University Press, 1975). Technologies involve two kinds of texts. First, there is a primary text that allows us to read. This is primary because it is the condition of possibility of others, in this notation called text 1. The second text is that which includes signs or like material and equals some form of information. The primary text, text 1, is not only interpretive but is also causal, in the sense that it not only creates the conditions of possibility for reading but also shapes the signs and objects that appear causally. The causal character of this text 1 is derived from a radical embodiment of the humans using it and the technologies involved. This human embodiment is completely transparent to those using it or adept in using it. But this causality is not on a par with physical causality, where the effect is proportionate to the cause. It is rather a causality more similar to biological causality where an effect may be disproportionate to its cause, as when the prick of the spur on the flank of the horse produces an exuberant jump totally disproportionate to the cause. And vice versa—no matter how much a horse is pricked by the spur, sometimes it does not move. These two texts, a primary one, text 1, and a secondary one, text 2, are the texts we will be referring to throughout this chapter. The primary text has to do with the embodiment of certain acts needed to create; the secondary text refers to the signs originated by the primary text in the acts of its exercise and repetitions, like consolations, tears, and visions. It is also obvious how texts derived from imaginative embodiments differ radically from texts derived from cognitive embodiments, and why throughout history they have been antagonistic or subservient to one another. It is also obvious why a plurality of texts is a radical necessity and why theoretical uniformity is a crime against humanity.

8. Works on the imaginative are not many, but the interest of philosophers seems to move, suddenly, in this direction: Edward S. Casey, *Imagining: Phenomenological Study* (Bloomington, Ind.: Indiana University Press, 1976); Robert C. Neville, *Reconstruction of Thinking* (Albany, N. Y.: State University Press, 1981), especially the last four chapters; Thomas P. Hohler, *Imagination and Reflection: Intersubjectivity, Fichtes's Grundlage of 1794* (Boston: Martinus Nijhoff Publishers, 1982).

9. As a preparation for understanding these technologies at work in several cultures see my work: Antonio T. de Nicolás, *Meditations through the Ṛg Veda* (Maine: Nicolas-Hays, 1976); *Avatāra: The Humanization of Philosophy through the Bhagavad Gītā* (Maine: Nicolas-Hays, 1976); "Audial and Literary Cultures: The Bhagavad Gītā as a Case study," *Journal of Social and Biological Structures* 5: 269–88.

10. This kind of inquisition is always present even in circles of contemporary philosophical styles like phenomenology and hermeneutics where one would expect that such presence would not be welcome. Philosophers like Heideg-

ger, Ricoeur, Merleau-Ponty and even Husserl take as legitimate the manipulative control over people and things that scientific models have. They take for granted the pragmatic goals of science as being the control of natural phenomena and that therefore this end justifies the means of a fictive—nonhistorical—reconstruction of nature according to model systems of science that make the achievement of such a goal possible. This is a far cry from the understanding and application of phenomenology and hermeneutics Ortega practiced as the "sport of transmigration," or the ability to get at the roots of the activity itself of doing philosophy historically. Our human acts are originally cultural and therefore our journey should be to the roots. But instead we have seen a whole tradition jump on the waves of theories and carry with it a whole people.

11. Plato needs to be studied anew in reference to the dialectic, or transformation of knowing through reason and abstraction and knowing through the experience of the Forms. The dialectics I refer to imply these four moves: (a) turning the soul in a new and opposite direction; (b) using a different faculty; (c) finding different objects, that are *experientially* different, as light is to shadows; (d) producing a different kind of knowledge. These four moves are from the *Republic* 508e–11e, 532a–34e. In the *Phaedo* 67c–d, also 79e–81e, Plato describes knowledge as equalling the experience of the Forms and being independent from the normal knowledge derived from the body sensations. The Forms may be known only "after death" or by "practicing death," by accustoming the soul to "withdraw from all contact with the body and concentrate itself on itself . . . alone by itself." But, Plato, of course, was an adept in the mystery religions of his time and a great footnote to the practices of previous cultures.

12. See in particular chap. 6 of de Nicolás, *Avatāra*.

13. See de Nicolás, *Meditations through the Ṛg Veda,* chap. 6: "The Languages of Images."

14. It should be clear we are dealing with the primary text, text 1, where embodiment is the prerequisite for experience, just like reading is made possible by embodying the skills proper to it before meaning can appear.

15. I am at this time finishing an edition of Ignatius's collected spiritual writings under the title *Powers of Imagining* for the State University of New York Press.

16. The image of dismemberment is as old as the Ṛg Veda, 2500 B.C. The Dragon Vrtra is dismembered again and again for creation to take place. The dragon never dies. See de Nicolás, *Meditation through the Ṛg Veda,* chap. 4.

17. The function of the gods in Hinduism has the same mediating property as we describe here. The mandala of the god or goddess is the same mediating imaging to lead to the original experience, as the structure of the Gītā leads Arjuna, chapter by chapter, as a mediation to reach the original experience. See de Nicolás *Avatāra,* chap. 6.

Contributors

Arabinda Basu Professor of Philosophy, Sri Aurobindo International Centre of Education; Director, Sri Aurobindo Research Academy, Pondicherry, India.

P. Joseph Cahill Professor, Department of Religious Studies, University of Alberta, Edmonton, Alberta, Canada

Edward S. Casey Professor and Chairperson, Department of Philosophy, State University of New York at Stony Brook, Stony Brook, New York

David E. Cooper Reader in the Department of Linguistic and International Studies, University of Surrey, Guildford, United Kingdom

Antonio T. de Nicolás Professor of Philosophy, State University of New York at Stony Brook, Stony Brook, New York

William A. Earle Professor of Philosophy, Northwestern University, Evanston, Illinois

Marcia Hermansen Professor, Department of Religious Studies, San Diego State University, San Diego, California

Carl Albert Keller Professor of Science of Religions, University of Lausanne, Lausanne, Switzerland

Samuel G. Kibicho Chairperson, Department of Religious Studies, University, of Nairobi, Nairobi, Kenya

Viggo Mortensen Associate Professor, Institute of Ethics and Philosophy of Religion, University of Aarhus, Aarhus, Denmark

Evanghelos Moutsopoulos Professor of Philosophy, University of Athens and Athens Academy of Sciences, Athens, Greece

Christopher Olubunmi Oshun Lecturer, Department of Religious Studies, University of Ibadan, Ibadan, Nigeria

William L. Power Professor, Department of Religion, University of Georgia, Athens, Georgia

Michael Smithurst Lecturer, Department of Philosophy, The University of Southampton, United Kingdom

Contributors

Antoine Vergote Professor, Catholic University of Louvain, Louvain, Belgium

Michael von Brück Visiting Professor, Gurukul Lutheran Theological College and Research Institute, Kilpauk, Madras, India

Emilie Zum Brunn Researchist, Centre National Recherche Scientific, Paris and Ecole Pratique des Hautes Etudes, Paris-Sorbonne, France

Index

Index

Index

Index

Index

HIEBERT LIBRARY
3 6877 00076 6658